PARIS

PICNIC CLUB

MORE THAN 100 RECIPES
TO SAVOR AND SHARE

PARIS

PICNIC CLUB

SHAHEEN PEERBHAI & JENNIE LEVITT

ILLUSTRATIONS BY JENNIE LEVITT

STERLING EPICURE
New York

STERLING EPICURE

New York

An Imprint of Sterling Publishing Co., Inc.
1166 Avenue of the Americas
New York, NY 10036

Consuming raw or undercooked meats, poultry, seafood, shellfish, or eggs may
increase your risk of foodborne illness, especially if you have certain medical conditions.
The young, elderly, pregnant women, and anyone who may
be immunocompromised should not consume them.

ISBN 978-1-4549-2036-6

Distributed in Canada by Sterling Publishing Co., Inc.
c/o Canadian Manda Group, 664 Annette Street
Toronto, Ontario, M6S 2C8, Canada
Distributed in the United Kingdom by GMC Distribution Services
Castle Place, 166 High Street, Lewes, East Sussex, BN7 1XU, United Kingdom
Distributed in Australia by NewSouth Books
45 Beach Street, Coogee, NSW 2034, Australia

For information about custom editions, special sales,
and premium and corporate purchases, please contact
Sterling Special Sales at 800-805-5489
or specialsales@sterlingpublishing.com.

Manufactured in Canada

2 4 6 8 10 9 7 5 3 1

www.sterlingpublishing.com

Interior design by Christine Heun and Barbara Balch

CONTENTS

VIII

INTRODUCTION

Food has the power to bring people together, and food is what brought us together in Jouy-en-Josas, a small town tucked into the hillsides south of Paris, where Jennie was studying for an MBA at HEC Paris and Shaheen was attending Le Cordon Bleu. Before we even moved to France, we began writing to each other, and when we finally met, we knew we were kindred spirits. We soon began thinking of ways to cook together, which is how Friday Lunches—our little Paris Picnic Club—began.

Every Friday for a year, we created a delicious lunch in our tiny apartment for eighty hungry eaters. We cooked and baked in the quiet hours of the morning, serving up the spread to the local community. The setting couldn't have been better: a farm and dairy stood next door; the town baker delivered warm, crusty baguettes; and the colorful market in the town square of Versailles was only a short ride away. Our heads brimmed with ideas as we basked in the culinary playground that is France.

For each Friday Lunch, we cooked up a meal consisting of a sandwich, dessert, and drink, all made from scratch. Why Friday? Because indulging in a delicious picnic-style meal was a great way to greet the weekend that lay ahead. The concept was sustainable, too. We made the meals with locally sourced ingredients and created virtually zero waste because we cooked only as many meals as people pre-ordered. What started as an experiment to try new recipes to share with friends grew into a popular lunch spot in our little community. Soon we moved the operation to Paris, where we packed baskets full of delicious meals to share among friends at different parks and hidden spots across the city. From a picnic lunch between classes to a bustling restaurant of eighty guests, Friday Lunches became something of a phenomenon. Following this success came a dinner series in our homes, at which travelers from all over the world could book a three-course meal with us.

PICNICS

It's such a happy word—*picnic*. It combines all the emotions of getting together with the people we love over food in the most fun, casual setting. Picnics are spontaneous; they don't need endless planning and fussing. Picnics are easygoing and avoid the formality and decorum that white tablecloths and shiny silverware command. A picnic can take place anywhere: in your courtyard, at a park, by a lake, or even a little breather you take on a hike while devouring a beautifully layered sandwich.

This book encompasses the essence of what began as a picnic club and grew into a dinner party series, with small plates and sharing platters laid out just as comfortably across kitchen counters and dining tables as on a blanket or bench. It's a book about the joy and comfort of cooking for those we love, whether that means sharing an elaborate meal atop a thoughtfully set table or just splitting a sandwich on the train.

Karen, one of our regulars and now a good friend, reminisced about our pop-ups:

> When I moved to France to go to school, I didn't think that finding a good meal would be an issue, but somehow, in the outskirts of Paris, it was. That was until I quickly learned about Friday Lunches. It wasn't just a meal, it was an event. There was nothing better than seeing that pre-order Facebook post, "Hey Everyone, Our next Friday Lunch is on . . ." I read the meal description and started salivating right then and there. The hardest decision was whether to order one sandwich or two (one for later, of course). On days when lunch was served, we all headed to the Piano Bar, our on-campus lounge space, and hoarded around Jennie and Shaheen, who were careful in perfecting each sandwich with the right amount of each mouth-watering ingredient. . . . The atmosphere that they created was more than just "lunch." They always had a fun indie playlist going. Their food attracted everyone, so the place was packed with students and faculty. Meeting new people was easy, the conversation starters so simple: "How awesome is this sandwich?" or "The cake is still warm!" These ladies know their food, and they cook with love; it is apparent in every detail."

OUR COOKING

Simple, fresh, and respectful is how we describe our style. Our cooking has its ideas rooted in tradition, but not constrained by it. We like to do very little to the ingredients that we have chosen thoughtfully, using them at their peak and coaxing flavor from them with care and technique to transform them into the best versions of themselves.

We are ingredient crazy. We go to great lengths to learn about and buy ingredients of impeccable quality. In French, *terroir* literally translates to "land," but it refers not only to the soil where something grows, but also its people, their lifestyle, and their culture. That's why Alsatian cherries or chestnuts from the Ardèche taste so special. Generations of people have poured their lives into perfecting and protecting age-old techniques.

Our cooking takes inspiration from the vast combination of ingredients that you'll find in Paris. That means it's not limited to butter and foie gras, but abounds with the flavors of the Middle East (mint, za'atar, Aleppo pepper), Africa (dates, harissa), Italy (lemon, tomato, olive oil), East Asia (miso, Gochujang), India (countless spices), Spain (ham, almonds), and Latin America (yucca flour, lime, passion fruit).

We like to make food that makes people happy, that comforts and feels substantial. We don't dot our plates with sauces from squeeze bottles. We'd much rather heap generous spoonfuls onto a plate. Food isn't just nourishment; it's meant to be savored—be it sitting on the floor playing board games with friends or passing platters around a table. It feels really special to be a part of people's lives through food. We hope to create happy food memories for those around us and now—with this book—for you.

COOKING IN FRANCE

KITCHENS

A typical Parisian kitchen is not very big. A mere 10 feet (3m) if you're lucky and with the possibility to accommodate a toaster oven if you're luckier. The fridge and freezer unit, rolled into one, typically fits under the counter with just enough room for a bottle of milk, some cheese, and charcuterie. (Wine bottles can sit by the potted plant on the windowsill at the peril of passersby below.) This setup means that Parisians need to shop frequently, which allowed us to indulge in one of our favorite hobbies: exploring the beautiful produce at the markets.

MARKETS

We always begin at the market. Looking, touching, smelling, tasting our way through the various stands, we discuss ideas, flavors, textures, and colors. Plump violet asparagus in spring; punnets of strawberries and apricots in summer; piles of chanterelle, mousseron, and black trumpet mushrooms in fall; and hearty mounds of root vegetables in winter.

French markets feature some of the best produce in the world. People here care deeply about what they put

into their mouths. It's never just about producing a saleable product but selling the best product possible. To honor and cultivate that spirit, the French have competitions for pretty much everything: best baguette (the winning baker gets the honor of providing baguettes for the Elysées Palace for the year), best *boudin noir*, best *choucroute*, best what-have-you. This specialization is so inspiring: Take a single ingredient, such as rhubarb or chestnut, understand it completely, and diversify it by making a range of products from it.

Every time we moved into a new neighborhood, we had to build new relationships with local vendors—the baker who knows that you like your baguettes *bien cuite* (well done), the cheesemonger who has a new chèvre he knows you'll love, and the butcher who will happily give you a bag of bones for your soup. With the growth of our weekly pop-ups, we became such serious bread buyers that our local *boulanger* dropped off the baguette on a scooter—and threw in a few extra, too!

PARIS POTPOURRI

French cuisine immediately draws the image of food that has simmered in stocks all night long and bathed in butter and cream. But then we discovered a whole different side of the City of Lights, a Paris where you can sip piping hot, spicy Turkish lentil soup at 4 A.M. or feast on tacos al pastor in the bylanes of the Marais instead of the usual *oeufs mayonnaise* at the local bistro.

In Paris, we discovered multicultural communities in the outer *arrondissements* (or districts), where you'll find the best *banh mi* outside Vietnam, and where people will queue in the cold for an hour for the most comforting Moroccan couscous and succulent kebabs. Down narrow passages you'll find hidden Indian grocery stores. On a quiet street in a dodgy neighborhood sits a Sri Lankan shop where they will grate fresh coconut to order for you. The diversity of Paris made us delve deeper to explore the foods and ingredients that the city really eats.

PEOPLE

A love of food permeates Parisian culture. Vincent, our neighbor and now good friend, gave us canelé molds for

Christmas. He later invited us over for a home-cooked dinner of succulent pork filet mignon with chestnuts that his aunt had picked, shelled, and bottled. His Spanish girlfriend, Irene, made a beautiful platter of Iberico ham that she brought back from Barcelona. As we left, they gave us jars of jam from the same aunt, the label proudly featuring the name of the fruit, a photograph of her cooking it, and the year it was bottled. This sort of pleasure that people seek in food makes France a joy to live in.

OUR RECIPES

This cookbook is a collection of recipes that take inspiration from the diverse cuisines of Paris and marries them with the rich food cultures that now surround us in London and Bogotá. We are very passionate about what we cook, and that passion reflects in how we select our ingredients. We rely on a baker, butcher, and cheesemonger for bread, meat, and dairy and make everything else from scratch. You can source your meat and dairy from the deli counter of your local supermarket, and you can use the three bread recipes in this book (pages 73–76) to make your own loaves. The techniques—strongly influenced by classic French cooking—go beyond mundane croque monsieurs and molten chocolate cakes to showcase the contemporary cooking that we undertook in our tiny Paris kitchenettes. Employing these methods, peppered with flavors from the lesser-known ethnic pockets of Paris, will elevate both the ingredients and your cooking to make taste and texture transcendent. These are our favorite recipes.

PANTRY ESSENTIALS

Our favorite thing to do is cook, and our second favorite thing to do is to shop for groceries and kitchen things. It's incredibly exciting to browse the aisles of specialty food shops and ponder buying either the French Luque olives or the Italian Taggascia. Raw milk butter or the one flecked with seaweed? Honey from the pine forests or honey from Provence? Living in France spoiled us for choice. While it's fairly easy to find some ingredients all over the world, others are worth seeking out on your next trip to *la belle* France.

In this section, you'll find ingredients for which we have a special affinity. It's so easy to perk up flavors with citrus zest or a heaping mound of Parmigiano Reggiano. Good French butter will uplift practically any dish, and real vanilla beans will speckle your cakes prettily. Always use the best-quality ingredients—they may cost a little bit more, but they'll take you a long way.

SEA SALT
Fleur de sel is harvested on the shores of France. Some of the best comes from Guérande and Camargue. We also love the crunchy, Maldon sea salt flakes from Britain.

DRIED HERBS, SPICES, AND BLOSSOMS
Source Aleppo pepper, dried chrysanthemum, dried mint, dried peppers, Espelette pepper, hibiscus, saffron, Sarawak pepper, za'atar, and ingredients for our Dukkah (page 188) from international food shops.

PRESERVED VEGETABLES
Buy marinated artichokes, sun-dried tomatoes, assorted olives, and preserved sweet peppers in jars or by weight at the market to add extra punch to sandwiches and tartines.

MUSTARD
The two mustards we use most frequently in our kitchen are Dijon and the grainy kind. Maille is available the world over. In Paris, you can buy mustard from a hand-pumped tap at the Maille store at 6, place de la Madeleine, 75008 Paris. Pommery mustard is lovely, too, and comes in a range of flavors.

HONEY
The quality and variety of honeys in France are pleasantly overwhelming, ranging from light lemon to dark, woody chestnut. Open-air markets are the best place to sample them (with quite a spread at Marché d'Aligre, Place d'Aligre, 75012 Paris).

VINEGARS
Apple cider, Balsamic, white Balsamic, Banyuls, honey vinegar, red wine, and white wine varieties are staples.

Seek out small-batch fruit vinegars, such as rhubarb or quince, at markets or specialty shops to change things up.

OILS

You need at least two types of extra-virgin olive oils: the supermarket kind for cooking and a higher quality, more expensive one to eat with bread, to drizzle on a salad, or for a finishing touch to a dish. We're referring to the latter kind when we mention best-quality extra-virgin olive oil in this book. You could use any variety—grassy, fruity, or peppery—based on your taste. The best way to find your favorite is to taste lots of them at a specialty store. You will be surprised by the spectrum of flavors and the difference in flavor each region and season can bring. We also like to use a range of nut and seed oils in our recipes; dipping crusty bread in them feels somehow luxurious. In Paris, go to Huilerie J. Le Blanc (12, rue Jacob, 75006 Paris). La Tourangelle makes great almond, hazelnut, pistachio, truffle, and walnut oils.

NUTS

We like to use a lot of nuts in our cooking. That hearty crunch can lift many a recipe. It's especially worth seeking out bitter Valencia almonds or—the jewel of all almonds—the Marcona variety, also from Spain. Also look for Bronte pistachios from the Sicilian mountains around Mt. Etna, hazelnuts from Piedmont in northern Italy, and walnuts from the Périgord region of southwestern France. To bring out their maximum flavor, toast the nuts at 325°F (160°C) for 8 to 15 minutes depending on their oil and moisture content. For example, pine nuts toast quickly, usually in 8 to 10 minutes, while almonds need 15 to 17 minutes.

VANILLA BEANS

To understand how vanilla beans can be so distinct from one another, sniff your way through the Épices Roellinger spice shop (51 bis, rue Sainte-Anne, 75002 Paris). In their Cancale shop, they stock and age vanilla beans from twelve different countries in a controlled environment. G. Detou (58, rue Tiquetonne, 75002 Paris) has some of the plumpest Madagascar vanilla beans at excellent prices.

CHOCOLATE

There's never a substitute for good chocolate. Using great chocolate will vault your desserts to a new level. We use Valrhona chocolate for our cakes and baking. It comes in a variety of strengths and blends, ranging from the sweet and creamy white chocolate at 35 percent to the acidic brick red 64 percent Manjari to the intense dark and tannic 85 percent Abinao. If you want to buy just one bag, the 70 percent Valrhona Guanaja is an all-rounder. The ingredients on the label should read: cocoa beans/cocoa mass, sugar, cocoa butter, emulsifier (soya lecithin), natural vanilla. Avoid supermarket brands labeled only "baking chocolate" and any brand containing vegetable fat, which replaces the cocoa butter in cheap "chocolate."

FLOURS

In Paris, the organic store Naturalia is our playground when it comes to picking beautiful, ancient grain flours. With at least half a dozen wheat flour varieties and grinds, they honor gluten in all its glory. We like to blend flours for our recipes to add earthiness and unconventional flavor. For example, we substitute a portion of the wheat flour in a recipe with buckwheat, chestnut, polenta, rye, spelt, and other grains to create different flavors and textures.

BAKING INGREDIENTS

For cacao nibs, nibbed sugar, cocoa powder, candied chestnuts, chestnut paste and purée, and tonka beans, G. Detou (58, rue Tiquetonne, 75002 Paris) is a one-stop shop. Shaheen lives in London now but still continues to hop across the Channel to restock.

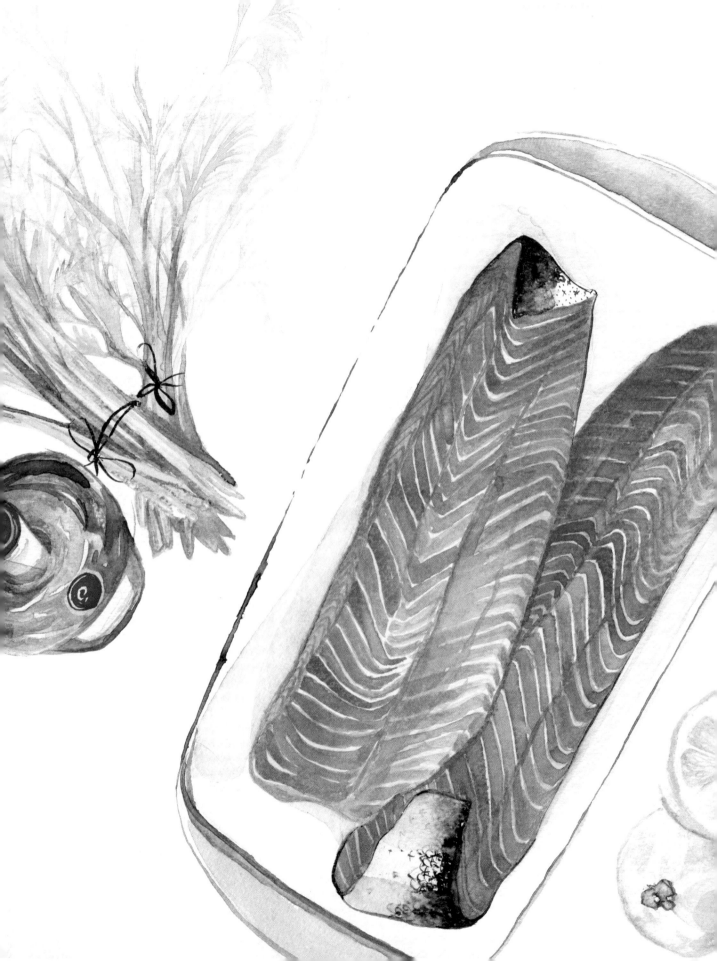

SMALL PLATES

Classic wine bars welcome you with effortlessly laid out platters of cheese, charcuterie, and crisp cornichons, which have a timeless charm of their own. And now, at the newer wine bars in Paris, helmed by young chefs with international experience, you are greeted with a thoughtful market-driven menu made up of plates to share.

The recipes for the small, flavorful plates in this chapter are inspired by the convivial meals and glasses of wine we've shared with our friends around the table. One of our favorite wine bars is L'Avant Comptoir, in the heart of the Saint-Germain-des-Pres neighborhood, where you can share elbow room, warm crusty bread, and glorious Bordier butter from Brittany with the person next to you. Our recipes celebrate the very spirit we've grown to love and cherish when we set out to enjoy an *apéro*.

FRENCHIE AREPAS

WITH CARAMELIZED PLUM JAM

We first discovered arepas soon after moving to Paris, when Jennie had just begun dating her husband, and he took us to a Colombian bistro near the famed Père Lachaise Cemetery. Eager to introduce us to the cuisine of his country, he chose the most universally appealing dish. Rounded patties of freshly ground maize seared with butter in a heavy iron skillet, arepas are wonderfully satisfying, with a solid savory appeal and a hint of sweetness from the corn. We've since learned that every region in Colombia and Venezuela boasts its own version of the South American treat, but our all-time favorite has semi-soft cheese kneaded into the dough itself and is stuffed with a bit more cheese, then pan-seared to create a delectable contrast between the hardened crust and soft, warm, cheesy center. We've French-ified the recipe by using semi-hard Comté, since it melts well and adds a subtle nuttiness to the arepa. We like to use a twenty-four month ripened cheese for its depth of flavor. You could also substitute Gruyère, sharp cheddar, or even Emmental, for a milder taste. You can make the arepas all in one go and then refrigerate the leftovers to reheat and eat later.

PREP TIME 15 minutes   COOK TIME 30–40 minutes   MAKES 10 small arepas

1 cup (150g) precooked yellow or white cornmeal (such as P.A.N.)

½ teaspoon sea salt

1 cup (100g) Comté cheese, shredded

1 cup (240ml) hot water

1 tablespoon melted butter + extra for smearing

2 tablespoons extra-virgin olive oil

In a bowl, combine the cornmeal, salt, and about half of the cheese. Pour the hot water over it, followed by the butter, then stir to combine until all of the cornmeal is well moistened. Add more water, a tablespoon at a time, if the dough feels a bit dry. Knead until it forms a smooth dough.

Keep a bowl of water handy for dipping your hands to help shape the arepas. Divide the dough into small balls (the size of a golf ball) and then flatten them between the moistened palms of your hands. Place more cheese in the middle, then gather the sides and pinch the dough in the middle so that the cheese is now stuffed inside the dough. Wet the edges of the arepas to smooth them out. Now flatten the dough again with the palms of your hands or use the bottom of a moistened glass.

Add a glug of olive oil into a large cast iron skillet over medium heat. Sear the arepas until you get a nice golden crust (about 6 to 8 minutes on each side). Repeat with the remaining arepas, adding extra olive oil when necessary.

Smear the warm arepas with cold butter and serve with plum jam (recipe on facing page). You can also eat them on their own with a sprinkle of sea salt or with guacamole.

CARAMELIZED PLUM JAM

Plums of every shade flood the markets in summer. Of all the varieties, we especially seek out two of them: the bijou yellow Mirabelle and the deceptively green, but incredibly sweet, Reine Claude. They are the perfect after-dinner dessert served with a few Pistachio and Cherry Financiers (page 121). Toward the end of the season we bottle the plums for the colder months. This plum jam recipe can be adapted to the kind of plums you are using. Try a tawny port, a red dessert wine, for dark, tart plums or a white dessert wine such as Late Harvest Riesling or Sauternes for lighter varieties of plum.

PREP TIME 10 minutes   COOK TIME 20 minutes   MAKES about 2½ cups

1½ cups (300g) sugar

2 pounds (1kg) ripe plums, pitted and coarsely chopped

¼ cup (60ml) tawny port

2 tablespoons lemon juice

1 vanilla bean

Zest of 1 lemon

Put a third of the sugar in a heavy saucepan over medium heat. Let the sugar melt, then add the next third and when most of it has melted and begins to turn light golden, add the remaining third of sugar. Stir gently with a spatula to make sure the sugar is cooking evenly. It will turn from a light golden to a dark caramel very quickly, so don't leave the pan unattended. When the sugar has a rich amber color and you see it bubbling lightly at the edges, take the pan off the heat and add the chopped plums, port, and lemon juice. At first, the mixture will bubble vigorously and the caramelized sugar will harden. This is normal. Return to the heat, and continue cooking. The sugar will melt again with the moisture from the plums.

Next, split a vanilla bean along its length with a paring knife, then scrape out the seeds. Add the bean and the seeds to the pan with the plums and stir to distribute evenly.

Cook for an additional 5 minutes, skimming off any foam that floats to the top. Remove from the heat and stir in the lemon zest. Let the vanilla bean continue to sit in the jam and infuse even after it's been bottled.

Pour the jam into sterilized jars, seal, and invert immediately to help form a vacuum. An opened jar of jam will keep for weeks in the fridge.

BRETON ARTICHOKES

Artichokes can be daunting to cook with their waxy, spiny leaves and a shape that looks more like a mace than a vegetable. You might even think it is a wasted effort to spend time cooking something you're going to throw away most of. But we urge you to cook with artichokes. We cook them in a flavorful court bouillon, a classic broth that is traditionally used in France to poach fish and seafood. In this recipe the cider court bouillon, perfumed with coriander seeds and lemon zest, helps bring out the natural flavors of the artichoke. The optional additional method of roasting the cooked artichokes is a slightly more elaborate way of preparing the French classic.

PREP TIME 15 minutes   COOK TIME 45 minutes–1 hour   SERVES 4

4 globe artichokes

2 cups (480ml) cider or dry white wine

1 bay leaf

3 garlic cloves, crushed

8–10 black peppercorns

8–10 coriander seeds

1 lemon, zest peeled and juiced

¼ cup (60ml) extra-virgin olive oil

Sea salt

For Optional Final Preparation

2 lemons

2 tablespoons extra-virgin olive oil

3–4 garlic cloves, germ removed and minced

Espelette pepper (mild red chili pepper powder from France)

Chopped fresh parsley

Prepare the Artichokes

Lay an artichoke on the work surface, with the thick stem protruding over the edge of the counter. Hold the artichoke down with one hand. With the other hand, push the stem downward to snap it off. It takes some strength, but it's worth the effort to get the fibrous bits out from the middle of the heart. If your stem isn't long enough to give you enough leverage, slice it off near the base of the artichoke. Next, if your artichoke has spiky leaves, trim them straight across with kitchen scissors. Repeat with the other 3 artichokes.

Place all the artichokes in a large pot of salted water with the cider or white wine. Add the bay leaf, garlic cloves, peppercorns, coriander seeds, and lemon zest and juice. Drizzle olive oil over the top of the water.

Once the water comes to a boil, cover the pot and reduce the heat to a simmer. Cook the artichokes for 40 to 45 minutes, until you can easily pierce through the middle of the base with a small knife. Another test to make sure the artichoke is cooked is to try to pluck out a leaf. If it comes away easily, it is cooked.

Once the artichokes are tender, remove them from the pot and let them sit bottom-up so that any cooking liquid can flow out. Then, when the artichokes are cool enough to handle, shake them off to dislodge any peppercorns and coriander seeds that might be caught inside.

At this point, you can either serve the artichokes whole, with aïoli or mayonnaise (see serving suggestions at the end) or continue to the next steps for a modern twist.

Preheat the oven to 425°F (220°C). Slice the artichokes through the center to split them in two. Using the pad of your thumb, firmly scoop out all of the inner purple leaves and the fuzzy bit that sits just above the heart (the "choke"). Give each of the artichoke halves a generous rub with a lemon (about half a lemon per artichoke), allowing the juice to pool in the cavity.

Over a medium-high flame, heat a heavy ovenproof skillet that can comfortably fit all of the artichoke halves (or as many as you want to eat at the moment). Swirl in the olive oil to coat the bottom of the pan in a thick layer, and then sauté minced garlic until it is faintly golden around the edges. Add the artichoke halves, flesh side down, to the pan. Remove the pan from the heat, swishing it back and forth so that the extra lemon juice deglazes the pan, and then pop the skillet into the oven. Roast the artichokes for about 15 minutes, or until the outside leaves are crisp. Remove and place them on a serving platter, inner sides facing up, and sprinkle with salt, Espelette pepper and chopped parsley before serving.

Serve with Tarragon Aïoli (page 196) or Lemon and Walnut Oil Mayonnaise (page 192) to dip on the side.

TIP To eat a whole artichoke, pluck out the leaves and draw your teeth along the base of each leaf to remove the flesh. Once you get to the fibrous leaves at the center of the artichoke, remove them along with the "choke." Eat the heart as is or cut it into cubes and drizzle it with olive oil and a sprinkle of sea salt, Espelette pepper, and chopped fresh parsley, just like they do at L'Avant Comptoir (3, carrefour de L'Odéon, 75006 Paris).

CHESTNUT TAGLIATELLE

WITH CHESTNUT AND ROSEMARY CÈPES AND WALNUT SAUCE

T he fall we moved to France, we discovered lush chestnut trees growing in the gardens right outside our apartment building. We'd go chestnut-picking downstairs, making sure to wear running shoes to avoid getting pricked by the horrible, spiky shells, and then come back upstairs to roast the chestnuts in the oven, eating them while they were still warm—almost too warm to peel. The first time we roasted chestnuts, we nearly called the *pompiers* (firemen), since we were too afraid to step into the kitchen while the chestnuts were exploding inside the oven. We didn't know we had to make an incision in the chestnut shells for the hot air to escape!

For this recipe, we like to use *cèpes* (porcini mushrooms), which come into season around the same time as chestnuts. You can use any other fresh wild mushroom for this recipe, if you'd like.

PREP TIME 1½ hours   COOK TIME 15 minutes   SERVES 4

Chestnut Pasta

1²/₃ cups (200g) all-purpose flour

²/₃ cup (150g) chestnut flour

6 egg yolks

Water, as needed

Extra-virgin olive oil, to coat pasta

Chestnut & Rosemary Cèpes

¾ pound (340g) cèpes, or other mushrooms

2 tablespoons extra-virgin olive oil

2 sprigs fresh rosemary

1 garlic clove, germ removed and crushed

²/₃ cup (75g) chestnuts, precooked and crumbled

1 recipe Walnut Sauce (page 198)

Parmigiano Reggiano, to taste (optional)

Sea salt and freshly ground black pepper

Chestnut Tagliatelle

Mix the flours together in a bowl. Make a well in the center of the flour, add the egg yolks, and break them up with a fork. Slowly draw in the flour from the sides as you bring the dough together. Add some water, a little at a time, as you knead the dough. The dough needs to be very firm, so add only a little water if absolutely necessary. Knead well until smooth. Cover in plastic wrap and refrigerate for 15 minutes.

Roll out the dough as thinly as you can. You could use a pasta machine, if you have one, or a rolling pin on a hard, smooth surface. Fold the pasta sheet on itself several times and, using a sharp knife or wheel cutter, cut it into ⅓-inch (1cm) wide strips. Fluff up the strips, sprinkle them with a bit of flour and then lay them on a tray lined with a kitchen towel, and let them dry in the fridge overnight or hang dry for 40 minutes (use clean metal hangers).

When ready to cook, bring a large pot of salted water to a boil. Add the pasta and cook for 4 to 7 minutes, until firm with still a bit of a chew. The cooking time depends on the size of your pasta as well as how dry it is. Strain the pasta in a colander. Reserve in a bowl and toss in olive oil, salt, and pepper. Keep covered.

Chestnut & Rosemary Cèpes

To prepare the cèpes, trim the base of each mushroom and scrape off as much of the earth as possible. If it is very dirty, peel a thin layer off the stem. With a damp cloth or paper towel, wipe the tops of the mushrooms. Cut them into ¼-inch (6mm) slices. Heat a pan to medium-high. Add a glug of olive oil and swirl to coat the pan. Add the rosemary sprigs and crushed garlic, and cook for a minute until fragrant. Add the mushrooms, making sure not to crowd them. Cook on high heat until the mushrooms are golden brown. Avoid stirring too frequently because this will prevent them from browning nicely. Season to taste with salt and pepper. Stir in the crumbled chestnuts. Discard the garlic and rosemary.

Assemble

Stir the pasta into the pan with the Walnut Sauce (page 198) and mix very well. Add shavings of Parmigiano Reggiano to this if you like and toss to coat. Spoon the pasta into serving plates and top with the chestnut and rosemary cèpes and freshly ground black pepper.

CRUNCHY CHICKPEAS
AND JERUSALEM ARTICHOKES
WITH TAHINI AND DATE DRIZZLE

Jerusalem artichokes, or sunchokes, are some of our favorite tubers because of their versatile texture and subtle nuttiness. Sliced raw in a salad, they lend a delicate crunch that complements fresh goat cheese and other crisp summer vegetables. When roasted, however, they release an earthy sweetness that's incredibly satisfying when paired with other savory elements, like these crunchy chickpeas. The flavors come together with a kick from the spicy, creamy, tahini and date drizzle. Serve the dish warm and make plenty as a snack for anyone lingering in the kitchen—they go fast!

PREP TIME 30 minutes   COOK TIME 40 minutes   SERVES 4

Crunchy Chickpeas

Extra-virgin olive oil

½ cup (60g) all-purpose flour

1 egg

1 tablespoon water

1½ teaspoons smoked sweet paprika

Small pinch of cayenne pepper

1 cup (65g) panko or bread crumbs

1 cup (200g) chickpeas, either canned or home-cooked

Jerusalem Artichokes

½ pound (225g) Jerusalem artichokes

1 garlic clove, germ removed and minced

Extra-virgin olive oil

Tahini and Date Drizzle

3 tablespoons tahini paste

1 small garlic clove, germ removed and minced

Zest and juice of 1 lemon

Water

¼ teaspoon cayenne pepper

2 tablespoons date syrup

Assemble

Juice of 1 lemon

4 ounces (110g) fresh frisée, chicory, or other firm leafy lettuce, stems removed and torn up

2 tablespoons fresh parsley, finely chopped

Extra-virgin olive oil

Sea salt and freshly ground black pepper

Crunchy Chickpeas

Preheat the oven to 425°F (220°C) and grease a baking sheet lightly with olive oil.

Prepare three dipping bowls to coat the chickpeas: The first with flour, salt, and pepper. The second with the beaten egg and a tablespoon of water. And the third with the paprika, cayenne pepper, and panko. Roll the chickpeas in the flour, then the egg wash, then the panko mixture, shaking off any extra coating at each step.

Place the coated chickpeas on the baking sheet, drizzle generously with olive oil and shake gently back and forth to coat.

Bake in the oven for 15 to 20 minutes, or until golden, shaking the pan halfway through.

Jerusalem Artichokes

Scrub the Jerusalem artichokes with a brush under running water. You could peel them if you like, but we like to keep the skin on. Cut them into about 1-inch (2.5cm) chunks and then toss together with the salt, pepper, garlic, and a drizzle of olive oil. Lay them in a baking pan and roast on a rack below the chickpeas for about 20 minutes. The Jerusalem artichokes are cooked when the skin looks puffed up and blistered and a knife can be inserted into the middle without much resistance, much like a potato.

Tahini and Date Drizzle

In a bowl, whisk together the tahini paste, garlic, lemon juice, lemon zest, and salt. As you whisk, the tahini will seize and thicken. Stir in a little water until the sauce has a smooth pouring consistency. Taste for seasoning. In another bowl, stir the cayenne pepper into the date syrup. Keep the tahini sauce and date syrup separate until ready to serve.

Assemble

Toss the chickpeas and Jerusalem artichokes together with half the lemon juice, and more salt and pepper if needed. Wash and dry the frisée lettuce and toss with salt, pepper, olive oil, and the remaining lemon juice. Place a handful of the lettuce at the bottom of a shallow serving dish. Spoon the chickpeas and Jerusalem artichokes into the dish. Drizzle with the tahini sauce, followed by the date sauce, and then sprinkle with fresh parsley. Serve warm.

PINK SALAD

with WINTER BITTERS, GRAPEFRUIT, and PEAR

This is the perfect winter salad that combines the flavors of beautiful, seasonal bitter greens with citrus and pears coated in a rich hazelnut oil. You could just as well use Granny Smith apples instead of pears for added tartness.

PREP TIME 10 minutes active time, 30 minutes rest   COOK TIME 5 minutes   SERVES 4

¼ cup (50g) sugar

¼ cup (60ml) water

1 sprig rosemary

1 grapefruit

2 heads tardivo radicchio

2 heads pink radicchio

2 tablespoons hazelnut oil

2 tablespoons extra-virgin olive oil

1½ tablespoons red wine vinegar

2 pears, cut into thin strips

4 tablespoons (40g) shaved Pecorino Romano

Zest of 1 lime

Sea salt and freshly ground black pepper

In a small saucepan, bring the sugar and water to a boil with the rosemary. Turn off the heat and let the syrup cool. Next, suprême the grapefruit: Top and tail the fruit with a knife so that it can sit flat on a cutting board. Using a sharp knife, cut the skin off from the top to bottom as you work around the fruit. Turn the fruit on the cutting board as you go along, trying to retain the round shape of the grapefruit as much as possible. Make sure to remove all of the white pith. Next, cup the fruit in one hand over a bowl and with the other hand, remove each section by cutting toward the core. Drop the segments into a bowl as you go along. Pour the rosemary syrup over the grapefruit, then set aside. Let the grapefruit segments infuse for 30 minutes. You can also do this the night before.

Separate, wash, and spin dry the bitter greens.

In a large bowl, make the vinaigrette by whisking the oils into the red wine vinegar. Season with salt and pepper. Drain the grapefruit segments. Mix in the remaining ingredients—the tardivo and pink radicchio, the pears, Pecorino Romano, and the drained grapefruit segments. Finally zest the lime over the salad and serve.

MARINATED SCALLOPS
WITH ZUCCHINI, AVOCADO, AND ALMOND RELISH

Come November, you will see *poissonneries* all over Paris display bright coral-colored scallops, unopened and alive. Only when you buy the scallops will the fishmongers prepare them for you, so they are incredibly fresh to use. When ordering, ask for the shells as well, to make a pretty presentation.

PREP TIME 20 minutes   COOK TIME 15 minutes   SERVES 4

Scallops

8 scallops in their shells

Juice of 1 lemon

Fleur de sel

Espelette pepper

1 tablespoon butter

Zucchini, Avocado, and Almond Relish

2 zucchini

4–5 sprigs parsley, leaves picked and finely chopped

Espelette pepper (mild red chili pepper powder from France)

2 teaspoons red wine vinegar

1½ tablespoons best-quality extra-virgin olive oil

1 avocado, cut into a tiny dice

Juice of 1 lemon

Fleur de sel

1 tablespoon butter

¼ cup (40g) almonds, chopped

Preparing the Scallops

Separate the scallops from the shells by running a knife close to the shell to dislodge the flesh. Gently pull out the coral, if attached, and any sinews on the scallop. Rinse the shells and flesh under cold running water to get rid of any residual sand. Dry the shells, and set them aside to use later. Lightly score the surface of the scallops in a crisscross pattern and refrigerate until ready to use.

Zucchini, Avocado, and Almond Relish

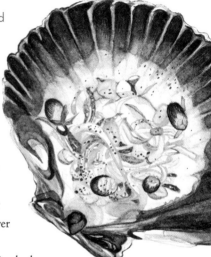

Julienne the zucchini, then place into a bowl and toss with the parsley, Esplette pepper, red wine vinegar, and olive oil. Let it marinate for about 5 minutes. We typically serve the scallop raw, but if you'd like you can also briefly sear the scallops on both sides over high heat.

Toss the diced avocado in the lemon juice, reserving a little bit to dress the scallops, a pinch of fleur de sel, and a bit of the olive oil.

Add the butter to a small saucepan and cook the chopped almonds until they are golden brown. Drain them on a paper towel and sprinkle with salt.

Assemble

To assemble the dish, place a scored scallop into a clean shell.

Squeeze a few drops of lemon juice on it and sprinkle with a pinch of fleur de sel and Espelette pepper.

Top with the zucchini relish followed by the avocados and almonds. Sprinkle with a little bit more of the Espelette pepper and finish with best-quality extra-virgin olive oil.

CURED SEA BASS

WITH ELDERFLOWER VINEGAR

A few pointers for curing fish:

+ The curing time of the fillet will depend on the thickness of the fish. Cure 10 minutes for a fillet that's ½-inch (1cm) thick, and an extra 10 to 15 minutes for every additional ½ inch (1cm) of thickness.

+ Always use coarse salt. It is absorbed more slowly into the fish than table salt and flavors it more evenly.

+ We like to use a 10:1 ratio of salt to sugar in the curing mix. As an example, for every 10 tablespoons of salt there is 1 tablespoon of sugar.

+ And finally, it is imperative that you get your hands on the freshest fish!

PREP TIME 10 minutes   CURING TIME 10–20 minutes   SERVES 4–6

1 cup (200g) coarse sea salt

1 heaping tablespoon (20g) sugar

2 teaspoons (10g) fennel seeds, toasted

Zest of 1 lemon

1 pound (450g) fillets of sea bass

Elderflower Vinegar (page 189)

Extra-virgin olive oil

Fresh elderflowers, for garnish

Crème fraîche, for serving

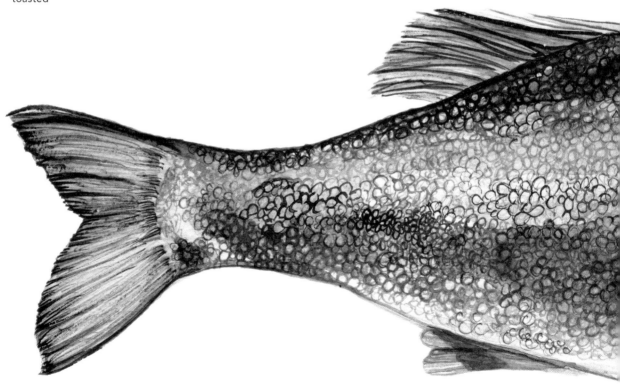

In a bowl, mix together the sea salt, sugar, fennel seeds, and lemon zest—this is your curing salt mix.

Remove the skin and any brown bits on the fish. Run your finger along the fillet to make sure there are no hidden bones. Use tweezers to pluck out any that you find.

Place the sea bass in a shallow baking pan and cover it with the curing mix. Leave it to cure as per the instructions at left (10 minutes for every ½ inch [1cm] of thickness).

Once cured, wash the salt off the fish and pat it dry with paper towels. Keep the fish refrigerated, and slice it only when you're ready to serve.

Using an extremely sharp knife, cut the sea bass into very fine slices at a very narrow angle, about 5–10 degrees. Cut only when you are ready to serve.

Lay the fish slices on a plate. Drizzle with a bit of the Elderflower Vinegar (page 189) and extra-virgin olive oil. Sprinkle with fresh elderflowers. Dollop a bit of the crème fraîche on the side and serve with Sourdough Crostini (page 30).

NOTE If you cannot find elderflowers near you, you can use white balsamic or champagne vinegar. For the garnish, you can use microgreens or chive blossoms.

SALMON GRAVLAX
WITH POMELO SEGMENTS,
SHAVED FENNEL, RED BEET SPROUTS, AND CITRUS VINAIGRETTE

On Rue Cler, in the middle of the posh 7th arrondissement and just blocks from the Eiffel Tower, Autour du Saumon prides itself on a meticulously sourced selection of European smoked fish. At any time of day, you're likely to find locals and tourists alike peering through the window and admiring the shop's display of bright coral Scottish salmon filets alongside wild eel and river fish from the sweet waters of France. Whenever we see a plump filet of salmon at the fishmonger, we're inspired to make our own cured salmon and spice it up with a little toasted coriander seed, orange zest, and gin. While you're putting this together you could treat yourself to a G&T—which has all of the same elements, minus the salmon, plus a thin slice of cucumber and tonic. *Tchin-tchin!*

PREP TIME 30 minutes   SERVES 4–6

1 teaspoon sea salt + extra for seasoning

1½ tablespoons fresh lemon or passion fruit juice

1 teaspoon Dijon mustard

1 teaspoon honey

6 tablespoons (90ml) extra-virgin olive oil

Freshly ground black pepper + extra for seasoning

3 ripe pomelos, zest reserved from ½ pomelo (optional)

1 large or 2 small fennel bulbs

1 pound (450g) Salmon Gravlax (on facing page)

Large handful red beet sprouts or microgreens

Sea salt and freshly ground black pepper

Prepare the vinaigrette by first adding a teaspoon of sea salt to the lemon or passion fruit juice. Whisk vigorously until the salt has dissolved. Stir in the mustard and honey, and then slowly drizzle in the olive oil until the mixture thickens. Add freshly ground black pepper to taste and the pomelo zest, if using, to give it a sharper citrus flavor.

Next, suprême the pomelo: Top and tail the fruit with a knife so that it can sit flat on a cutting board.

The pomelo has more white pith than a grapefruit, so you want to cut enough of the pith to expose the inside segment. Using a sharp knife, cut the skin off from the top to bottom as you work around the fruit. Turn the fruit on the cutting board as you go along, trying to retain the round shape of the pomelo as much as possible. Make sure to remove all of the white pith. Next, cup the fruit in one hand over a bowl and with the other hand, remove each section by cutting toward the core. Drop the segments into a bowl as you go along. You will be left with the fibrous core that you can squeeze to extract any extra juice left in the pomelo.

Prepare the Fennel

Trim the stalk and fronds of the fennel. You can use the fronds to mix in with the dill for your next batch of gravlax or homemade stock (page 184–185).

Cut the fennel bulb vertically in half. Scoop out the tough core and discard it. Slice the fennel halves diagonally, making sure to keep the slices as thin as possible—or use a mandoline, if you have one.

Assemble

Arrange the Salmon Gravlax on a plate, each slice slightly overlapping the next. Toss the pomelo segments and fennel shavings in half of the vinaigrette. Drizzle the remaining vinaigrette over the fish and and then top with the pomelo and fennel.

Sprinkle the sprouts or microgreens on top of the salmon and season lightly with a small pinch of sea salt and black pepper.

SALMON GRAVLAX

PREP TIME 30 minutes   CURING TIME 24 hours   SERVES 6–8

1 large salmon fillet (about 2 pounds/1kg), skin on

10–12 sprigs fresh dill, or a mixture of dill sprigs and fennel fronds

3 tablespoons (45g) light brown sugar

5 tablespoons (75g) coarse sea salt

¼ cup (60ml) gin or vodka

Grated zest and juice from 1 large lemon

½ teaspoon freshly ground black pepper

½ teaspoon coriander seeds, toasted and ground

Start preparing the gravlax 24 hours before you want to serve it. Pat the salmon dry with paper towels and remove any noticeable bones. Cut the fish crosswise through the middle.

Remove the dill leaves from the stalks. Wrap the leaves in a moist paper towel and store in the refrigerator to use the next day.

Chop the dill stems finely and mix together with the brown sugar, sea salt, gin (or vodka), lemon zest and juice, black pepper, and coriander in a shallow ceramic or glass casserole dish. This is your curing mixture.

Place both halves of the salmon fillet in the dish and rub them all over with the curing mixture. When the fillets are thoroughly coated, place one fillet skin side down and the other on top, skin side up, so that the fleshy sides of both fillets are touching each other.

Cover the fish with plastic wrap and refrigerate for 12 hours, turning it over after 6 hours, so that the fillet that was on the bottom is now on top (and vice versa). The curing mixture will draw moisture out of the salmon flesh, so flipping it allows both fillets to have equal exposure to the seasoned liquid that collects at the bottom of the dish.

Remove the salmon from the refrigerator and scrape the curing mixture off the fillets. Chop the reserved dill leaves and press into the flesh of the salmon fillets. Wrap the fillets tightly against each other, as before, with sufficient plastic wrap (making sure that the package is airtight). Lay the package flat in the refrigerator for an additional 12 hours, flipping it over after 6 hours. (Place the package in a dish, if you like, to catch any liquid if the package leaks.) Unwrap the fish over the sink, discard the plastic wrap, and pat the fish with paper towels to dry it.

Use a very sharp knife to thinly slice the salmon on the diagonal. Once you have sliced half of the piece of salmon, flip it around and use your other hand to firmly hold the skin, for better leverage, while you slice the fish diagonally. Repeat with the other fillet.

OYSTERS

I did it. I finally did it. I ate raw oysters.

I set a goal for myself to eat oysters when I first visited Paris in 2010 and saw beautiful platters of *fruits de mers* on display outside bistros, but I never summoned the courage and got back on the plane before trying them. I imagined raw oysters to be active and squiggly, with bits of ocean grit. I imagined that on putting the oyster in my mouth, it would jump up and down in there before I could swallow it.

A few years later, when Jennie and I were walking around Marché des Enfants Rouges in the Marais we came upon a tiny restaurant that was selling oysters from Arcachon—one of the best types of oysters in France. Thinking this just might be the day to finally experience raw oysters, we decided to get a plate of them, with the disclaimer that I might back out at the nth hour.

A plate of six oysters arrived at the table. On another plate was a shot glass filled with red wine vinegar and finely chopped shallots, a wedge of lemon, some crusty bread, and a tiny wheel of sweet butter. My heart raced.

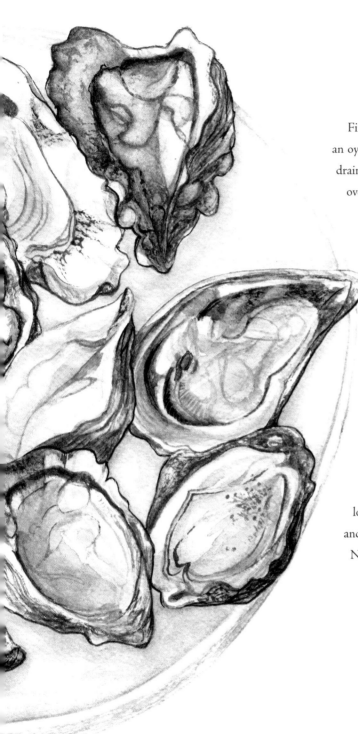

First, I watched Jennie, a recent oyster convert, eat an oyster. She detached it from the shell with her fork, drained off a bit of the liquor, and squeezed some lemon over it before sliding the whole thing into her mouth. She smiled, and I felt a bit of relief.

My turn. I picked up an oyster from the bed of seaweed it was sitting on and opened the shucked bivalve very carefully—almost like a delicate jewelry box. I struggled a bit, trying to detach the oyster from the bottom shell. With a brief squeeze of lemon juice, I popped the oyster into my mouth.

How was it? Fun. Exciting. And above all, liberating. I finally got over my fear of eating raw oysters. The flavor wasn't fishy and the oyster didn't dance in my mouth! I actually loved it. Absolutely. Utterly. I loved the flavor of the citrus with the sweet flavor of the oyster. I loved the feeling of the slippery oyster in my mouth, and I loved the taste of the ocean. I loved it all.

Now, to make up for lost time.

—Shaheen

OYSTERS WITH PICKLED RHUBARB

Although serving oysters with a wedge of lemon and finely chopped shallots in red wine vinegar is a classic, we like making things pretty with some pickled rhubarb. We like to use pink winter rhubarb for its beautiful color and delicate stems, as opposed to the more fibrous summer variety. Shucking oysters takes a bit of practice, but soon enough you will get the hang of it—sometimes, the oyster is just very stubborn and it takes extra prodding to open it up, but don't let that dissuade you. Oysters produce a briny liquid called "oyster liquor." The oyster shell should be filled with it; if it isn't, it's possible that the oyster is dead and should be discarded. It's usually easy to spot a bad oyster because the flesh isn't shiny and it has a foul smell. A little trick to know if a mollusk is very fresh: touch the black collar that surrounds its shell with the tip of a knife—if it shrinks a little, you're in business!

PREP TIME 15 minutes   SERVES 2–4

12 oysters in their shells
1–2 stems Pickled Rhubarb (recipe follows)
Coarse sea salt

Shuck the Oysters

You need a good oyster knife and a thick dish towel before you're ready to start shucking.

Use the dish towel to hold the oyster firmly, curved shell facing down, in one hand.

With the other hand, insert the tip of the oyster knife either into the hinge of the shell or along the perimeter between the top and bottom of the shell, wherever you can slip the tip of the knife inside for a bit of leverage.

Using some pressure, twist the knife back and forth until the shell snaps open, then scrape the knife along the top of the upper shell to detach the flesh from the muscle.

Remove any small pieces of shell that might have broken off and fallen inside the oyster as you were shucking it, being careful not to lose any of the flavorful "oyster liquor." Detach the flesh at the bottom of the shell as well.

Serve

Chop the Pickled Rhubarb into tiny cubes. Place 3 to 6 oysters, in their half shells, per plate on a bed of coarse sea salt. Spoon the rhubarb over the oysters. Serve with crusty bread and sweet butter.

PICKLED RHUBARB

PREP TIME 15 minutes   COOK TIME 5 minutes   PICKLING TIME 2–4 days   MAKES 1 pint jar

1 pound (450g) rhubarb

1 tablespoon (15g) sea salt

1 tablespoon (15g) sugar

2 cups (480ml) water

15–20 black peppercorns

4–5 thin slices fresh ginger

Wash, cut, and trim the rhubarb and pack it tightly into a sterilized jar.

Bring the salt, sugar, and water to a boil with the peppercorns and ginger. Turn off the heat and let it cool completely.

Pour the brine into the jar of rhubarb, making sure to submerge the rhubarb completely. The rhubarb will tend to float up. To make sure the rhubarb is well coated throughout the pickling process, give the jar a little shake every day

Let the rhubarb mixture sit at room temperature for 2 to 4 days, checking it every day. You'll know the rhubarb is ready to be used when it looks translucent and can easily be pierced with a knife without exerting much pressure. The sourness of the rhubarb will depend on the ambient temperature and the amount of time you let it steep in the brine. The longer the time, the more sour it will be. Pickled Rhubarb can be refrigerated for up to a month.

COLD-OVEN CHICKEN

This recipe for chicken—made with a mere handful of ingredients—seems too simple to result in such a spectacular dish, but the magic is all in the method. Once the chicken has been thoroughly rubbed with salt, it is packed into a cast iron pot with the aromatics, and then placed in a cold oven. The heat is then turned up, and in the end what you get is the most succulent chicken you have ever tasted. The juices brown, the garlic softens, and the chicken is incredibly moist and packed with flavor.

PREP TIME 10 minutes active, 15 minutes rest   COOK TIME 35 minutes   SERVES 4

4 free-range chicken breasts, bone in and skin on

Coarse sea salt, for rubbing the chicken

2 tablespoons extra-virgin olive oil

1 head garlic, cloves separated and peeled and germ removed, but kept whole

2 sprigs fresh rosemary

2 sprigs fresh thyme

4–5 fresh sage leaves

Peel and juice of 1 lemon (the yellow part of the peel only)

Sea salt and freshly ground black pepper

Rub the chicken all over with salt. Pull the skin up and rub the salt into the flesh, and then pull the skin back over it. Let the salted chicken rest for 15 minutes.

Coat the bottom of a cast iron pot (or an ovenproof pot) with a lid with olive oil. Add the garlic cloves, rosemary, thyme, sage, and lemon peel. Place the chicken breasts on top, skin side up. Squeeze the lemon juice over them, and then season with salt and pepper. Cover the pot with the lid.

Place the pot in a cold oven. Turn up the temperature to 450°F (225°C) and roast the chicken for 35 minutes, removing the lid for the last 15 minutes to brown the skin. To make sure the chicken is cooked, the flesh shouldn't be pink on the inside or should measure 165°F (75°C). Remove the pot from the oven and let it cool. Carve the breast off the bone to serve either whole or sliced with spoonfuls of the pan juices and garlic.

The cooking time for thighs is 45 minutes, and if you are roasting a whole chicken, it is 1 hour.

TIP While we use chicken breasts, you can also prepare a whole chicken or just thighs with the same method. Just increase the cooking time according to the instructions at the end of the recipe. When using the chicken in salads or for Potage d'Hiver (page 22), discard the herbs, shred the chicken into the pot, and coat it in its juices.

LATIN KARAAGE

Karaage is special. It's not your regular fried chicken. It is chicken coated in potato starch that yields the most exquisite golden crust. Karaage has a delicate crunch to it—the kind that makes you wish for a lot more crispy bits. In our version of karaage, we use yucca flour, instead of potato starch, to give it a Latin twist. To make the most of its unique texture, lift the chicken thighs and breasts out of the oil at least once during frying. This allows the chicken to cool and the crust to harden. Then, plunge the chicken pieces back into the oil for a final crisping. According to a Japanese friend, the rule of thumb is 5 minutes for five pieces.

We suggest serving the chicken over a smear of mayo and then topping it with a drizzle of your favorite hot sauce, a squeeze of lime, and fresh cilantro leaves for garnish.

PREP TIME 10 minutes active, 2–6 hours to marinate   COOK TIME 20 minutes   SERVES 4–6

2 garlic cloves, germ removed and mashed to a paste

2 inch (5cm) piece fresh ginger, peeled and grated

½ tablespoon light brown sugar

½ teaspoon coriander seeds, toasted and ground

3 tablespoons soy sauce

4 teaspoons sake (Japanese rice wine)

½ pound (225g) chicken thighs (boneless and skinless), cut into 1-inch (2.5cm) chunks

½ pound (225g) chicken breast (boneless and skinless), cut into 1-inch (2.5cm) strips

Vegetable oil for frying

1 cup (120g) yucca flour or potato starch

Sea salt and freshly ground black pepper

½ cup Classic Mayonnaise (page 187)

Hot sauce

Fresh limes, quartered

Fresh cilantro leaves

In a small bowl, mix together the mashed garlic, ginger, brown sugar, and coriander. Whisk in the soy sauce and sake until mixed thoroughly. Divide the marinade between two bowls. Toss the thighs and breasts separately to coat. Cover with plastic wrap and refrigerate for 2 to 6 hours.

When ready to prepare, heat two inches of vegetable oil in a deep frying pan over medium-high heat. It should be 350°F (180°C). To test whether or not the oil is hot enough, toss in a scrap of onion or garlic. The oil should bubble vigorously around the vegetable.

Combine the yucca flour (or potato starch) with salt and pepper. Coat all the chicken pieces lightly and evenly. Fry the chicken in batches, according to the size of the pan (be careful not to crowd the pieces), until the chicken is deep golden on all sides. To get a great crispy texture and golden color, lift the chicken pieces out of the oil briefly at least once during frying. Let them cool on a wire rack or in a colander. Be sure to fry the breasts and thighs separately to avoid overcooking the breasts. If you follow the five pieces for 5 minutes rule, you will find that the chicken gets cold by the time you get through all of the batches. We keep a toaster oven at 280°F (140°C) to keep the pieces warm for serving.

Set the chicken atop a smear of mayonnaise. Garnish with hot sauce, a squeeze of lime, and fresh cilantro leaves.

POTAGE D'HIVER

POTATO-LEEK SOUP WITH SHREDDED GARLIC CHICKEN

This recipe marries the classic French vichyssoise (essentially, a potato and leek soup) with its colorful Colombian counterpart, *ajiaco*. The trick to *ajiaco*, as any good Colombian cook will tell you, is to use three different types of potatoes that have varying textures. Traditionally used varieties are *criolla*, *pastusa*, and *sabanera*, but here we've given other options that work well. The soup's unique richness is created from the disintegration of soft potatoes that form the base of the soup, while firmer varieties of potatoes give the dish another degree of texture. In lieu of native Colombian *guascas* (an earthy, slightly acidic herb), we stir in chopped sorrel at the last minute, just before serving. We also use a dollop of crème fraîche, when serving, to help cool down the soup. Other toppings, such as shredded chicken, cilantro, etc., are meant to be placed on the table in separate little dishes and left up to the diners' whimsy to add to their bowls of soup. *Buen provecho!*

PREP TIME 30 minutes   COOK TIME 2½–3 hours   SERVES 4–6

8 cups (2 liters) Basic Vegetable Stock (page 184) or Chicken Stock (page 185)

2–3 ears of corn, broken or cut into halves

2 tablespoons extra-virgin olive oil

2 tablespoons (30g) salted butter

2 large leeks, white and pale green parts, minced

½ pound (250g) waxy golden potatoes (such as new potatoes), peeled and cut into 1-inch (3cm) cubes

½ pound (250g) all-purpose potatoes (such as Yukon Gold), peeled and cut into 1-inch (3cm) cubes

½ pound (250g) firm white potatoes (such as Idaho russet), peeled and cut into 1-inch (3cm) cubes

2 bay leaves

Big handful fresh sorrel

Sea salt and freshly ground black pepper

Toppings

2 Cold-Oven Chicken breasts (page 20), shredded

1 sliced avocado

Capers

Fresh cilantro

Crème fraîche

Heat the stock and cook the corn in the stock before making the soup. If you'd like the corn charred, you can either grill the cobs or cook them on the stovetop right before serving. (If you want a snack while you're getting everything ready, grill some extra corn and rub it with half a lime dipped in a mix of chili powder and salt—this was Shaheen's monsoon snack growing up in Bombay.)

Add a glug of olive oil to a large heavy pot over medium heat. Add the butter. Once sizzling, stir in the leeks and cook them until they're very soft but not browned (about 10 to 15 minutes).

Add the stock, potatoes, and bay leaves. Season with salt and pepper. Bring the soup to a boil and then reduce the heat to a gentle simmer. Let it cook until the white potatoes are very tender and the waxy golden potatoes have dissolved completely (about 2½ hours). Skim the foam from the top whenever it forms. If the potatoes are soft but not completely broken down, you can use an immersion blender briefly. If the soup thickens too much, add extra stock as necessary. Just before serving, stir in the sorrel leaves

Ladle the soup into bowls and place half a corn cob in each bowl.

Serve the soup along with shredded Cold-Oven Chicken breasts, avocado slices, capers, cilantro, and crème fraîche for garnish.

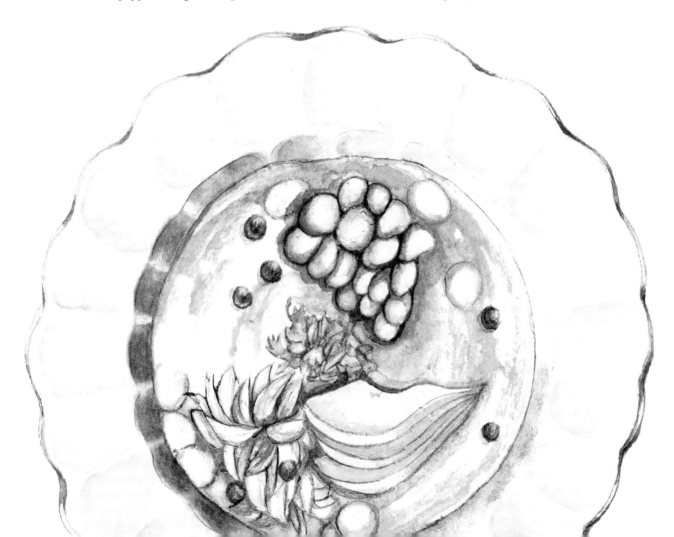

FOIE GRAS ROYALE

WITH ARUGULA, BASIL, FRESH FIGS, IBERICO HAM, AND BUTTER CROUTONS

Right in the heart of Paris sits Les Halles, the namesake Métro station for the central food market of Paris that once stood there—the market that has been immortalized by Émile Zola in *The Belly of Paris* and in black and white by the famed photographer Robert Doisneau. An important street for us is Rue Montmartre—for cooking equipment, baking supplies, and a little shop through a courtyard called Foie Gras Luxe (26, rue Montmartre, 75001 Paris), where we generally buy our guilty pleasure. For a bit more of a wander, you can walk up to Rue Montorgueil and soak in the atmosphere of the busy food-filled street. This recipe for foie gras custard is a version of what Shaheen learned to make at Alain Ducasse. It has a wonderful silken texture. A ladleful of the custard per ramekin is plenty because of its sheer richness. The greens and figs bring freshness, the croutons add a much needed crunchy contrast to the smooth custard, and the Iberico ham takes the indulgence level up even higher. *Mon Dieu!*

PREP TIME 30–40 minutes   COOK TIME 30 minutes   SERVES 4–6

Foie Gras Custard

- 4 ounces (112g) raw foie gras
- 1 cup (240 ml) light cream
- 2 eggs
- 1 egg yolk
- ½ teaspoon sea salt
- Melted butter, to coat the ramekins

Croutons

- 2 slices of white bread
- 1 tablespoon (15ml) extra-virgin olive oil
- 3 tablespoons (45g) butter, cut into cubes + more as needed

To Serve

- 1 tablespoon white balsamic vinegar
- 1 tablespoon extra-virgin olive oil
- 1 tablespoon hazelnut oil
- Handful baby arugula
- 6–10 fresh basil leaves
- 4 fresh figs, quartered
- 4–6 slices Iberico ham
- Sea salt and freshly ground black pepper

Foie Gras Custard

To make a smooth foie gras custard, it is important to devein the foie gras (you could also buy deveined and vacuum-packed foie gras from speciality food stores). In the middle of each lobe, there's a thick main vein that breaks up into tiny branches. For the purpose of this recipe it's okay to have the foie gras broken down because we are going to purée it all. Work with your fingers to probe for the main vein, feeling from the underside of the lobe to find the structure of the branches. (You can use the tip of a paring knife to help you move the flesh out of the way without breaking the web.) Remove the vein with the greatest care to avoid breaking the branches, and then discard it.

Preheat the oven to 250°F (120°C). In a small saucepan, heat the cream until warm—it does not need to boil.

In a bowl, add the eggs, egg yolk, foie gras, and salt and stir together. Pour the warm cream into the bowl. Blend the mixture with an immersion blender. Pour it into a clean bowl through a fine mesh sieve.

Brush 4 to 6 ramekins or 4 small individual cocottes with butter and divide the foie gras custard among them leaving some room at the top for the garnishes. Cover tightly with plastic wrap. Make sure the plastic doesn't touch the surface of the custard. Carefully place the ramekins in a baking dish filled with water about a third of the way up.

Bake for 25 to 30 minutes, or until set. Keep warm.

Croutons

Cut the crusts off of the sliced white bread. Then cut the bread into tiny cubes. It is helpful to use bread that is a few days old. For perfectly clean cuts, freeze the bread for a few hours before slicing. Heat a nonstick frying pan on medium heat and add a splash of olive oil and all of the butter. When the butter has foamed up, add the pieces of cubed bread and stir until evenly coated in fat. Continue to stir the bread and cook until it's a crispy, golden brown. Depending on how dry the bread is, it may absorb more or less fat. If you see that the croutons aren't sizzling, but are browning unevenly from the heat of the pan, then add another couple tablespoons of butter. Once cooked, drain the croutons on paper towels.

Assemble

Make a vinaigrette by stirring together the white balsamic vinegar, salt, and pepper. Drizzle in the oils in a thin stream and whisk until a thick emulsion forms.

In a bowl toss the arugula, basil, and figs with the vinaigrette. Place a handful of the salad on one side of each ramekin of foie gras, a slice of Iberico ham on the other side, and sprinkle some butter croutons over the top, while still leaving room for the foie gras custard to peek through.

PECAN CRUSTED RACK OF LAMB
WITH PARSNIP PURÉE AND CHIPS

You can ask your butcher to prepare the lamb for you so that the bones are "frenched"—the meat is cut away from the ends of the rib and a large part of the bone is exposed. Make sure the bones are absolutely clean of any meat, otherwise tiny bits will burn and the rack won't look pretty.

PREP TIME 30 minutes   COOK TIME 25 minutes   SERVES 4–6

1 frenched rack of lamb with 12 chops (about 2 pounds/1kg)

3 tablespoons extra-virgin olive oil, divided

2 cups (350g) Basic Vegetable Stock (page 184)

1 sprig fresh rosemary

½ cup (50g) pecans, finely chopped

3 garlic cloves, germ removed and finely chopped

1½ tablespoons fresh rosemary leaves, finely chopped

1 tablespoon fresh thyme leaves, finely chopped

1 tablespoon fresh flat-leaf parsley leaves, finely chopped

Zest of 1 lemon

1 tablespoon (15ml) maple syrup

1 tablespoon extra-virgin olive oil

2 teaspoons Dijon mustard

Sea salt and freshly ground black pepper

Preheat the oven to 400°F (200°C). One hour before cooking, remove the lamb from the refrigerator and trim off any silver skin (the white-and-silver-colored membrane that covers the bone side of the rack) and visible stamp marks. If the lamb is very fatty, trim off excess fat, but be sure to leave at least ¼ inch (5mm) on the meat to keep it from getting too dry while it cooks. Score the fat side in a crisscross pattern. Wrap foil around the exposed bones to keep them from burning. Place the meat in a baking dish and season it with salt and pepper.

Heat 1 tablespoon of olive oil in a large, heavy skillet and brown the lamb on all sides. Return the lamb to the baking dish. Keeping the skillet hot over medium heat, make a jus: Add a ladleful of the stock to the hot pan and swirl it around to deglaze the browned bits in the bottom of the pan. Scrape it lightly, if necessary. Bring the mixture to a boil, and then add the remaining stock. Add the sprig of rosemary to the pan and reduce the mixture to a quarter of the original volume. When reduced, season the jus with salt and pepper. Pass the jus through a fine mesh sieve to remove any bits, and keep it warm until ready to serve.

Mix together the pecans, garlic, rosemary, thyme, parsley, lemon zest, 1 teaspoon salt, pepper, maple syrup, and 1 tablespoon of olive oil. Rub the fatty side of the lamb with Dijon mustard and then pat on the pecan mixture so that it adheres to the mustard.

Place the rack, pecan side up, on a baking dish in the middle of the oven.

Roast the lamb for about 15 minutes for medium rare or until an instant read thermometer reads 120–125°F (49–52°C). Turn off the heat and let the meat sit for another 5 minutes before removing it from the oven. Let it rest, covered, for another 5 to 7 minutes before slicing.

When ready to serve, slice each lamb chop individually and plate it with parsnip purée and chips. Pour a little bit of the jus on the lamb or serve it on the side.

PARSNIP PURÉE AND CHIPS

PREP TIME 10 minutes   COOK TIME 30 minutes   SERVES 4

1 pound (450g) parsnips

2 sprigs thyme

1 bay leaf

8–10 black peppercorns

6 tablespoons (90g) butter

Water, to cover

Peanut oil for deep-frying the chips

Sea salt and freshly ground black pepper

For the Purée

Reserve 1 parsnip for the chips.

Peel and chop the remaining parsnips into 1-inch (2.5cm) pieces. Tie the thyme, bay leaf, and peppercorns in a muslin cloth. It is an extra step, but it is worth the trouble to avoid having to pick through the cooked parsnips for the black peppercorn and tiny leaves of thyme.

In a saucepan, add the chopped parsnips, about half the butter, salt, and the herb-and-peppercorn packet. Add enough water to cover the parsnips completely.

Cook on a simmer for about 20 minutes or until the parsnips are completely tender.

Drain the parsnips and purée them. When they've cooled a bit, stir in pieces of the remaining cold butter. Keep warm.

For the Chips

In a saucepan, heat about 2 inches (5cm) of oil over medium heat. Bring it up to 285°F (140°C) and then turn the heat down to low to maintain the temperature. You can also test if the oil is hot enough by adding one slice of parsnip. If it floats to the top and bubbles around the edges, the oil is ready. Thinly slice the parsnips directly into the saucepan with the help of a mandoline and fry until light golden.

Drain on paper towels and season with salt and pepper.

PORK BELLY WITH ROASTED RED KURI SQUASH
AND PISTACHIO PARSLEY PESTO

Three elements: Buttery, melting pork belly. Velvety, sweet, maple-roasted kuri squash. Crunchy pistachio pesto packed with flavor.

For one of our largest events at HEC (École des Hautes Études Commerciales) Paris, we cooked this pork belly with an Asian twist, served it in steamed buns (400 of them!), and loaded them with pickled cucumbers, cilantro, fermented hot sauce, and roasted cashews. We cooked through the night while Arjun, Shaheen's husband, was our kitchen apprentice, cashier, and runner rolled into one. We worked for twenty-three hours straight and then, when it was all done, we couldn't feel our feet.

The pork belly is easy to make—you just need to plan ahead because of the overnight curing process. Also, because the process is fairly lengthy, it is probably better to make a large quantity. You can use as much as you need and then freeze the rest for later. We have put it to use as a topping for soups, a sandwich filling, and even chopped up into an omelette.

PREP TIME 20 minutes active, 6–8 hours rest   COOK TIME 3 hours   SERVES 8

Pork Belly

- 2 pounds (900g) slab pork belly, skin and bones removed
- 3 tablespoons coarse sea salt
- 3 tablespoons sugar
- 2 bay leaves
- 4–5 sprigs fresh thyme
- 6 garlic cloves, germ removed
- 12–15 black peppercorns

Roasted Kuri Squash

- 2 red kuri squash (Japanese squash or Baby Red Hubbard squash)
- 4 garlic cloves, germ removed and crushed
- 4 sprigs rosemary
- 2 teaspoons Espelette pepper, Aleppo pepper, sweet paprika, or 1 teaspoon ground cayenne
- 2 tablespoons maple syrup
- 3 tablespoons extra-virgin olive oil
- Sea salt and freshly ground black pepper
- Pistachio Parsley Pesto (page 193)

Pork Belly

Place the pork belly in a shallow roasting pan.

Mix the salt and sugar together and rub it over the meat. Cover with plastic wrap and leave to cure in the refrigerator for 6 to 8 hours.

The next day, preheat the oven to 440°F (225°C). Drain off any liquid that has pooled in the pan. Rinse the meat with cold water and pat it dry.

Place the meat in a clean roasting pan. Tuck the bay leaves, thyme, garlic, and peppercorns under the meat.

Roast the meat in the oven for 40 to 45 minutes until it is golden brown. If it is browning too quickly, cover the pan with aluminum foil. Next, turn the heat down to 240°F (120°C) and continue to cook for another 60 to 90 minutes; when you cut into a piece of the meat from the side, it should be soft and fall apart. Let the meat cool.

To get perfectly clean cuts of the pork belly, tightly cover the meat in plastic wrap and refrigerate it until chilled.

Cut the pork belly into thick slices, about 3 inches (7.5cm) in length, with a sharp knife. Just before you are ready to serve, brown the meat on both sides in a hot pan. You don't need to add any oil—there is enough fat in the pork.

Once browned, lay the rectangles on paper towels briefly to soak up the excess fat, and then transfer the meat to a serving plate.

Roasted Kuri Squash

Preheat the oven to 400°F (200°C). Cut the squash in half, then scoop out the seeds, and discard them. (There's no need to peel the squash—the skin helps retain the shape of the squash while it's roasting and can easily be removed later. The skin may be edible, too, depending on the squash.)

Next, cut each half into ½-inch to ¾-inch (1.5 to 2cm) crescents. In a bowl, mix together the garlic, rosemary, pepper or paprika, maple syrup, and olive oil. Season the mixture with salt and pepper. Toss together with the squash.

Lay the pieces of squash in a baking pan lined with parchment paper, making sure the pieces don't touch each other. Pour out any loose spice mixture on top of the squash.

Roast for 25 to 30 minutes, flipping the pieces halfway through the cooking time.

Assemble

On each plate, lay 2 slices of pork belly and 3 to 5 slices of the roasted squash (depending on the size). Spoon some of the Pistachio Pesto on the side and serve.

CLASSIC STEAK TARTARE

WITH SOURDOUGH CROSTINI

We prefer the texture of hand-cut filet mignon, rather than ground beef steak, for our tartare. The trick to cutting the steak into very small cubes is to freeze it first, for 45 minutes to 1 hour, allowing it to firm up a bit. Serve it with plenty of crostini on the side.

PREP TIME 20 minutes active, 1 hour in the freezer   SERVES 4

1 tablespoon Dijon mustard

1 teaspoon sherry vinegar

7 tablespoons red onion, finely diced

2 tablespoons fresh flat-leaf parsley leaves, finely chopped

2½ tablespoons capers, drained

1 teaspoon paprika (sweet or smoked)

½ teaspoon lemon zest

Small pinch cayenne pepper, or to taste

4 tablespoons (60ml) best-quality extra-virgin olive oil + extra for greasing molds

1 pound (450g) filet mignon, cut into ¼-inch (6mm) dice

4 small organic egg yolks

4 cornichons, thinly sliced

Small handful fresh chives, finely chopped

Sea salt and freshly ground black pepper

In a bowl, whisk together the Dijon mustard, sherry vinegar, onions, parsley, capers, paprika, lemon zest, cayenne pepper, ½ teaspoon sea salt, and ¼ teaspoon black pepper. Once well combined, drizzle in olive oil while whisking to create a uniform emulsion. Taste for seasoning and add additional salt, pepper, and more spice to taste. Add the meat to the bowl and toss thoroughly to coat.

Divide the meat mixture equally into four parts and, using a round ring mold (lightly brushed with olive oil), place the tartare onto the center of each plate. Carefully remove the ring. If you don't have a ring you can use a

steel ½ cup measure brushed with olive oil or you can lightly grease your hands with a little olive oil and form a mound in the center of the plate.

In the center of each portion of tartare, gently place a raw egg yolk.

Scatter the sliced cornichons around the plate, drizzle with olive oil, and sprinkle with the chopped chives. Serve immediately with Sourdough Crostini.

SOURDOUGH CROSTINI

PREP TIME 5 minutes   COOK TIME 10 minutes
SERVES 4–6

½ White Country Loaf (page 73) or 1 baguette

Extra-virgin olive oil

Sea salt

Preheat the oven to 400°F (200°C). Slice the bread diagonally and arrange it in a single layer on a baking sheet. Brush the bread lightly on both sides with olive oil and sprinkle it with sea salt. Bake the bread for about 10 minutes, flipping it halfway through, until it is toasted, but still slightly soft in the middle.

ASPARAGUS, GREEN GARLIC, HAZELNUTS, AND FETA

Come April, you will find the open-air markets of Paris abloom with bunches of asparagus in green, violet, and white hues. The French have a particular affinity for the white variety, which they revere for its tenderness and sweet undertones. This recipe works for any color or thickness of asparagus. Thick stalks take slightly longer to cook than young, skinny stalks, which only require a couple of minutes in the pan.

PREP TIME 10 minutes   COOK TIME 10 minutes   SERVES 4

¼ cup (60g) hazelnuts, reserving some for garnish

1 tablespoon (15ml) extra-virgin olive oil

3 tablespoons (45g) butter

1 pound (450g) fresh asparagus

1 bunch wild garlic or garlic ramps

Juice of 1 lemon

4 ounces (112g) fresh feta

Sea salt and freshly ground black pepper

Preheat the oven to 325°F (160°C). Toast the hazelnuts on a baking sheet in a single layer for 12 to 15 minutes, or until they're golden brown throughout. Let the nuts cool slightly, then rub off the papery skin. Chop coarsely.

In a large skillet over medium heat, combine the olive oil and butter, swirling the pan until the butter melts and starts to foam. Add the asparagus to the pan and increase the heat to medium-high. Sauté, shaking frequently, for about 4 minutes, or until the asparagus is tender enough to pierce through yet crisp to the bite. Add the wild garlic to the same pan and give it a quick stir until it softens and becomes fragrant. Add the lemon juice, scraping the bottom of the pan with a wooden spoon.

Divide the asparagus among the plates and then pour the remaining liquid from the pan over the top. Crumble the feta and sprinkle the remaining chopped hazelnuts over the top. Finish off with salt and pepper.

TIP Because wild garlic and garlic ramps have such a short season, you can substitute with scallions when you can't find them. You'll need to cook the scallions longer to get a nice char before mixing them with the rest of the ingredients.

SQUASH, CHESTNUT, AND RICOTTA RAVIOLI

WITH SAGE BROWN BUTTER AND ALMONDS

We have a special fondness for chestnuts, so as soon as Shaheen learned to make this recipe at Alain Ducasse at The Dorchester, we exchanged notes on Skype and got down to making it in our own kitchens in London and Bogotá. All of the flavors work together in such harmony—the subtle bitterness of the Amaretti cookies melds beautifully with the squash and also helps bind the other ingredients in the dish.

PREP TIME 1 hour   COOK TIME 1 hour 15 minutes   SERVES 8

Squash, Chestnut, and Ricotta Ravioli

- 1 small butternut squash (about 1½ pounds/675g), deseeded and cut in half
- 3 tablespoons extra-virgin olive oil
- 1 tablespoon honey
- 4 sprigs thyme
- 1 tablespoon butter
- 2 garlic cloves, germ removed and finely chopped
- 1 bunch baby spinach leaves (about 100g), ribs removed
- ½ cup (120g) cooked chestnuts, finely chopped and divided
- ¼ cup (60ml) dry white wine
- ½ cup (120g) Amaretti cookies
- ⅔ cup (150g) ricotta
- ¼ cup (45g) Pecorino Romano, finely grated
- 1 egg yolk
- Zest of 1 lemon
- ¼ teaspoon grated nutmeg
- 1 pound (450g) Fresh Egg Pasta dough (page 199)

Egg Wash

- 2 egg yolks
- 1 tablespoon milk

Sage Brown Butter

- 1½ sticks (12 tablespoons/170g) salted butter
- 10–12 fresh sage leaves

Assemble

- ⅓ cup (80g) almonds, toasted and roughly chopped
- ½ cup (90g) Pecorino Romano

Sea salt and freshly ground black pepper

Squash, Chestnut, and Ricotta Ravioli

Preheat the oven to 400°F (200°C). Place the butternut squash, cut side up, on a baking sheet and drizzle with olive oil and honey. Season to taste with salt and pepper and scatter thyme sprigs across the tops of the squash halves. Bake until soft, about 45 minutes. Remove the squash from the oven and let cool slightly before scooping out the flesh directly into a food processor.

While the squash is roasting, prepare the Fresh Egg Pasta dough (page 199).

In a medium skillet, heat 1 tablespoon butter and a glug of olive oil over medium heat. Add the chopped garlic and cook until fragrant, about 1 minute. Place the spinach leaves in the skillet and cook, stirring frequently, until wilted. Add half of the chopped chestnuts and pour in the white wine. Reduce the wine by two-thirds, or until it has been mostly absorbed by the chestnuts and spinach. Remove the skillet from the heat and set it aside to cool.

Add the remaining chestnuts, Amaretti cookies, ricotta, Pecorino Romano, egg yolk, lemon zest, and nutmeg to the food processor. Pulse until smooth. The mixture should be firm and hold its shape when you scoop it out with a spoon. If it's too soft, add more chestnuts and ricotta. Give the wilted spinach and chestnuts a quick chop and stir into the squash mixture. Season to taste with sea salt and freshly ground black pepper.

Make the egg wash by whisking together the yolks and milk.

Roll out the ravioli sheets according to the instructions in the pasta dough recipe. Place 2 long ravioli sheets side by side and drop heaping teaspoon-size mounds of the filling, about 2 inches (5cm) apart, on one of the sheets. Brush the egg wash on the dough around the filling. Place the second sheet directly on top of the first. Using your fingers, gently press on the dough around each mound, to push out any trapped air and form a seal. With a fluted pastry wheel or a knife, cut the pasta between the squares to form individual ravioli. (Save the scraps for rolling out extra dough, if needed.) Make sure the edges of the ravioli are well sealed before cooking.

Cook the ravioli in salted boiling water, a few pieces at a time, until the pasta floats to the top and the dough is translucent, about 5 to 7 minutes. Repeat in batches as necessary. Drain the pasta and set it aside in a bowl with a little bit of olive oil to prevent the ravioli from sticking to each other.

Sage Brown Butter

Melt the butter over medium heat in a heavy bottomed pan. Once the butter is melted, add the sage leaves and cook until crispy. Remove the sage and reserve on the side. Continue to cook the butter on a low heat until the milk solids in the butter turn golden. Take the pan off the heat immediately as the butter will turn darker in its own heat.

Assemble

Transfer the brown butter to a large sauté pan over low heat and toss the cooked ravioli to coat. When warmed through, transfer to plates and garnish with crispy sage and almonds. Serve with shavings of Pecorino.

SHARING PLATTERS

There's something so endearing (and so Parisian) about friends and acquaintances stuffed like sardines into a tiny space to share a great meal. There is a dynamic ebb and flow of people in the kitchen, trying the food, bringing us wine, and sharing their family recipes with good music and happy chatter. From sharing Thanksgiving with multicultural friends to the final good-bye party, when we danced late into the night, we've made many such happy memories in Jennie's 10th arrondissement attic. And when the crowds got too big for us to fit into a 300-square foot space, we moved the party to a favorite park, where we cooked picnic-style meals and made the loveliest Citrus-Scented Baklava, which our friends still rave about after all these years.

We hope these recipes will bring your near and dear ones together around sharing platters or in the kitchen to make happy memories of your own.

APPLE, FENNEL, AND KOHLRABI SALAD

WITH SHAVED MANCHEGO AND CANDIED WALNUTS

This salad really comes alive with the texture and bite of a firm, aged Manchego and the spicy crunch of candied walnuts. Don't be shy with the black pepper—it works brilliantly with the honey. For this, we like to take the effort to crush or coarsely grind black pepper by chopping with a sharp knife or pounding in a mortar. Or if you have a Peugeot pepper mill, you can simply set it to the coarsest grind.

As for the fennel, apple, and kohlrabi, it's important to keep the slices really thin for the perfect crunch. When buying fennel, look for the fattest and whitest bulbs—they'll give you the greatest yield and a firm and crispy texture. The thinner bulbs aren't as flavorful and are quite fibrous all the way through.

PREP TIME 20 minutes   COOK TIME 15 minutes   SERVES 4–6

Candied Walnuts
- ½ cup (50g) walnuts, halved
- 1–2 tablespoons honey

Apple Cider Vinaigrette
- ½ tablespoon apple cider vinegar
- ½ tablespoon Dijon mustard
- ¼ teaspoon fennel seeds, toasted and ground
- ½ tablespoon honey
- 3 tablespoons best-quality extra-virgin olive oil

- 2 fennel bulbs
- 2 Granny Smith apples
- 1 large kohlrabi bulb
- 1 small package (200g) mixed baby lettuce
- 3 ounces (85g) 12-month Manchego, thinly shaved

- Sea salt and freshly ground black pepper

Candied Walnuts

Preheat the oven to 350°F (175°C).

Place the walnuts in a small bowl and toss to coat lightly with honey, salt, and pepper to taste. Line a baking sheet with parchment paper and spread the walnuts on it. Roast for 10 to 12 minutes, tossing the nuts halfway through to ensure even cooking. Slide the sheet of parchment paper onto a cooling rack and spread the nuts out in a single layer to cool.

Apple Cider Vinaigrette

Combine the vinegar, mustard, fennel seeds, and honey in a small bowl. Add salt, and then slowly whisk in the olive oil until the mixture thickens and takes on a shiny appearance. Add black pepper to taste.

Trim the stalk and fronds of the fennel. You can use them as an aromatic in a Basic Vegetable Stock (page 184) or Fish Stock (page 185). Cut the fennel bulb vertically in half. Scoop out the tough core and discard it. Slice the fennel halves diagonally, making sure to keep the slices as thin as possible. Halve and core the apples, and cut them into thin slices. Remove any knobby bits from the kohlrabi, cut it into quarters, and then into thin slices. If you have a mandoline, it is a lot quicker to get perfectly thin slices of apple, fennel, and kohlrabi.

Add the fennel, apple, and kohlrabi slices, along with the lettuce, half the candied walnuts, and half the Manchego to a large mixing bowl. Toss to coat with the vinaigrette, starting with half and then adding little by little to ensure that you don't overdress the salad.

Transfer the salad to a vinaigrette-coated serving bowl. Top with the remaining walnuts and Manchego. Serve immediately.

QUINOA SALAD
WITH BUTTERNUT SQUASH, POMEGRANATE, FETA, AND HAZELNUTS

This method comes straight from a Bolivian friend of ours who grew up in the Andes eating quinoa. The perfect texture is one that retains a little bit of a bite at its core even after it's done cooking. First, rinse the quinoa several times. Quinoa has a natural soapy coating that acts as an insecticide. It should be rinsed off, or the quinoa will taste bitter when you cook it. Boxed quinoa is usually prerinsed, but give it a few good rinses anyway, just to be sure. Rather than cooking quinoa in plenty of water, and then draining it, as you would if you were preparing pasta, quinoa should be treated like rice: bring it to a rolling boil in exactly two times the amount of stock as quinoa. You then reduce it to a gentle simmer and let the quinoa cook, until it has absorbed all of the stock and has just about popped open. Overcooking, along with under-rinsing, can make quinoa taste bitter and destroy the perfect chew that makes it such a lovely and versatile seed.

PREP TIME 30 minutes   COOK TIME 45 minutes   SERVES 4–6

1 medium butternut squash, deseeded and cut into 1½-inch (4cm) cubes

5 tablespoons extra-virgin olive oil, divided

1 teaspoon fresh thyme leaves, chopped

¾ cup (85g) hazelnuts

1½ cups (250g) quinoa

3 cups (720ml) Basic Vegetable Stock (page 184)

2 medium leeks (white and light green parts only), sliced into thin rounds

2 cups (100g) fresh arugula

4 ounces (112g) feta

¾ cup (100g) pomegranate seeds

Hazelnut Oil Vinaigrette

1 tablespoon (15ml) white balsamic vinegar

¼ cup (60ml) hazelnut oil

Sea salt and freshly ground black pepper

Preheat the oven to 425°F (215°C). In a large bowl, combine the cubed squash with 3 tablespoons olive oil, thyme, and salt and pepper. Spread the squash cubes on a baking sheet in a single layer and roast for 25 to 30 minutes, until the squash is golden and tender.

After removing the squash, lower the heat to 350°F (275°C). Toast the hazelnuts in one layer on a baking sheet, until they're fragrant and the skins look dark and papery. Remove the hazelnuts from the oven, let them cool slightly, and then rub them between the palms of your hands to remove the skin. Don't worry about skin that's firmly stuck.

Prepare the quinoa by rinsing it several times under cold water and then draining it.

Heat the vegetable stock in a pot. Bring it to a simmer.

Add 2 tablespoons of olive oil to a medium-size saucepan and sauté the leeks until they're just golden (about 10 minutes). Season generously with pepper (hold off on the salt), and then add the quinoa, sautéing until it starts to toast with a nutty fragrance. Stir frequently and make sure it doesn't stick to the bottom of the pan. Add the hot stock to the pan and give the quinoa a good stir. Place the lid on the pan and turn up the heat to high. Once the stock is boiling vigorously, turn down the heat and continue to cook the quinoa until it has absorbed all of the liquid, about 10 to 15 minutes. You'll know the quinoa is done, and has just the right texture and bite, when it looks like it has popped open, with its "tail" out.

Remove the quinoa from the heat and let it sit, covered, for about 10 minutes. Spread the quinoa in a thin layer on a baking sheet or a shallow bowl to let it cool quickly.

While the quinoa is cooling, prepare the vinaigrette by first whisking together the white balsamic vinegar and salt to taste. Once the salt is dissolved, whisk in the hazelnut oil. Season to taste with black pepper and additional salt as necessary.

Once the quinoa has cooled, toss all ingredients (except the feta and a few pomegranate seeds) to coat with the white balsamic vinaigrette. Crumble the feta directly on top and finish with a sprinkle of pomegranate seeds, salt, and pepper.

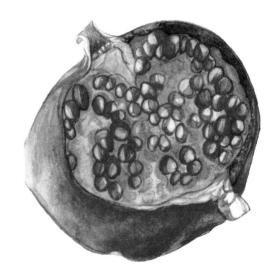

ROASTED SPICED EGGPLANT

WITH MOORISH TOMATO SAUCE, FRESH GOAT CHEESE,
AND CILANTRO LEAVES

France is a country with an unabashed love of ham and boasts an exhaustive variety of smoked and cured and herb-crusted haunches. And although hams were featured regularly on our sandwich menus, the roasted eggplant still emerged as a favorite among our customers, both vegetarian and otherwise. This version of roasted eggplant, infused with the spice and warmth of our slow-cooked tomato sauce and topped with creamy goat cheese and cilantro, leaves nothing to be desired. You can ask Karen, our resident eggplant lover.

PREP TIME 15 minutes   COOK TIME 1 hour   SERVES 6–8

3–4 garlic cloves, germ removed and minced

¼ cup (60ml) extra-virgin olive oil

4 medium eggplants

8 sprigs fresh thyme

2 cups (480ml) Moorish Tomato Sauce (opposite)

4 ounces (112g) fresh goat cheese

Fresh cilantro leaves

Sea salt and freshly ground black pepper

Preheat the oven to 400°F (200°C). Mix together the garlic and the olive oil.

Slice the eggplants in half lengthwise. Score the flesh in a diagonal crisscross pattern to make 1-inch (3cm) cubes. Gently splay open the halves to rub the garlic oil into the slits. Drizzle generously with olive oil and season with salt and pepper.

Arrange the thyme sprigs on a baking sheet. Place the eggplants, cut side down on the thyme sprigs, and roast it for 40 minutes.

Flip over the eggplants so that the cut sides face up, and then spread the tomato sauce (recipe on facing page) over them evenly. Cook the eggplants for an additional 10 to 15 minutes or so until the tomato sauce begins to bubble.

Remove the eggplants from the oven and serve them on a platter and sprinkle each half with fresh goat cheese and cilantro.

MOORISH TOMATO SAUCE with CUMIN, ORANGE ZEST, and CINNAMON

In many Mediterranean cuisines, cinnamon is a key complement to meat and other savory delights. It adds an unexpected hint of warmth and comfort to stews and roasts. Often times, Jennie's Kurdish neighbor would cook lamb redolent with cinnamon that perfumed the corridors of the entire building. We never got a taste of it, but whenever we cook with cinnamon we are reminded of cooking together in the 10th arrondissement of Paris.

PREP TIME 10 minutes   COOK TIME 45 minutes–1 hour   MAKES about 2 cups

3 pounds (1.4kg) fresh ripe tomato or 2 15.5 ounce (400g) cans

1 large orange, zest and juice

1 teaspoon cumin seeds

¼ cup (60ml) extra-virgin olive oil

1 sprig fresh rosemary

4 sprigs fresh thyme

2 medium onions, finely chopped

4 garlic cloves, germ removed and finely chopped

1 fresh Serrano or red jalapeño pepper (stem removed, deseeded, and finely chopped)

1 small red bell pepper (stem removed, deseeded, and finely chopped)

6 pieces of Tomato Confit (page 197), finely chopped

1 tablespoon honey (optional)

1 cinnamon stick

1 bay leaf

Sea salt and freshly ground black pepper

Prepare the tomatoes by first cutting them in half lengthwise. With a coarse grater, keep your hand very flat and grate each tomato half until you reach the skin. Repeat for all the tomatoes and discard the skins (or use them for a stock later on). Reserve the pulp.

With a sharp vegetable peeler, peel a large strip of orange zest, making sure to avoid the bitter white pith. Juice the orange.

Heat a medium-size saucepan over medium heat and toast the cumin seeds until they're fragrant, about 3 to 5 minutes. Remove the cumin seeds from pan and, while they are still warm (and crumble easily), pound them finely in a mortar and pestle or crush them with a rolling pin.

Return the saucepan to medium-high heat. Add the olive oil and then the rosemary and thyme. Give the mixture a good stir and then add the onions, garlic, chili pepper, red bell pepper, tomato confit, and ground cumin. Cook for about 10 minutes, until the onions begin to brown around the edges. Add the orange juice to deglaze the pan, scraping up any brown bits that have stuck to the bottom. Once the juice has reduced by about half, add the tomato pulp, orange zest, cinnamon stick, bay leaf, a teaspoon of sea salt, and a pinch of black pepper.

Bring the sauce to a boil and then immediately reduce the heat to a gentle simmer. Let the sauce cook, uncovered, until it is reduced and thickened, about 30 to 40 minutes. The fresh tomatoes will take longer than the canned tomatoes. Discard the rosemary stalk, thyme twigs, cinnamon, and orange zest. Taste to season with additional salt, pepper, and honey (if too acidic).

CASABLANCA COUSCOUS

North African communities from Morocco, Tunisia, and Algeria have a strong presence in the outer arrondissements of Paris, and that's where we go to get our fix of couscous and kebabs. Before heading back into the Métro, it is de rigueur to stop at one of the local corner shops—small spaces crammed with everything from pots and pans to every nut imaginable, tubs of fresh feta, and harissa galore.

Jennie learned this method of preparing couscous on a weekend trip to Casablanca. Unlike the semi-instant method of drowning the grains in boiling water, and then fluffing back up with a fork, this approach yields beads of semolina that burst with a flavorful richness that you have probably never experienced in couscous before. The grains are traditionally steamed at intervals over a simmering pot of water, within a basket of tiny holes called a *couscoussier*. It works much like a double boiler, but the inner pan is perforated for the steam to pass through. When the couscous is quickly removed and diligently rubbed by hand with alternating dashes of olive oil and sea salt, the grains are coaxed into realizing their true flavor. Our method is an adaptation inspired from the original that is not quite as time consuming but still renders an incredibly delicious and delicate result. It is best to use high-quality extra-virgin olive oil because its flavor is prominent—we prefer really green, fresh-tasting olive oil, but a spicy variety could also do the trick.

PREP TIME 30 minutes   COOK TIME 30 minutes   SERVES 6–8

Couscous

- 1 teaspoon (6–8 threads) saffron
- 2/3 cup (100g) raisins
- 2 cups (350g) couscous
- ¼ cup (60ml) extra-virgin olive oil
- 2 tablespoon (60g) salted butter, softened
- A handful of fresh mint leaves, cut into thin strips

Vegetables

- 2 medium leeks (white and light green parts only), finely diced
- 1 orange or yellow bell pepper, cut into ¼-inch (6mm) dice
- 2 medium zucchinis, sliced into ¼-inch (6mm) rounds
- ¾ cup (100g) almonds, toasted and cut in half

  Sea salt and freshly ground black pepper
  Extra-virgin olive oil

Couscous

Put the saffron in a small bowl and pour about 2 to 3 tablespoons of boiling water over it. Cover. Let it steep gently for 5 to-10 minutes until the water turns a bright color.

In a separate bowl, cover the raisins with boiling water and allow them to rehydrate as you prepare the couscous.

Place the couscous in a wide ceramic bowl (the bigger the better to give yourself adequate working space and to avoid spilling hundreds of miniature grains) and spread them evenly across the bottom. Bring 4 cups of water to a boil and then reduce the heat to a simmer. Keep the water at a gentle simmer while you prepare the couscous.

Drizzle the saffron-infused water over the couscous and then add the boiling water, one-quarter cup at a time. Let the couscous cool for a minute or two. Add a small pinch of salt and a dash of olive oil and then rub the couscous between the palms of your hands in a circular direction. Work through all of the couscous, rubbing continuously during each addition of water, to ensure that you spread the ingredients throughout. Repeat at least 5 times with the boiling water, olive oil, and salt. (You may not need all of the water. Typically, it's one-and-a-half times the amount of couscous. The amount used depends on the size of the grain, the temperature of the water and how quickly the couscous cools in the large mixing bowl.) Just before the last addition of boiling water, season to taste with salt and pepper. Continue until the grains have just lost their hard center but still have plenty of texture and bite.

Once the couscous has absorbed enough liquid so that it is tender and just slightly firm, rub in the butter until thoroughly mixed.

Vegetables

Heat a large heavy skillet over medium-high heat and then swirl in 2 tablespoons (30ml) of olive oil. Stir in the leeks and cook until golden. Remove the leeks from the pan. Add the yellow or orange peppers to the pan and reduce the heat to medium. Add more oil if necessary. Stir occasionally until the edges start to brown and the peppers have softened. Finally, remove the peppers. Swirl in additional olive oil and sear the zucchini rounds (about 2 to 3 minutes on each side). Remove from the heat.

Assemble

In a large bowl or platter, toss the couscous together with leeks, pepper, zucchini, almonds, drained raisins, and mint leaves before serving. Finish with a drizzle of olive oil. The dish can hold its own, but it is really good alongside Slow-Roasted Rosemary Lamb (page 52).

CARAMELIZED ONION, THYME, AND MARJORAM TART

WITH FRESH GOAT CHEESE

Caramelizing onions takes time, but is well worth the effort. The key is to find the right balance between stirring the onions with enough regularity, so that they don't stick to the pan and burn, and giving them time to rest so they caramelize and take on some color. It is important to use a heavy-bottomed pan that will conduct heat evenly, to prevent burning. To make the onions a little bit richer, we sometimes like to finish them off with a good dollop of double cream.

PREP TIME 30 minutes, 30 minutes rest   COOK TIME 1½ hours   SERVES 6–8

Tart Dough

- 1½ cups (180g) all-purpose flour
- ½ teaspoon salt
- 5 ounces (145g) unsalted butter, chilled and cut into ¼-inch cubes
- 4–5 tablespoons ice water

Onion and Thyme Filling

- 3 tablespoons (45g) salted butter
- 2 tablespoons extra-virgin olive oil
- 8 yellow or red onions, peeled and thinly sliced
- 5 sprigs fresh thyme + extra for garnish
- 2 tablespoons balsamic vinegar
- 2 teaspoons fresh marjoram leaves, chopped
- 3 ounces (85g) fresh goat cheese
- Sea salt and freshly ground black pepper

Egg Wash

- 1 egg yolk
- 1 teaspoon cream

Make the tart dough

Mix the flour and salt in a large bowl.

Add the cubed butter and swiftly rub it into the flour with your fingertips, making sure the butter doesn't heat up and soften. Alternatively, you can use a food processor to pulse the dough for about 30 seconds until the dough resembles coarse crumbs. It is okay to have chunks of butter in the dough—this will help create a very flaky, rich tart.

Slowly incorporate the ice water, little by little, until you can form a crumbly ball of dough. If there are lots of small pieces that won't incorporate, add a touch more water to bring them together into a cohesive mass.

Wrap the dough in plastic wrap and flatten it into a thick disk to make the dough more compact. Refrigerate the dough for at least 30 minutes before rolling it out.

Onion and Thyme Filling

Add the butter and olive oil to a heavy-bottomed saucepan set over medium heat.

Once the butter has melted and starts to foam, add the onions and thyme. Cover the pan and sauté over medium heat until the onions are softened and begin to brown. Stir frequently until the onions have reduced significantly and have caramelized to a dark golden brown (about 40 to 45 minutes total). Continue to brown and mix, repeatedly, until the onions have reduced significantly and are entirely golden brown. There should be no excess liquid in the bottom of the pan.

Add the balsamic vinegar to the onions in the pan, stir to coat, and cook for another 5 minutes.

Season the onion mixture with salt and pepper and toss in the marjoram leaves. Stir and cook for another minute. Remove the mixture from the heat. Let it cool and then remove the thyme stems.

Assemble

Preheat the oven to 375°F (185°C).

On a well-floured surface, roll out the disk of chilled tart dough into a 13–14-inch-wide (33–36cm) and ⅛-inch-thick (3mm) circle.

Transfer the rolled-out dough to a baking sheet lined with parchment paper (or a tart pan) and let it firm up in the fridge for about 15 minutes if it is too soft to handle.

Spread the cooled onions over the center. Leave a good inch or two around the edge so you have ample dough to fold up around the onions.

Fold the edges up and over the onion filling. Brush the folded dough with the beaten egg and cream mixture. Bake the tart for 40 to 50 minutes, until the crust is golden brown.

Once you remove the tart from the oven, immediately crumble the fresh goat cheese over the onion filling, allowing it to melt just slightly. Top with a pinch of fresh thyme and serve warm with a green salad.

COCONUT FISH STEW
WITH SPICY PIRÃO

We like to think of this stew—a slightly spicy, hearty soup of tender white fish, poached in a mildly sweet base of coconut milk, tomato, cilantro, and ginger—as a Bouillabaisse-meets-Brazilian curry. The soul of the dish is Spicy Pirão, a unique hot sauce whose kick is balanced by savory undertones of sautéed garlic and a punch of fresh lemon.

PREP TIME 30 minutes   COOK TIME 45 minutes   SERVES 4–6

¼ cup (60ml) extra-virgin olive oil

1 medium fennel bulb, cored and thinly sliced on the diagonal

1 small onion, thinly sliced

1 leek (white and light green parts only), finely chopped

5 garlic cloves, germ removed and minced

¾ pound (340g) Yukon gold potatoes, peeled and sliced into ¼-inch (6mm) rounds

¼ cup (60ml) dry white wine

1 14-ounce can (414ml) sweet coconut milk

2 pounds (1kg) firm white fish (sea bass, grouper, red snapper), cut into 2-inch (5cm) chunks

3 tablespoons Spicy Pirão (recipe at right)

1 cup (240ml) Fish Stock (page 185) or Basic Vegetable Stock (page 184)

½ pound (225g) ripe cherry tomatoes, halved

Marinade

2 ½-inch (6cm) pieces of ginger, peeled

2 large ripe tomatoes, roughly chopped

1 medium onion, diced

2 garlic cloves, germ removed and minced

3 tablespoons fresh cilantro leaves, chopped

3 tablespoons lime juice

Spicy Pirão

1 small potato (50g), peeled and quartered

½ cup (120ml) Fish Stock (page 185) or Basic Vegetable Stock (page 184)

2 tablespoons (30ml) extra-virgin olive oil

3 hot red peppers (habanero, Serrano, red jalapeño, etc.), ribs and seeds removed and cut into large chunks

6 cloves of garlic, germ removed and crushed but kept intact

3 tablespoons lemon juice

½ teaspoon lemon zest

½ teaspoon coarse sea salt + extra

¾ cup (180ml) extra-virgin olive oil

Assemble and Serve

2 fresh limes

A handful of cilantro leaves, chopped + extra whole leaves for garnish

Sea salt

Espelette pepper (or hot chili pepper)

Marinade

Grate the ginger using a fine grater or Microplane. Squeeze the grated ginger pulp as hard as you can to extract all of the juice and then discard the fibrous pulp. Place the tomatoes, onions, garlic, cilantro, ginger, and lime juice in a blender or food processor. Process until broken down to small pieces.

Pour the marinade into a large ceramic or glass container. Place the fish in the marinade, cover the container, and leave to marinate at room temperature for 20 minutes. Five minutes before cooking, add a teaspoon of salt to the mixture.

Spicy Pirão

In a small pot, cook the potato in the stock until it is tender and the stock has reduced.

Heat 2 tablespoons olive oil in a small skillet over medium-high heat. Once the oil is hot, add the chili peppers and garlic. Sauté, stirring frequently, until the edges of the garlic start to turn golden. Add the lemon juice and scrape a wooden spoon across the bottom of the skillet to dislodge any brown bits that have formed. Remove the skillet from the heat and let cool.

Place the contents of the skillet in a blender or a food processor along with the potato in its stock, lemon zest, and salt. Blend until smooth.

Gradually drizzle ¾ cup (180ml) olive oil into the blender while it is on, as if making a mayonnaise, adding stock as necessary to smooth the emulsion.

Transfer the resulting pirão to another container and keep it at room temperature until ready to serve. Season to taste with additional sea salt and Espelette pepper.

Coconut Fish Stew

In a large saucepan, heat ¼ cup olive oil over medium-high heat, add the sliced fennel, onions, and leeks and cook until translucent (about 7 to 10 minutes), stirring frequently. Then add the minced garlic and sauté until fragrant, about 2 minutes.

Stir in the potatoes until well coated with the olive oil and mixed with the other ingredients. Deglaze the pan with the dry white wine. Bring the wine to a boil, lower the heat to a simmer and reduce the liquid to about 1 tablespoon.

Add the coconut milk and stir to combine with the other ingredients in the pan. Bring to a simmer and then add the fish in its marinade, 3 tablespoons Spicy Pirão and ¾ to 1 cup of the stock to the pan. Season to taste with sea salt and add the cherry tomatoes and chopped cilantro. Cover the pan and cook until the fish is white and flaky, about 7 to 10 minutes.

Assemble

Serve the fish in a warmed shallow dish and top with a generous dollop of Spicy Pirão. Garnish with fresh cilantro leaves and serve with sliced lime on the side.

POULET BASQUAISE
WITH BUTTER RICE

B asque-style chicken, made with lots of tomatoes, peppers, and a generous pinch of Espelette pepper is a simple recipe, yet it is so stunning. If you want to be diligent, peel the bell peppers (if they are the kind that soften easily) with a vegetable peeler to keep the skins from floating in the sauce. The rice, although so simple, deserves a special mention. With all the buttery flavor and sweet bite of soft onion, it makes good on its own, too.

PREP TIME 15 minutes   COOK TIME 45 minutes   SERVES 4

Poulet Basquaise

3 pounds (1.3kg) whole free-range skinless chicken, broken down to 4 large pieces

2 teaspoons Espelette pepper (or hot chili pepper)

2 pounds (900g) tomatoes

3 tablespoons extra-virgin olive oil

2 yellow onions thinly sliced

2 red bell peppers thinly sliced

1 yellow bell pepper thinly sliced

4 garlic cloves, germ removed and minced

2 bay leaves

¼ cup (40g) grams Kalamata olives

Butter Rice

1 tablespoon extra-virgin olive oil

3 tablespoons (45g) butter

1 yellow onion, finely chopped

2 cups (350g) long grain rice (e.g., Basmati)

2¼ cups (525ml) Chicken Stock (page 185)

Parsley leaves, chopped to garnish

Sea salt and freshly ground black pepper

Poulet Basquaise

Rub the chicken with a tablespoon of salt and a teaspoon of Espelette (or hot chili) pepper. Bring a large pot of water to a boil and have a large bowl of ice cold water on hand. Score an X at the bottom of the tomatoes and plunge them into the pot of boiling water for about 1 minute. Then, transfer the tomatoes to the bowl of cold water. Peel off the skins and chop the tomatoes coarsely.

Add 3 tablespoons of oil to a large saucepan, and then cook for 3 to 4 minutes on each side on moderate heat until browned. Remove from pan and reserve to add back to the dish later.

Next, add a little more olive oil if necessary and then the sliced onions to the same pan. Add the sliced red and yellow peppers immediately, followed by the bay leaves and remaining Espelette pepper. Cook the peppers for 6 to 8 minutes until softened.

Stir the chopped tomatoes into the pan. Cook for 10 minutes. Season with salt and pepper.

Next, stir in the browned chicken and Kalamata olives. Coat with the sauce. Cover the pan, turn down the heat and let it simmer for 20 to 25 minutes.

Butter Rice

For the rice, first cut a circle of parchment paper to the size of the pan. Make a small hole in the center as well.

Heat a medium-size saucepan. Add a tablespoon of olive oil and the butter. Stir in the chopped onions and cook until softened.

Next, add the rice to the pan (make sure you don't wash or soak it). Now cook the rice with the onions, stirring constantly. The rice should be coated with the butter and turn translucent. It shouldn't stick to the bottom of the pan.

Add the chicken stock to the pan. Stir in a teaspoon of salt and bring the mixture to a boil. Place the sheet of parchment on top of the rice. Then turn the heat down to low and cook covered for 12 to 15 minutes.

Serve

To serve, place the rice in a bowl and the Poulet Basquaise in a serving platter. Garnish with chopped parsley.

KOREAN CHICKEN SALAD
WITH PICKLED CABBAGE, CUCUMBERS, PEANUTS, AND CILANTRO

Walking up Rue Sainte-Anne, you will chance upon K-Mart (6–8, Rue Sainte-Anne, 75002 Paris), the incredibly well-stocked Korean supermarket in Paris. Here's where we go when we want to tinker with ingredients we've never used before: seaweed seasoning for rice, corn tea, tubs of homemade banchan (vegetable-based side dishes), Korean red chili flakes, and whatnot. This is where we discovered the flavorful fermented red-chili-and-bean-paste, tobanjan. In this recipe, you could use Youki tobanjan instead of the gochujang, if you manage to get your hands on it.

As for the chicken, rather than poaching the breast, we use an unconventional (and convenient) roasting method in which you start cooking the chicken in a cold oven (see Cold-Oven Chicken page 20). This raises the temperature of the chicken slowly and is the secret to yielding the most tender results.

PREP TIME 45 minutes active, 15 minutes rest   COOK TIME 35 minutes   SERVES 6–8

Korean Chicken

- 4 free-range chicken breasts, bone-in with skin on
- 2 tablespoons (30g) gochujang or tobanjan
- Extra-virgin olive oil for coating the pot
- 1 head of garlic, germ removed and minced
- 1 3-inch piece of ginger, peeled and grated
- Stems from ½ cup cilantro sprigs
- Juice of ½ lemon

Vinaigrette

- 1 tablespoon rice wine vinegar
- 1 tablespoon honey
- Juice of ½ lemon
- 1 tablespoon (15g) gochujang
- ¼ cup mix of sesame and vegetable oil
- Sea salt

Pickled Cabbage and Cucumbers

- 1½ cups pickled cabbage and cucumber mix (recipe at right)
- ½ cup (65g) peanuts, toasted
- ½ cup (30g) chopped cilantro leaves

Pickling Mix

- ¼ cup (60ml) rice wine vinegar
- 1 tablespoon sugar
- 1 teaspoon salt
- ½ teaspoon coriander seeds, lightly toasted and ground
- 1 inch piece of ginger, peeled and grated
- 1 hot green chili, finely chopped
- 1 medium Chinese cabbage, thinly shredded
- 2 large cucumbers, deseeded and cut into thin strips
- Sea salt and freshly ground black pepper

Korean Chicken

Rub about ½ teaspoon salt and the gochujang into the chicken.

Lightly coat the bottom of a cast iron pot with olive oil and then sprinkle with garlic cloves and ginger. Top with the cilantro stems and then set the chicken breast on it, skin side up. Squeeze the juice of half a lemon all over the skin and then sprinkle generously with sea salt and pepper.

Place the chicken breast in a covered pot in the oven. Turn up the temperature to 450°F (225°C) and cook for 35 minutes, removing the lid for last 15 minutes. Remove the pot and let it cool.

Once the chicken is cool, shred it into small, bite-size pieces with your fingers.

Vinaigrette

Whisk together the rice wine vinegar, honey, lemon juice, gochujang, and sea salt until well combined. Slowly drizzle in the oil until the mixture thickens. Taste for seasoning and add additional vinegar, honey, or salt, as necessary, to create a delicate balance of sweet, savory, sour, and spice.

Pickled Cabbage and Cucumbers

Whisk together all the ingredients for the pickling mix, except for the cabbage and cucumbers, until the sugar and salt have dissolved.

Toss together the cabbage and cucumbers with the pickling mix, making sure to coat evenly. Cover with plastic wrap and let it sit for 15 minutes, turning the mixture over every 5 minutes. Drain off any of the excess liquid before serving.

Assemble

Toss the shredded chicken, pickled cabbage and cucumber, half of the peanuts, and half of the fresh cilantro in vinaigrette until lightly but evenly coated. Once ready to serve, sprinkle with the remaining peanuts and fresh cilantro.

SLOW-ROASTED ROSEMARY LAMB

WITH LATE HARVEST RIESLING YOGURT-FETA SAUCE

There is so much to love about this recipe—the flavor from the garlic, the potatoes soaked in lamb juices, and the sweetness from the confit tomatoes concentrated in flavor from hours of cooking. This recipe is the coming together of decidedly French flavors and techniques that are brightened with cumin and parsley. When Shaheen lived near Algerian *boulangeries* in the 19th arrondissement, we'd buy Kesra, a traditional semolina flat bread, and use it to mop up all the meat juices.

PREP TIME 20 minutes   COOK TIME 3–4 hours   SERVES 6–8

3–4 pounds (1.5kg) lamb, cut into large chunks, from the leg or shoulder

3 teaspoons cumin seeds

¼ cup (60ml) extra-virgin olive oil

8–10 cloves garlic, germ removed and minced

6 shallots, divided, chopped into small dice

3.5 ounces (100g) lardons or diced pancetta (smoked or unsmoked, whichever you prefer)

1½ cups (350ml) dry white wine

6–8 fresh sprigs rosemary, divided

1 bay leaf

2 pounds (1kg) potatoes, cut into large pieces

¼ cup fresh parsley, chopped + extra for garnish

12–15 pieces of Tomato Confit (page 197 or sun-dried tomatoes

Sea salt and freshly ground black pepper

Late Harvest Reisling Yogurt-Feta Sauce (recipe at right)

Trim the pieces of lamb to get rid of the excess fat and silver skin. If the lamb has a stamp mark on it, trim that off as well.

Toast the cumin seeds in a small skillet over medium heat until fragrant, about 3 to 5 minutes. While still warm, grind half of the seeds to a fine powder in a mortar and pestle or with a rolling pin. Leave the other half whole to use later.

Season the lamb chunks all over with freshly ground black pepper, ground cumin, and sea salt. In a large cast iron casserole heat about 3 tablespoons of the olive oil over medium-high and brown the chunks of lamb until all sides have a nice brown sear—don't crowd the pieces or they won't brown well. Repeat in batches, adding more olive oil as necessary. Reserve the lamb chunks in a large bowl.

Keep the casserole on the burner and add the garlic and half of the shallots and the lardons (or pancetta) to the pan. Cook until golden around the edges. (If using pancetta or another cut of bacon with less fat, you may need to add a bit olive oil here). Add the white wine and half of the rosemary and the bay leaf, and let the wine reduce by half. Remove from the heat.

Add the mixture to the large bowl with the lamb and potatoes, the remaining diced shallots and cumin seeds, the parsley, and tomato confit. Toss well to coat and season to taste with salt and pepper.

Return the lamb and potato mix to the casserole, including any juices that may have collected at the bottom of the bowl. Arrange the meat and potatoes so that they are evenly spaced in a large Dutch oven (cast iron pot)—this is important because the potatoes will gradually absorb the other flavors in the dish. The bay leaf and half of the rosemary sprigs should sit at the bottom of the casserole in the cooking liquid.

Place the lid on the dish and cook in the oven at 300°F (150°C). After 30 minutes, remove the lid and spoon the cooking liquid over the lamb and potatoes. Put the lid back on. Repeat again after 30 minutes. Cook the lamb and potato mix covered for another 1½ to 2 hours.

To check to see if the lamb is ready, remove a piece and try to cut it with the side of a fork. The meat should break apart easily. It should be moist, too.

Once cooked, toss the meat in its juices and add the remaining half of the rosemary. Place the lid back on and return to the oven for another 10 minutes. Then, remove from the oven and let it rest for 15 minutes.

Depending on how fatty the lamb is, there might be rendered fat on the surface of the liquid, so tilt the pan slightly and spoon out the excess fat.

Serve the lamb and potatoes directly in the casserole with Late Harvest Riesling Yogurt-Feta Sauce (recipe below) on the side and a simple green salad made with a lemon-mustard vinaigrette. If plating, remove the rosemary and bay leaf first. Smear a generous spoonful of the yogurt-feta sauce on the bottom of the plate and top with a mound of the lamb and potatoes. Garnish with chopped parsley.

LATE HARVEST RIESLING YOGURT-FETA SAUCE

For years we had been serving our rosemary lamb with a nice, lemony tzatziki. We ventured to try something different only recently—a reduction of dessert wine to give the sauce some sweetness and a little feta to intensify the tanginess of the yogurt. For this recipe, it's best to use a sweet, light-colored wine like Late Harvest Riesling or Sauterne, which will not discolor the yogurt.

PREP TIME 5 minutes   COOK TIME 15 minutes   MAKES 1½ cups

1 tablespoon butter
1 garlic clove, germ removed and minced
1 small shallot, finely chopped
½ cup (120ml) Late Harvest Riesling
2 sprigs fresh thyme
1½ cups (250g) thick, full-fat Greek yogurt
¼ cup (40g) feta, crumbled
2 teaspoons lemon juice
Sea salt and freshly ground black pepper

Melt the butter in a small saucepan over medium heat. Add the minced garlic clove and shallot, sautéing until golden around the edges. Add the Late Harvest Riesling and thyme and bring to a boil. Lower the heat to a gentle simmer and reduce by half.

Remove from the heat and discard the thyme sprigs. Once cool, mix together with Greek yogurt, feta, and lemon juice. Season to taste with salt and pepper.

ALIGOT
WITH MERGUEZ SAUSAGE AND HARISSA

ligot—rich creamy mashed potatoes taken up a notch with the addition of cheese—is the perfect winter comfort food. We first discovered *aligot* at a Christmas market on the streets of Paris. It was quite the spectacle, as the the vendor stretched the big spoonful of the warm, elastic potato-and-cheese mash over his head—only to drop it and and stretch it out again. It was a feat that attracted all the passersby to line up for a plate of Toulouse sausage with a giant dollop of *aligot*. We make ours with spicy merguez sausage and lots of our homemade version of Harissa (page 191).

PREP TIME 15 minutes   COOK TIME 1 hour   SERVES 4

Harissa Vinaigrette

- ¼ cup Harissa (page 191)
- Zest of 1 lemon
- 1 teaspoon freshly squeezed lemon juice
- 1½ tablespoons extra-virgin olive oil

Aligot

- 1 pound (450g) potatoes for mashing, peeled
- 3 tablespoons salted butter
- 1 tablespoon) crème fraîche
- 3 garlic cloves, germ removed and minced to a paste
- ¾ pound (275g) Tomme d'Auvergne, Gruyère, or Appenzeller, grated
- Pinch of freshly grated nutmeg

- 1 tablespoons extra-virgin olive oil for the pan
- 8 Merguez sausages
- Fresh cilantro for garnish
- Sea salt and freshly ground black pepper

Prepare the harissa vinaigrette by whisking together all ingredients. Season to taste with salt.

Preheat the oven to 450°F (230°C).

Place the peeled potatoes in a large pot of salted water and bring to a boil over high heat. Once the water has boiled, cook the potatoes for an additional 20 to 30 minutes, depending on their size and density. (To tell if they are done, you should be able to insert a fork easily into the center of the potatoes, but they shouldn't break apart.)

When the potatoes are ready, remove them from the stove and drain them. In a stand mixer, or in a large bowl with a hand masher, beat the warm potatoes to a mash. Mix in the butter, crème fraîche, garlic, and a pinch of pepper to make a smooth, silky purée.

Place the mixture in a medium-size, thick-bottomed saucepan and set it over low heat on the stove. Add in the grated cheese and nutmeg; stir until well combined.

With a wooden spoon, stir the potato mixture in figure eight motions. Continue to stir the over low heat for about 15 minutes. You'll know that the mix is ready when it starts to pull away from the edges of the pan and has taken on a more elastic, thicker texture. Keep the *aligot* warm in a bain marie.

Heat a pan with olive oil and brown the sausages over medium heat. Switch to turning them over when you see that the sausages have taken on enough color, instead of moving them constantly.

Dollop the warm *aligot* onto four small plates. Top with merguez sausage, drizzle with the harissa, and garnish with fresh cilantro leaves.

FENNEL, LEEK, PUY LENTILS, AND SAUSAGES

WITH BASIL PISTOU

Classic French training will ingrain two things in a cook: (1) remove the germ of the garlic before using it; and (2) always have bay leaf and thyme at hand to make a bouquet garni. It's amazing how using just these three ingredients can make a dish taste so decidedly French. We use Toulouse, Montebéliard, or Morteau sausages for this recipe, but any fresh sausage with a good amount of fat will work just as well. Just make sure there aren't any bread crumbs in the meat. You can tweak this recipe as the seasons change. Stir in some black kale or flowering Brussels sprouts in the winter or add sorrel or green beans in the summer. And if you want to make the Toulousains proud, use a liberal amount of goose fat instead of olive oil.

PREP TIME 20 minutes   COOK TIME 45 minutes   SERVES 6–8

Fennel, Leek, Puy Lentils, and Sausages

- 4 tablespoons extra-virgin olive oil
- 4 Toulouse sausages
- 2 fennel bulbs, trimmed and each cut into 4–6 wedges
- 1 leek, sliced into thin rings
- 1 small carrot, cut into small cubes
- 1 clove garlic, germ removed and minced
- 2 ounces (55g) smoked pancetta or lardons (dry-cured pork belly)
- ½ pound (225g) Puy lentils or green lentils
- 1 bay leaf
- 4–6 sprigs fresh thyme
- 3 cups (750ml) Chicken Stock (page 185)
- Sea salt and freshly ground black pepper

Basil Pistou

- 1 clove garlic, germ removed and minced
- 1 anchovy fillet, chopped
- 1 bunch of basil leaves, torn into small pieces
- ¼ cup (60ml) extra-virgin olive oil
- Sea salt

Heat a pan with some of the olive oil and brown the sausages over medium heat. Turn them over only when you see that the sausages have taken on enough color. Once the sausages are browned evenly, remove them from the pan. Place the fennel in the same pan, and brown the wedges on both sides. The moisture from the fennel will begin to deglaze the pan.

Add a little olive oil to the pan, if needed. Add the leeks, carrots, garlic, and pancetta or lardons, and cook until the leeks have softened.

Stir in the Puy lentils and cook for 3 to 4 minutes until the lentils are coated with fat. Add the bay leaf and thyme.

Pour over enough chicken stock just to cover the lentils. Season with salt and pepper. Cook covered over low heat for 10 minutes.

After 10 minutes, give the lentils a stir, then top with enough chicken stock to keep them submerged. Cut the sausages into large chunks before placing them back in the pan, with the browned fennel around them, and continue to cook for another 15 to 20 minutes. When cooked, the lentils should have a bit of a bite, and a knife inserted into the fennel should slide through it without any resistance.

Basil Pistou

In a large mortar, grind the garlic with a pinch of salt and the anchovies until it forms a paste. Add the basil by the handful and grind the leaves against the side of the mortar until they've broken down. Gradually stir in the olive oil until it's incorporated.

Serve

Serve the lentils and sausages in the pan, along with a dollop of the basil pistou.

ANCHO AND APPLE CIDER PORK SHOULDER

WITH PICKLED PLUMS, SHALLOTS, AND CRÈME FRAÎCHE MASHED POTATOES

There are a plethora of world ingredients to be found in Paris, and La Grande Epicerie (38, rue de Sèvres, 75007 Paris) is one of our favorite places to begin exploring. It is an incredibly large department store dedicated to food. There are honeys, jams, confections, cheeses, walls of water, and yogurts as far as the eye can see. It is hard to leave La Grande Epicerie without Bordier butter, their *confiture du lait*, and a jar of Christine Ferber's jam. As much as we can find pretty much anything we want in Paris, Mexican cuisine is vastly underrepresented. After living abroad for several years now, we have learned what to stock up on when we go home. When Jennie goes back to Phoenix, she returns with a sack of dried chiles and the famed chipotle chiles in adobo sauce—the real ones from local Mexican shops, rather than the mass-produced variety. Ancho chiles add a unique smokiness that's hard to substitute and work in perfect harmony with the flavors of apple cider, orange zest, fresh oregano, and thyme.

PREP TIME 30 minutes   COOK TIME 4 hours   SERVES 6–8

Spice Paste

- 1 dried guajillo chile, deseeded and torn up
- 1 dried ancho chile, deseeded and torn up
- 3 cloves
- 1 inch cinnamon stick
- ½ teaspoon cumin seeds
- ½ teaspoon coriander seeds
- 10–15 black peppercorns
- ⅓ cup (80ml) boiling water
- 3 chipotle chiles in adobo
- 1 head of garlic, peeled, germ removed
- 2 teaspoons fresh oregano leaves + extra for garnish
- 1 tablespoon honey
- 3 tablespoons extra-virgin olive oil

Pork Shoulder

- 4½ pounds (2kg) pork shoulder, boneless with excess fat removed
- 2 medium carrots, cut into large chunks
- 2 stalks of celery, cut into large chunks
- 2 medium onions, cut into large chunks
- 1 bay leaf
- 1 cinnamon stick
- 1 long strip of orange zest
- 5–6 sprigs fresh thyme
- 2 cups (475ml) apple cider
- 1 cup (240ml) freshly squeezed orange juice
- ¼ cup (60ml) tequila or apple cider

  Fresh oregano leaves for garnish
  Sea salt and freshly ground black pepper

Spice Paste

Toast the dried chiles, cinnamon, cloves, cumin, coriander, and peppercorns in a preheated oven at 300°F (150°C) until fragrant, about 8 to 10 minutes. Place the mixture in a small bowl and cover with the boiling water. Let steep for 10 minutes.

Blend the chile mix along with the chipotles in adobo, garlic, oregano, and honey until smooth. In the blender or by hand, drizzle in the olive oil until it incorporates. You should have a thick, dark paste. Season with salt.

Pork Shoulder

Rub the paste on the pork shoulder, being sure to coat all of the surface area. Place it in the fridge for at least 2 hours or, preferably, overnight.

When ready to cook, remove the pork from the fridge and bring it to room temperature.

Preheat the oven to 400°F (200°C). Place the pork shoulder in a medium-size Dutch oven (cast iron pot) with a lid. Surround the pork with the carrots, celery, onions, bay leaf, cinnamon stick, orange zest, and thyme. Pour the apple cider and orange juice around the meat in the pot.

Cook the pork uncovered for 1 hour; then flip the meat over and cook the meat on the other side for another 40 minutes.

Flip the shoulder back to its original side, cover it with the lid, lower the oven temperature to 325°F (160°C), and cook until the meat can easily be separated with a fork (after 2 or more hours). Make sure that the level of liquid in the casserole stays about a third of the way up the height of the pork shoulder. If it's low, add more cider or orange juice.

Remove the pork from the oven and let it rest, covered, for 20 to 30 minutes.

Transfer the pork to a cutting board and use a spoon to break it up into large chunks. Place the meat on a serving platter or in shallow bowl.

Strain the remaining contents of the pan. Discard the aromatics (orange zest, cinnamon stick, thyme, bay leaf) and vegetables. Pour about ½ cup of the pan juices over the pork shoulder to keep it moist and reserve the rest.

Place the roasting pan on the stove over medium-high heat. Once the fat leftover from the pork is sizzling, add the tequila or apple cider to deglaze the bottom of the pan and scrape up any browned bits. Add the reserved pan juices back into the pan. Let the mixture cook until it is reduced by half.

Serve

Pour the jus over the pork and serve alongside Pickled Plums and Shallots (page 60) and Crème Fraîche Mashed Potatoes (page 61). Garnish with fresh oregano leaves.

PICKLED PLUMS AND SHALLOTS

While traditional Mexican dishes are typically served with pickled red onions, we have opted for pickling shallots and plums together. We like to cut the shallots into delicate wedges—when served on top of the pork they add a beautiful pop of bright pink. Depending on your preference, you can use sweet or tart plums or a mixture of the two.

PREP TIME 10 minutes, 1 hour rest   COOK TIME 10 minutes   MAKES 3 1-pint jars

1 teaspoon fennel seeds

2 star anise

¾ cup (180ml) red wine vinegar

¼ cup (60ml) apple cider vinegar

¼ cup (50g) sea salt

½ cup (100g) packed light brown sugar

½ cup (120ml) water

2 pounds (900g) firm red plums, cut into ¼-inch wedges

6–8 shallots, thinly sliced

Lightly toast the fennel seeds and star anise in a preheated oven at 300°F (150°C) until fragrant, about 5 to 7 minutes.

Combine the vinegars with the salt and sugar, and whisk together until both have dissolved. Add the water, plums, shallots, and toasted spices.

Refrigerate the mixture for one hour, or preferably longer, to get a really bright pink color in the shallots. Stir the mixture every 20 minutes or so.

CRÈME FRAÎCHE MASHED POTATOES

WITH CHARRED CORN AND SHARP WHITE CHEDDAR

Few things are more comforting than a great mashed potato. Here we incorporate a crème fraîche—the decadent staple of Norman cuisine—with some sharp English cheddar and charred corn kernels, reminiscent of a summer barbecue. If you cannot find crème fraîche, use sour cream with a good tablespoon of heavy cream stirred into it. When making large quantities, a great trick for mashing potatoes is to throw them into a stand mixer! As long as they are still warm, the whisk attachment will break them down and leave you with just a few chewy chunks that make it seem as if the potatoes have been mashed by hand. If you are a stickler for a smooth mash, then pass the cooked potatoes through a fine-mesh drum sieve first.

PREP TIME 20 minutes   COOK TIME 30 minutes   SERVES 6–8

- 3 pounds (1.4kg) mashing potatoes, peeled and cut into 1-inch (3cm) chunks
- 4 ounces (112g) unsalted butter
- 1 cup (200g) crème fraîche
- 2.8 ounces (80g) sharp white cheddar, grated
- ½ cup (120ml) whole milk
- 2 tablespoons extra-virgin olive oil
- 2 cups (350g) raw corn kernels
- Sea salt and freshly ground black pepper

Add the potatoes to a large pot of salted water and bring to a boil. Partially cover the pot, reduce the heat to a simmer, and cook until a fork can easily be inserted into the potatoes.

Remove the potatoes from the water and immediately transfer them to a stand mixer fitted with a whisk attachment. Gradually mix in the butter and crème fraîche until they are well integrated and the potatoes are mostly smooth, using a spatula to scrape down the sides in between additions. If you're using a handheld masher, add the butter and crème fraîche gradually as well, to help break down the potatoes.

Add the grated cheese to the potato mix and continue to whisk or mash, until it is incorporated—the heat from the potatoes should melt the cheese.

Add the milk as needed to loosen up the potatoes, especially if you plan to reheat them or keep them warm, rather than serve the potatoes immediately.

In a large heavy skillet over medium-high heat, drizzle in the olive oil and then sauté the corn kernels until they're cooked through and slightly charred, about 5 minutes.

Stir the corn kernels into the potatoes, season with salt and pepper, and serve warm.

ROAST BEEF
WITH ROSEMARY PEPPERCORN CRUST AND HORSERADISH JUS

The trick to carving thin, neat slices is to wrap the roast beef tightly in plastic film and refrigerate it for at least an hour, better still overnight.

PREP TIME 20 minutes   COOK TIME 2 hours   SERVES 6–8

Roast Beef

7 pounds (3kg) boneless rib of beef

1½ tablespoons coarse sea salt

2 tablespoons crushed black peppercorns

5 garlic cloves, germ removed and minced

4 tablespoons fresh rosemary leaves, finely chopped

1 tablespoon fresh thyme leaves, finely chopped

4 tablespoons fresh flat-leaf parsley leaves, finely chopped

¼ cup (60ml) extra-virgin olive oil

Horseradish Jus

2 medium onions, sliced into medium rounds

1 cup (250ml) red wine

2 cups (500ml) Basic Vegetable or Beef Stock (page 184)

1 inch (2.2cm) horseradish, grated or 1 tablespoon grated horseradish from a jar

Sea salt and freshly gound black pepper

Roast Beef

Remove the rib roast from refrigerator 2 hours before cooking. Mix the coarse sea salt, peppercorns, garlic, rosemary, thyme, parsley, and olive oil. Rub the mixture over the entire surface of the beef.

Preheat the oven to 475°F (245°C). Place the rib roast (fat side up) in a roasting pan, discarding any liquid that has collected. Place the roasting pan, uncovered, in the upper part of the oven and cook for 10 to 15 minutes until well browned. Turn the temperature down to 275°F (135°C) and move the roast to the middle rack in the oven. For medium rare, cook until a meat thermometer reads 115°F (46°C), after about an hour and a half. The temperature will continue to rise when you remove it from the oven.

Remove the pan from the oven, transfer the beef to a board, and tent it loosely with aluminum foil. Let the meat rest for 20 minutes before carving.

Horseradish Jus

While the beef rests, make the jus. Reserve the pan juices, while leaving 2 tablespoons of the rendered fat in the pan. Sauté the onions in the fat in the roasting pan over medium-high heat until browned (about 10 minutes), stirring every few minutes. Deglaze the pan with the wine and let it reduce slightly before adding the stock and reserved juices. Cook the jus for an additional 5 minutes. Add the horseradish and season with salt and pepper.

Serve the beef with the jus and Escoffier Potatoes (at right).

TIP You can easily make a sandwich or tartine with the leftovers. Drizzle about 1½ tablespoons of the horseradish jus over each slice of toasted bread. Top with Onion Jam (page 104) and then the roast beef, folded over. Spoon another tablespoon of jus over the roast beef. and crumble your favorite blue cheese over the top and garnish with fresh chives.

ESCOFFIER POTATOES

Turning to Escoffier for comforting classics never fails. This recipe stems from Escoffier's *Pomme de terre fondantes*. The idea of melting, soft potatoes bathed in a little bit of water and a lot of butter that turns to browned butter after the water has evaporated, is beyond inviting. Typical of his style, Escoffier's instructions are very fluid and the ingredient list merely mentions 12 potatoes. We've created this recipe building on his technique. We hope Escoffier would be proud.

The garlic deserves a special mention. As it cooks, it softens and browns, and eating it is like chewing on a really good caramel that sticks to your teeth in the most pleasant way. You can add heaps more to the pan and use it to smear on toast. We have made the potatoes with and without their skins and liked them both. The ones with skin brown better and have a nice chew. If you are not sure how you'd like to make the potatoes, just make a mixed batch.

PREP TIME 5 minutes   COOK TIME 1 hour   SERVES 4

8–10 cloves of garlic, germ removed

1½ pounds (750g) small potatoes, such as fingerling

1 sprig rosemary or thyme

4 ounces (112g) butter

Sea salt

Preheat the oven to 375°F (190°C).

Remove any papery skin from the garlic cloves, leaving only a single layer of the shiny skin intact. With the tip of a knife make a small incision through the skin.

Scrub the potatoes clean. You can peel them or leave the skins on.

Place the potatoes in a cast iron skillet or an ovenproof pan so that they fit snugly together. Add the rosemary or thyme and garlic cloves. Sprinkle with coarse sea salt. Pour ¼ cup of water into the pan around the potatoes.

Dot the potatoes with cubes of butter. Put the pan on the stovetop and bring the water to a boil, then transfer the pan to the oven and cook for 30 minutes. Take the pan out of the oven and gently flatten the potatoes, taking care not to break them. Cook for another 15 minutes.

By now, all the water in the pan should have evaporated. Spoon the melted butter from the pan over the potatoes. Turn the oven up to 425°F (220°C) and continue to roast the potatoes until the butter is brown and sizzling. Remove the potatoes from the pan. Drizzle the remaining butter over the potatoes and let them rest for 10 minutes until the butter is absorbed.

TURKISH POT ROAST

This recipe is based on Jennie's mom's classic pot roast—a seared, slow cooked rump roast with a web of marbled fat that allows the meat to tenderize and fall apart on its own. We've added Turkish spices to the mix to give it an earthy kick. If you cannot find Aleppo pepper, we recommend substituting with a combination of smoked paprika, red pepper flakes, and a pinch of cayenne pepper.

PREP TIME 20 minutes   COOK TIME 3½–4 hours   SERVES 6–8

2 teaspoons cumin seeds

2 teaspoons black peppercorns

4.4 pounds (2kgs) marbled chuck roast (shoulder roasting joint)

3–4 tablespoons extra-virgin olive oil

8 garlic cloves, germ removed and minced to a paste

2–3 teaspoons Aleppo pepper

3 medium onions, peeled and cut into thick rounds

1 carrot, cut into thick rounds

1 large stalk of celery, cut into chunks

½ cup (120ml) dry red wine

3–4 cups (750ml–1L) Basic Vegetable Stock (page 184), Chicken Stock (page 185) or Beef Stock (page 184)

Sea salt and freshly ground black pepper

Preheat the oven to 350°F (175°C).

In a small heavy pan, toast the cumin seeds and black peppercorns until fragrant (about 2 minutes). Transfer the mix to a mortar and pound it to a fine grind with the pestle and combine with a tablespoon of sea salt.

Pat the meat dry with a paper towel, then spread evenly with the spice mixture. Let the meat sit at room temperature for 30 minutes before searing.

In a large Dutch oven (cast iron pot), heat the olive oil over a medium flame. Sear the meat on all sides until it turns a nice, deep golden brown.

Remove the meat and let it rest on a large plate. Now, rub it with the garlic paste and Aleppo pepper.

Increase the heat to medium-high and sear the onions, carrots, and celery in batches, being careful not to crowd the pan.

Remove the vegetables and deglaze the pan with red wine. Once the mix is bubbling and reduced, return the meat to the center of the pot and scatter the vegetables around it. Pour (warmed) stock to about halfway up the meat. Once the liquid comes to a gentle boil, cover the dish and transfer it to the oven.

Cook the meat for 1 hour 45 minutes. Reduce the heat to 325°F (155°C) and cook for an additional hour.

Check to see if the meat falls apart easily when probed with a spoon. If it doesn't, cook for an additional half hour.

Remove the roast from the oven and let it rest for 10 to 15 minutes. Discard the vegetables.

Break the meat into large pieces and transfer to a platter. You can pour the pan juices on top or reduce the jus on the stovetop, over medium-low heat, to make a richer, thicker sauce.

KALE SALAD

While kale's popularity has steadily been on the rise in the United States, Parisians have only recently warmed up to it. You can now find it in most farmers' markets, where there's been a revival of *legumes oubliés*, or the forgotten vegetables of yesteryear. The robust and fibrous consistency of kale allows it to resist sogginess over time, so you can prepare a greater quantity of it, knowing that it will keep for a few hours in the fridge and still have plenty of texture.

PREP TIME 20 minutes   COOK TIME 5 minutes   SERVES 6–8

¼ cup (35g) pine nuts

1 large bunch (about 200g) of common curly green kale

½ cup (70g) dried currants (or dried cranberries), coarsely chopped

1 small red bell pepper, deseeded and stem removed, cut into ¼-inch dice

½ cup (65g) pomegranate seeds

1 cup (70g) Parmigiano Reggiano, finely grated

Sea salt and freshly ground black pepper

Lemon Vinaigrette

Juice of 1 lemon

¼ cup (60ml) best-quality extra-virgin olive oil

Toast the pine nuts in a skillet until golden, about 3 to 5 minutes.

Wash and spin the kale and then remove the center stalk. Roll the leaves into a tight bundle and slice them as thinly as possible.

To make the lemon vinaigrette, whisk together the lemon juice and half a teaspoon of salt. Slowly add the olive oil in a steady drizzle until the mixture thickens. Season to taste with salt and pepper.

Twenty minutes before serving the salad, toss the kale strips in the lemon vinaigrette and let it sit. Add the vinaigrette little by little (you may not need to use all of it), so that the kale is evenly coated but not dripping. Let the dressed kale rest for 10 minutes while you prepare the other ingredients for the salad.

Next, rehydrate the currants by pouring boiling water over them in a small bowl. Cover the bowl and let it sit for 10 minutes. Drain the currants.

Just before serving, add the currants, diced red pepper, toasted pine nuts, pomegranate seeds, and grated Parmigiano Reggiano to the kale. Toss well to combine. Add more vinaigrette if needed.

BREAD, ETC.

When buying bread always select one that has *au levain* (in France) or sourdough in the name. This means that a sourdough pre-ferment was used to make the bread. Bread made with natural leaven has more flavor, is easier to digest, and keeps longer. If you slice into a regular baguette (one made without a starter), you will see that it has a cottony-white, inelastic texture because it has been fermented rapidly with yeast; it's the kind of bread that is excellent to pluck at and feed to pigeons at the park. The *baguette tradition,* on the other hand, has a webbed texture with irregular size air holes. The color of the bread is a translucent gray, and when you try to pull out a bit of the crumb, it resists, demonstrating that it has a distinct chew.

One time we visited Veronique Mauclerc's charming bakery in the 19th arrondissement of Paris (now closed), where the organic bread was baked in one of the last remaining wood-fired ovens in Paris. We asked the shopkeeper to recommend a loaf of bread and expected to be pointed to a best seller. Instead, she asked us what we intended to eat with the bread. *Pain Nordique,* for example, which is made with malted barley, linseed, sunflower seeds, and sesame seeds, is good with salmon, while fig bread, made with T80, a more delicate version of whole wheat all-purpose flour, would be great with blue cheese. This attention to pairing bread with food inspired us to make breads that would pair well with tartines.

For making a sourdough bread, you only need flour, water, and salt. A crucial fourth ingredient is time, which works its magic in creating and nurturing the wild yeast.

A sourdough loaf is a labor of love. You need to make a sourdough starter, feeding it regularly over a period of days, until it's ready to be used. Or you could ask your local sourdough bakery to give you some to jumpstart your baking. This starter will transform the most basic staple to a loaf so incredible that it needs nothing more than a smear of sweet butter or a dip of peppery olive oil to be thoroughly enjoyed.

The three recipes in this section are distinct from one another in texture as well as technique. The Pain de Mie (page 75) is made with baker's yeast; the Buttery Hazelnut Loaf (page 76) is made with a blend of sourdough pre-ferment and yeast; and the White Country Loaf (page 73) is a 100 percent sourdough loaf that, hopefully, will inspire you to gt baking using the ancient principles of slow fermentation.

SOURDOUGH BREAD

You are never too far away from a *boulangerie* in Paris. When I lived in Montmartre, arguably the area in Paris with the highest concentration of excellent *boulangeries*, I was spoiled for choice. Montmartre is where most of the winners of the annual *La Meilleure Baguette de Paris* invariably come from. The winner of this prestigious competition supplies baguettes to the Elysées Palace for the year. There were two bakeries on either side of my building—one was owned by a master MOF (*Meilleur Ouvrier de France*, the highest honor conferred to a craftsman in France) baker, and the other looked like it'd been there for at least half a century, with Old World interiors and grumpy old ladies. My favorite bakery, Maison Landemaine, was just outside the Métro Jules Joffrin. I'd happily shuffle my choices among these three, and when I craved *Pain des Amis*, I'd hop on bus 56 to Du Pain et des Idées for their beautiful bread and their *escargot chocolat-pistache*, a flaky chocolate and pistachio *viennoiserie*.

In my early days in France, whenever I'd stop at Max Poilâne, I'd only buy a *pain au chocolat* or croissant because I was reluctant to buy the entire *miche* (country loaf). I'd never be able to go through an entire loaf, I thought. Soon enough I discovered that you can buy bread in halves and quarters or even point to how large a piece you'd like. That changed everything. I was eating bread with glorious abandon. On another visit, I saw a

SOME OF OUR FAVORITE
BOULANGERIES IN PARIS:

◆ **Du Pain et des Idées**
   34, rue Yves Toudic, 75010 Paris

◆ **Maison Landemaine**
   shops dotted across Paris

◆ **Liberté**
   39, rue des Vinaigriers, 75010 Paris

◆ **Boulangerie Gana**
   54, rue Oberkampf, 75011 Paris

man ask for two slices of bread. At first, I thought I was mistaken. I lingered to watch the shopkeeper carefully cut two slices of bread and place them on a scale in order to draw up the bill. I was amazed at the value given to just two humble slices of bread, making me realize that in France, bread is truly an integral part of the culture.

Over time, I've grown to appreciate the finer textures and flavors of bread achieved through slow fermentation: A dark, crisp crust. An irregular, almost gray, but shiny webbed crumb. I have eaten some incredible bread in France. Bread that doesn't need any embellishments, although a smidgen of sweet, raw butter elevates the experience.

—Shaheen

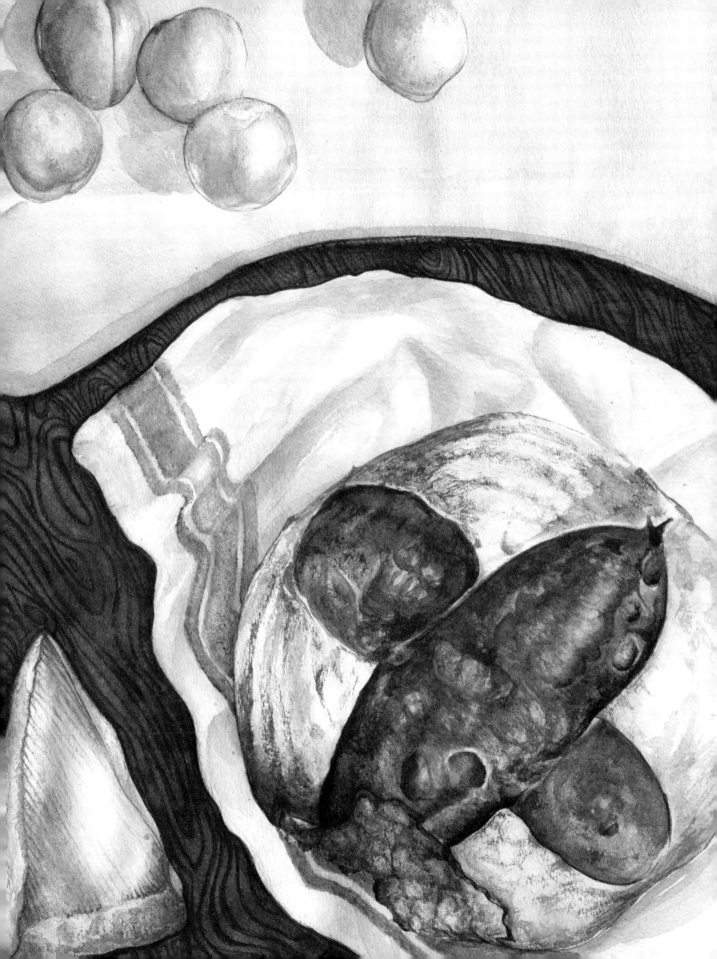

CREATE AND MAINTAIN YOUR SOURDOUGH STARTER

There are a lot of factors that go into making a sourdough bread. The time taken for resting and proofing, the flour, the water, the temperature, and the technique all play a part. And even when you think you have figured it all out, a slight change in the weather or in the amount of salt added can make a huge difference. This is not to dissuade you from bread-making—quite the contrary. These challenges are what make it all the more fun.

1 A sourdough starter is what you need to make your loaf. To create your own starter, begin with two ingredients.

> ¾ cup (90g) whole wheat flour
> ¾ cup (90g) water

In a glass jar, mix together the flour and water and let it sit, loosely covered, on the counter. In a couple of days' time you will notice a few stray bubbles, and then vigorous bubbles in another day or so. This is a sign of life in the starter.

2 Begin to "feed" the starter at this point. This means that from now on, you'll take a part of the mature starter and add to it, discarding the rest.

> ¼ cup (30g) of the starter
> ⅔ cup (75g) whole wheat flour
> ⅔ cup (75g) water

Mix the starter, whole wheat flour, and water together and leave it at room temperature. With each feed, you can mark the initial level with a rubber band to observe the change in volume of the starter. The natural yeast and bacteria will work on the fresh ingredients, and your mixture will rise, hit its peak, and then fall back down over the course of a few hours. The time it takes depends on the flour you're using, the temperature of the water, and the room temperature. You will also notice how the smell changes, from neutral when it's freshly mixed, to pleasantly acidic and yogurty to alcoholic after vigorous fermentation. Feeding it at about the same time every day will train the starter, and it will set itself into a pattern. Whenever you take a portion of starter to feed, discard the balance of the starter. Some people use the discarded portion for pancakes or waffles.

3 We begin with a liquid starter, because water encourages the growth of yeast and bacteria. After 3 to 4 days of feeding the liquid starter, it's time to change the ratio of water and flour to make it into a firm starter with a hydration of about 60 percent. This simply means that for every 100 parts of flour, there are 60 parts of water. Every baker has his or her own favorite method of either using a firm or liquid starter in making bread. Right now, we're very happy with how our breads turn out, using a firm starter.

4 To convert to a firm starter, mix together these ingredients just as you would for a regular feed, but with these ratios:

- ¼ cup (30g) of your liquid starter
- ½ cup (120g) whole wheat flour
- ½ cup (60g) + 1 tablespoon water

5 From now on, to maintain the starter, use the following ratios to feed the starter. You can feed it up to twice daily if you're baking regularly, or you can keep the starter refrigerated up to two weeks between baking sessions. Again, remember that you're only using a small portion of the existing starter, and you're discarding the balance of the starter you have on hand.

To maintain the starter, mix together the following ingredients and form them into a ball. Keep the ball covered in a jar so that a crust doesn't form.

- 1 tablespoon + 1 teaspoon (20g) starter
- ¾ cup + 2 teaspoons (100g) whole wheat flour
- ½ cup (60g) water

REFRESHING A STARTER. If you are leaving town or don't plan to bake for a few days, you can refrigerate or even freeze your starter. Give it a feed for two days before mixing the dough again.

6 Once you have a healthy starter going, you can begin to bake bread in a week from the time you created the starter.

If you feed your starter every day in the morning, give it an extra feed the night before you want to mix it into bread dough to increase its activity, and then use the starter the next morning. A starter is ready for use when it has doubled in volume and has a very webbed look when you pull the ball of the starter dough apart.

You can add other flours to the starter instead of whole wheat flour while feeding it. Rye is quite popular, because it makes the starter a lot more active. You will also see the result in the crumb of the bread when baked—the air pockets are a lot more intense.

HYDRATION is the amount of water you add to the dough. It is always expressed as a percent of the total amount of flour. For example, if the total amount of flour for a loaf weighs 1 pound (454g) and you are adding 12 ounces (340ml) water, the loaf is 75 percent hydrated. As you establish more ease and rhythm with your dough, you can work your way up to more hydration, which also means your bread can get the larger holes that bakers covet, and which demonstrate their mastery of technique. The higher the protein or gluten content in the flour, the more it can stretch to hold air. If there's too much air, the holes (bubbles in the dough) can collapse, leading to a dense, overfermented bread.

BREADMAKING TOOLS

Bench Scraper
This solid stainless steel tool is essential to help maneuver dough and lift it from the work surface.

Lame
You must always score the dough at an angle. This is a tool for scoring dough. You can also make your own with a coffee stirrer and a steel blade (refer to diagram).

Bannetons
These molds give a shape during final proofing to the loaves you bake. Two types of bannetons are widely available: one is made with rattan and the other with wood pulp. The swirled pattern of rattan bannetons helps give the loaf an attractive striped appearance. Wood pulp bannetons don't leave a pretty pattern on the loaf but are much easier to work with, because even high hydration doughs don't stick to them, making unmolding bread from the bannetons a breeze. For the recipes in this book, a 2-pound (1kg) banneton works best.

Dutch Oven (cast iron pot)
This is the piece of equipment that makes crusty bread a reality in home ovens. It replicates the effects of a professional steam oven. Preheating the pot for 30 minutes before you start baking is very important. And when you put the loaf in, bake it with the lid on for half the baking time. During this time, the loaf will steam in its own moisture and result in a bread that will rise better because the skin is moist and not sealed or crusted, enabling the bread to open up beautifully and to attain maximum volume.

WHITE COUNTRY LOAF

This is the most basic white loaf. You can play around with different types of flours such as rye, einkorn, spelt, buckwheat, and khorasan (also known as kamut). Bear in mind, though, that whole grain flours will give you a dense crumb. Each grain will lend its own unique flavor. Remember, timing depends on room temperature—the hotter it is, the faster the fermentation, so use any of our suggestions regarding timing as a guide rather than following them rigidly. The more you work with sourdough, the better you will get at playing with time so bread-baking works around your schedule (rather than the other way around). You can also control the timing element by using cold water on hot days.

PREP TIME 24 hours   BAKE TIME 50 minutes   MAKES 1 loaf

2 ½ cups (320g) water

1 cup (120g) starter

3⅓ cups (400g) unbleached bread flour/strong wheat flour, plus more

Rice flour

1½ teaspoons (8g) salt

Mix
In a bowl, add all but ¼ cup of the water, at about 80–86°F (27–30°C). Add the sourdough starter to the bowl and mix to disperse evenly in the water. Then add the flour and stir until hydrated. It's okay for it to look like a rough, shaggy mass.

Autolyse
Let this mixture sit for at least 30 minutes before you proceed to the next steps.

Knead
Next, mix together the remaining water with the salt and add it to the dough. If using a mixer, use a dough hook to mix the ingredients until they come together to form a smooth dough that pulls away from the sides of the bowl. If working by hand, stir the dough first with a wooden spoon and then knead it in the bowl.

Bulk Rise
Put the dough in a clean bowl and cover it with a cloth. Let it sit at room temperature for 2 to 3 hours for the bulk rise. Every 30 to 40 minutes, stretch and fold the dough over itself by pulling one side of the dough, then tucking it under. Rotate the bowl with one hand while you pull and stretch every corner of the dough, a total of 4 to 5 times. During the bulk rise the dough gains strength and stretches to a thin membrane without breaking as it pulls away from the bowl—indicating good gluten development.

Pre-Shape
Transfer the dough to a lightly floured work surface and stretch and fold the dough, just like you did when it was in the bowl. The flour should only be on the outer surface of the dough—do not add excess flour to the inside. Once you've stretched the dough and gathered it to the middle (like an envelope), flip the bread over and cup it to form a ball by rolling it on an un-floured part of the counter, building tension at the point to which the dough sticks to the work surface.

Bench Rest

Let it sit for 15 minutes. The dough will spread a bit, but it should have rounded, definite edges. If the edges are droopy, give them another stretch and fold to develop the gluten.

Final Shape

Repeat what you did in the pre-shaping: pull and stretch the dough from all four sides as if you were forming an envelope, then place all of the stretched ends toward the center of the dough and pinch them together in the center. Then flip it over so the seam is now in contact with the work surface. You want the dough to stick to the work surface at the bottom, so avoid using flour on the counter, and try to work quickly with a bench scraper instead. Flour the top of the dough lightly (the side on the top after flipping the dough over). Use your hands, or one hand and a bench scraper if you find that easier, to guide the movement of the dough as you pull it toward you and shape the dough into a ball. The dough should be stuck to the surface but should not leave dough bits behind. It should move as you guide it. This tension at the bottom of the dough creates a taut outer surface that when scored at the time of baking opens up beautifully. If you overdo it, the tension breaks and you may have to let the dough rest for a bit then start over with the final shaping.

Flour the surface of the dough and transfer it to a banneton that has been dusted with a mixture of equal parts of white wheat flour and rice flour.

Final Rise

Let the dough have a final rise in the banneton, loosely covered with a cloth, for 12 to 18 hours in the fridge. When you touch the surface of the dough it should spring back.

Bake

Half an hour before you are ready to bake, put the Dutch oven (cast iron pot) in the oven and turn up the temperature to the highest setting. Put the Dutch oven in the oven and turn up the temperature to the highest setting. After 30 minutes, remove the Dutch oven and place the dough inside it. Score the top of the dough with a lame or a blade. Be careful not to burn yourself.

Put the lid on the pot and bake the dough for 20 minutes at 475°F (250°C). Then reduce the temperature to 440°F (225°C), remove the lid and bake it for another 20 to 25 minutes until the dough has browned and the top appears to be blistered.

Transfer the bread from the pot to a wire rack and let it cool for an hour before slicing.

WEEKLY BAKING SCHEDULE

If you want to bake a loaf of bread on a Sunday morning,
we suggest following a schedule like this one:

FRIDAY	9AM	Remove starter from fridge and give it a feed
	9PM	Give the starter another feed
SATURDAY	9AM	Mix the dough
	9:30AM	Autolyse complete
	9:30AM–noon	Bulk fermentation—fold the dough
	Noon–12:30PM	Pre-shape and bench rest
	12:30PM	shape loaf, place into prepared banneton
	12:40PM	final proof in the fridge
SUNDAY	7–8AM	Remove from the refrigerator and bake

PAIN DE MIE

This classic white bread is made using a Franco-Japanese technique and is as light and fluffy as a cloud. Tang Zhong is a technique that originated in Japan and is used to create a gel that gives bread a soft crumb by helping it retain moisture longer without the use of preservatives.

PREP TIME 3 hours   BAKE TIME 45 minutes   MAKES 1 loaf

Tang Zhong
SCANT 2 tablespoons (25g) all-purpose flour
½ cup (115g) water

Dough
1 teaspoon (6g) instant yeast
½ cup (110g) milk
3 cups (350g) all- purpose flour
½ cup (115g) tang zhong
¼ cup (50g) sugar
1½ teaspoons (7g) salt
1 egg
2 tablespoons (30g) powdered milk
2 tablespoons (30g) butter

Tang Zhong
Make the tang zhong the night before or at least 6 hours ahead of when you want to make your loaf. In a pan, whisk together the flour and water and heat it gently, until it reaches 150°F (65°C) and thickens to form a glue-like paste. Make sure not to bring it to a simmer. Transfer the mixture to a small bowl, cover it, and refrigerate overnight. If you are pressed for time let it cool at room temperature for at least 4 to 6 hours.

Dough
In a bowl, dissolve the yeast in warm milk (about 105°F, or 40°C).

Add the flour and the rest of the ingredients, as well as the tang zhong.

Knead the mixture to form a smooth, elastic dough.

Let the dough rise for at least 2 hours, or until it has doubled in volume.

Divide the dough into 4 to 5 equal portions and then shape each portion into a ball.

Tuck the balls of dough into a large loaf pan brushed with butter.

Let the dough rise one-and-a-half times in volume.

Place the loaf pan in a preheated oven at 175°C (350°) for 35–45 minutes, until the bread has baked through and the internal temperature is 195°F (90°C). Remove from the pan once cool enough to handle. Cool completely on a wire rack before slicing.

BUTTERY HAZELNUT LOAF

Sourdough bread is leavened by the natural bacteria and yeast in the air, water, and flour. Sometimes, a little extra baker's yeast added to the dough helps the bread achieve an excellent volume in a shorter time, while still drawing benefits of flavor and texture from slow fermentation. With this butter-and-milk-powder-enriched hazelnut loaf, you will be on your way to making a silky soft crumb and a crisp, thin crust. It will give you the confidence to leave out all the yeast and make a loaf that has been entirely leavened by a sourdough starter.

PREP TIME 4½ hours   BAKE TIME 40 minutes   MAKES 1 loaf

3⅓ cups (400g) unbleached bread flour/strong wheat flour

SCANT 1 cup (225ml) water

⅓ cup + 2 tablespoons (100g) sourdough starter

¼ teaspoon (2g) instant yeast

1 tablespoon (20g) milk powder

1½ teaspoon (8g) sea salt

4 tablespoons (60g) butter

1 cup (150g) hazelnuts

In a bowl, mix together the flour, water, starter, and yeast until the flour is moistened. Let the mixture rest for 10 minutes and then add the milk powder, salt, and butter. Mix the dough by hand or on a low speed in a stand mixer until the dough comes together to form a shiny ball. Finally, mix in the hazelnuts until they are uniformly distributed.

The next steps to handling the dough are exactly the same as the White Country Loaf (page 73). Only the timing is different: autolyse: 10 minutes; bulk rise: 2 hours; final rise: 2 hours; baking time: 40 minutes.

TIP There are three different types of yeast on the market: instant, active dry, and fresh. To convert among these, the quick ratio is 1:2:3 (1 part instant equals to 2 parts active dry equals to 3 parts fresh).

FENNEL SEED CRACKERS

We add a little bit of spelt flour to our dough, but you can substitute whole wheat or plain all-purpose flour just as easily. Sometimes, we swap the fennel with anise seeds for a bit of a change. Most important tip: don't forget to sprinkle the crackers with plenty of flaky sea salt right before baking them (there's nothing worse than under-salted crackers!).

PREP TIME 15 minutes active, 15 minutes rest   BAKE TIME 25 minutes   SERVES 6–8

1⅔ cups (200g) all-purpose flour

½ cup (60g) spelt flour

⅔ cup (150g) cold butter, cubed

1 teaspoon (5g) fine sea salt

5 tablespoons (25g) fennel seeds

3 tablespoons (30g) confectioners' sugar

3 tablespoons (45g) cold water (as needed)

Fleur de sel or Maldon sea salt

Preheat the oven to 350°F (175°C).

Put both flours, the butter, and sea salt together in a bowl. Rub the butter into the flour swiftly with your fingertips until the mixture resembles coarse crumbs.

Scatter the fennel seeds evenly into the bowl. Stir in the confectioners' sugar. Next, add the water, a little at a time, until the dough comes together. If the dough is too dry add a little more water.

Don't overwork the dough or the crackers will be tough. Once it comes together, flatten the dough into a disk, wrap it in plastic, and refrigerate for 15 minutes.

Cut two pieces of parchment paper to the size of your baking pan. Place the dough between them and roll it out as thinly as possible. Transfer the rolled-out dough, with the parchment paper, onto your baking tray. Peel off the top sheet of parchment and sprinkle the dough with plenty of sea salt and gently push it in with a rolling pin.

Score the surface of the dough with a knife where you want to break off the crackers, and bake it for 20 to 25 minutes until golden.

Remove from the oven and let it cool. It will crisp up as it cools. Break into shards.

CIDER JELLY

This recipe comes from a Breton restaurant in Paris, Chez Michel, where Shaheen interned. There the cheese course was quite a spectacle—they wouldn't just lay out preproportioned pieces of cheese. Instead, they presented a large wooden board with a display of 5 to 6 large slabs of different seasonal cheeses, and cider jelly was always served on the side.

PREP TIME 5 minutes   COOK TIME 20 minutes   SERVES 6–8

⅓ cup (65g) pectin
2½ cups (500g) sugar
3 cups (750ml) apple cider

Mix the pectin with about ½ cup (100 g) of the sugar and give it a good stir.

In a saucepan, add the cider and pectin and sugar mixture and bring to a boil. Cook for 2 to 3 minutes over high heat.

Then add the remaining sugar and cook for another 2 to 3 minutes until completely dissolved.

To Store

Ladle the jelly into sterilized jars filled very close to the top (to have very little air) while it's still hot and place the jars in a canner, making sure that they are completely covered with water. Bring the water to a boil. Leave the jars in the boiling water for at least 10 minutes. Remove the jars and let them cool. Properly sealed jars can last up to 1 year in the pantry.

If you want to use the jelly immediately, pour the mixture into a flat, stainless steel tray and let it cool completely before neatly cutting it into squares for the cheese board. Refrigerate the leftovers.

CHEESE

A good cheese plate reflects different milks, textures, strengths, regions, and seasons to offer a well-rounded experience. It can be as simple or elaborate as you like. Have a minimum of three types of cheese on offer and make sure to serve them at room temperature.

Fresh goat cheese rolled in herbs or ash is perfectly mild. Have a spreading knife and a small pot of runny honey on hand to accentuate the flavors. For a slightly ripened goat cheese, we love a coin of Rocamadour that tastes of artichokes.

Have a wheel of a soft cheese with a bloomed rind on the plate. The edible rind of cheeses like Brie, Camembert, and Brillat-Savarin have a fuzzy texture, hence the name bloomed rind. Ask your cheese monger for a ripe wheel that will ooze richness when cut into.

Soft cheeses with a washed rind are an acquired taste—they can be identified by an orange-colored rind and pungent smell. Alsatian Munster is notoriously smelly. Other examples are Livarot, Maroilles, and Epoisses.

Pressed cheeses could be cooked (Gruyère, Comté) or uncooked (Manchego, Pecorino, or Cheddar). These can be served presliced on the platter. They are generally sweeter and less acidic.

And finally, include a wedge of creamy blue-veined cheese like Roquefort or Gorgonzola on the board to complete it.

If you are sitting around the table in the fall, you could even bake the wheel of Mont D'Or in its box. To do this, score the rind in a criss-cross fashion then slip in a few slices of garlic and a splash of dry white wine. Bake for 20 minutes at 340°F (170°C) and serve with crusty bread.

Our all-time favorite cheese platter will have a 24-month Comté, a perfectly ripe Brillat-Savarin, Rocamadour, and Stilton with grapes, Cider Jelly (at left), and Fennel Seed Crackers (page 77).

TARTINES

Tartines are what got this book started. We ran a little weekly pop-up in France, where we would cook a meal every Friday and have our friends come over for a lunch that promised to make everyone happy and give them something to look forward to all week. Word spread quickly and soon enough it became a restaurant-size operation feeding eighty customers during each meal. For our lunches, we served up a meal of a baguette sandwich, a drink, and dessert, all made by us with produce from the farm next door and cured meats from Italian co-ops and our neighborhood charcutier; baguettes were dropped off by our local boulanger on his little Vespa.

Because it may not be easy to find a good baguette quite as easily as it is in France, we re-created our most popular recipes as open-face sandwiches, or tartines. And because good bread is non-negotiable, you can re-create the perfect sourdough White Country Loaf (page 73) to make the tartines.

While tartines are pretty and delicate, we recommend piling high all of the ingredients of a tartine recipe and making it into one hearty sandwich to carry on the go. You could just as well skip the bread and make the toppings into a salad.

HOW WE TOAST OUR BREAD

When making tartines, we recommend cutting a good rustic sourdough loaf, like our White Country Loaf (page 73) into slices of medium thickness just when you need them. Brush the bread lightly with extra-virgin olive oil on one side before toasting it in a cast iron skillet over medium heat for a minute on each side. This way, the bread gets warm and crunchy and is more receptive to soaking up flavors. The idea is to have a thin, golden, toasted surface that is still warm when the spread is smeared onto the bread. This way it will soak up flavors without becoming soggy. Use the side that has not been brushed with olive oil to smear the spread (which will invariably have some fat component in it) and build the tartine.

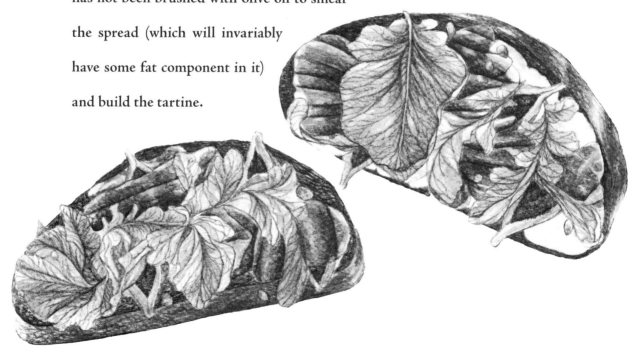

ZUCCHINI, ROASTED PEPPERS, ARTICHOKES,

BASIL PESTO, AND TOMATO CONFIT MAYONNAISE

Ossau-Iraty is a sheep's milk cheese that hails from the Basque region. If you can't find it, Manchego or even Pecorino Toscano is an excellent substitute. In this recipe, when cooking the zucchini, we wait till the very end of the cooking process to add the salt. This way, the zucchini stays crisp and retains its watery crunch.

PREP TIME 20 minutes   COOK TIME 15 minutes   MAKES 4 tartines

4 slices of bread, toasted

¼ cup (60g) Basil Pesto (page 186)

4 slices (100–125g) cooked ham

2 Roasted Peppers (page 194)

4–6 pieces (150–200g) marinated artichokes, well drained

A handful of arugula

2 ounces (60g) Ossau-Iraty or any firm sheep's milk cheese, shaved

Sea salt and freshly ground black pepper

Garlic Zucchini

1 tablespoon extra-virgin olive oil

1 clove garlic, germ removed and minced

1 zucchini

1 teaspoon dried oregano

Tomato Confit Mayonnaise

2 pieces of Tomato Confit (page 197) or sun-dried tomatoes

3 tablespoons Classic Mayonnaise (page 187)

Garlic Zucchini

Add the olive oil to a pan over medium heat, then add the minced garlic. Cut the zucchini diagonally into ¼-inch (6mm) thick slices and stir them into the pan. Cook the mixture until the zucchini has softened and has a few charred spots. Finally, crumble the dried oregano and add it the pan to coat the zucchini. Cook for another minute before taking the pan off the heat. Salt to taste.

Tomato Confit Mayonnaise

Chop the tomato confit into tiny cubes and stir it together with the mayonnaise.

Assemble

To assemble the tartine, spread the toasted bread with the basil pesto. Begin layering with the ham, zucchini, mixed roasted peppers, and artichokes. Finally, toss the arugula and shaved Ossau-Iraty with the tomato confit mayonnaise and gently place on top.

ASPARAGUS AND VALENÇAY
WITH BÉCHAMEL

Asparagus and Valençay, an unpasteurized goat cheese with a creamy yellow interior and an ash-coated exterior, come into season together in early spring. Legend has it that the cheese, which was once shaped like a perfect pyramid, is now made with a flattened top because when Napoleon returned to the castle of Valençay, after an unsuccessful expedition in Egypt and saw the cheese, it reminded him of the pyramids and he cut off the top with his sword in a fit of rage. When making this tartine you could also slip in a slice of cooked ham below the layer of béchamel to make it even more substantial and reminiscent of a croque monsieur.

PREP TIME 15 minutes   COOK TIME 20 minutes   MAKES 4 tartines

4 slices of bread, toasted

1 bunch asparagus, tough ends removed

3 tablespoons extra-virgin olive oil

4 tablespoons (60 g) salted butter

1 pyramid of Valençay (220g), or ½ pound (225g) of any ash-coated goat cheese

A handful of shaved Gruyère

½ cup alfalfa or sunflower sprouts

2 medium red radishes, thinly shaved

Sea salt and freshly ground black pepper

Béchamel

1 tablespoon butter

1 tablespoon all-purpose flour

¾ cup (200ml) cold whole milk

¼ teaspoon freshly grated nutmeg

½ teaspoon Dijon mustard

¼ teaspoon sea salt

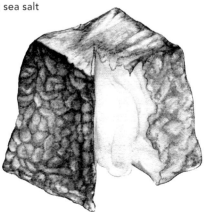

Béchamel
Melt the butter in a heavy-bottomed saucepan over medium heat. Whisk in the flour and continue to cook for 2 to 3 minutes, whisking vigorously, until the roux is fragrant and turns faintly golden. At this point, drizzle in a thin stream of the milk, whisking all the while. Once the milk has incorporated into the roux, increase the heat to medium-high and add the freshly grated nutmeg and Dijon mustard. Continue to cook until the sauce thickens. Season with salt and pepper.

Asparagus
In a large, heavy skillet over high heat (or under a broiler on high), sear the asparagus until charred but still very firm (about 4 to 5 minutes). Set aside.

Assemble
Butter both sides of all four slices of bread (½ tablespoon each side) and arrange them on a baking sheet. Spread the béchamel over all four slices of bread so that they are well coated. Dot with slices of Valençay and then arrange the asparagus on top, diagonally. Sprinkle with Gruyère, salt, and pepper. Broil until the cheese is toasted and just starting to blister. Remove and garnish with alfalfa sprouts and shaved radish.

WILD MUSHROOMS
AND POACHED EGGS
WITH ST. MARCELLIN AND CHIVES

A good mix of wild mushrooms doesn't need more than a nudge from garlic and lots of chopped parsley mixed in at the end of cooking. If you have some white wine or apple cider handy, you could even add a dribble, once the mushrooms have browned, to deglaze the pan and add extra flavor. Turn up the heat and reduce completely.

We like to use St. Marcellin, a cheese that's fairly firm when young and gets increasingly oozy as it matures. St. Félicien is very similar and you could use either of the two.

PREP TIME 20 minutes   COOK TIME 20 minutes   MAKES 4 tartines

Wild Mushrooms

10 ounces (300g) fresh wild mushrooms (such as chanterelles, girolles, trompettes, mousserons)

2 tablespoons extra-virgin olive oil

1 clove garlic, germ removed and minced

4 sprigs fresh thyme

1 tablespoon fresh parsley, chopped

Poached Eggs

4 organic eggs

4 tablespoons white wine vinegar

Assemble

2 pieces of St. Marcellin or 1 piece of St. Félicien (about 6 ounces/170g)

4 slices of bread, toasted

1 tablespoon chives, chopped

Sea salt and freshly ground black pepper

Wild Mushrooms

Brush any dirt off the mushrooms and trim as necessary. If the mushrooms are large, cut them into slices of about ½-inch (1cm). If they are small, keep them whole. Heat a large pan over medium heat and add the olive oil. Add the garlic, followed by the thyme a minute later. Turn up the heat and add the mushrooms, making sure that they don't crowd, or else they will steam instead of getting a good sear. Let the mushrooms cook for 2 to 3 minutes before you turn them over. Season with salt and pepper. Discard the sprigs of thyme, and stir in the parsley.

Poached Eggs

Start with very fresh eggs. Fill a medium saucepan with water and vinegar to more than half its capacity. Bring the water to a boil, then turn down the heat to a very gentle simmer. Create a whirlpool in the pot with a large spoon. Crack an egg into a cup and gently drop the egg into the simmering water. Cook the egg for 3 minutes and then remove it with a slotted spoon. Lay the egg on a paper towel and snip off any flailing bits of whites.

Assemble

Place thin slices of St. Marcellin or St. Félicien, whichever you're using, on the toasted bread. Spoon the hot mushrooms on the cheese so that it melts it a bit. Place the poached egg on the mushrooms. Season with salt and pepper and sprinkle with chives. Serve hot.

EGGPLANT KATSU
WITH QUICK-PICKLED VEGETABLES

Thanks to the influx of Japanese chefs in Paris, we're lucky to experience a taste of Tokyo in the city. From the udon restaurants with lines down the street, to the luxe, curtained dining rooms in St. Germain, the precision and craft of the Japanese way of handling ingredients shines through. This tartine is inspired by a meal at Abri (92, rue du Faubourg Poissonnière, 75010 Paris), where they serve a special sandwich menu for lunch.

PREP TIME 30 minutes   COOK TIME 30 minutes   MAKES 4 tartines

4 tablespoons Japanese-style Kewpie mayonnaise or Classic Mayonnaise (page 187)

4 slices of bread, toasted

1½ cups (125g) Gouda, sliced or shredded

Cilantro for garnish

Vegetable oil for frying

Sea salt and freshly ground black pepper.

Eggplant Katsu

2 medium eggplants, sliced into ½-inch (1cm) thick rounds

2 eggs, beaten

2 cups panko

Quick-Pickled Vegetables

½ tablespoon sea salt

1½ teaspoons sugar

¼ cup (60ml) rice wine vinegar

½ small red cabbage, thinly sliced

4 radishes, thinly sliced

Japanese-Style Omelet

2 teaspoons mirin

2 teaspoons soy sauce

2 teaspoons sugar

6 eggs, lightly beaten

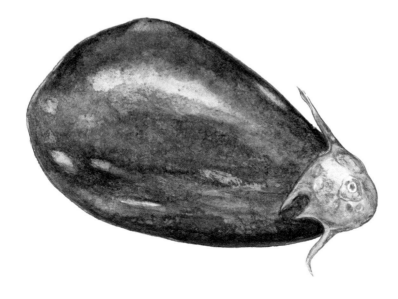

Eggplant Katsu

Prepare the egg wash by combining the beaten eggs with a teaspoon of water. Season with salt and pepper. Dip the eggplant slices into the egg wash and then turn them over in the panko a couple of times to coat.

Coat the bottom of a frying pan with vegetable oil and set it over medium-high heat. Cook the panko-coated eggplant rounds until golden, about 3–5 minutes on each side. Drain on a plate lined with paper towels.

Quick-Pickled Vegetables

Whisk together all the ingredients for the pickling mix, except the cabbage and radishes.

Toss together the cabbage and radishes with the pickling mix, making sure to give the vegetables an even coating. Cover with plastic wrap and let the mixture rest for 15 minutes, turning it over every 5 minutes. Drain off any of the excess liquid before using.

Japanese-Style Omelet

Add the mirin, soy sauce, and sugar to the lightly beaten egg. Season to taste with salt and pepper. Heat about 1 tablespoon of the vegetable oil in a frying pan over medium heat. Add the egg mixture and cook, stirring frequently, until it has just set, but is still soft.

Assemble

Spread 1 tablespoon of mayonnaise on each slice of toasted bread. Top with a handful of pickled vegetables, one-quarter of the scrambled egg mixture, and 3 slices of the Eggplant Katsu. Carefully place the Gouda on top of the mounded tartine and place it under the broiler for 2 to 3 minutes, until the cheese melts. Garnish with fresh cilantro and serve warm.

TIP: Japanese greens like mizuna and sisho make excellent additions to the sandwich, If you can get your hands on some.

GRAVLAX, CAPERS, SORREL,
AND CERVELLE DE CANUT

Cervelle de Canut literally translates to "Brains of a weaver." Thankfully, it is way more innocuous than it sounds. Cervelle de Canut is a tangy dip made with fromage blanc and packed with herbs, served as an appetizer, along with toasted bread, at *bouchons* (restaurants) in Lyon. It packs a punch with some sorrel and home-made gravlax piled up high.

PREP TIME 20 minutes   COOK TIME 5 minutes   MAKES 4 tartines

1 red onion, cut into thin rings

4 slices of bread, toasted

1 small bunch sorrel

2 ounces (60g) of Salmon Gravlax (page 15) per tartine

2 tablespoons capers

Sea salt and freshly ground black pepper

Cervelle de Canut

½ pound (225g) fromage blanc (or Greek yogurt)

2 tablespoons heavy cream

1 small shallot, finely chopped

1 clove of garlic, germ removed and minced

1 tablespoon parsley, chopped

1 tablespoon chives, chopped

1 tablespoon tarragon, chopped

2 tablespoons walnut oil

Put the slices of red onion into a bowl filled with ice water and let them sit for at least 20 minutes. This will help reduce their pungency.

Cervelle de Canut

In a bowl, mix together all the ingredients. Stir in the walnut oil. Season with salt and pepper. It makes an excellent dip with toasted White Country Loaf (page 73), too.

Assemble

Smear the Cervelle de Canut generously on the toasted bread and arrange the sorrel leaves on top. Place the sliced gravlax on the sorrel, then finally top with red onions and capers. Finish with salt and pepper. Serve with more Cervelle de Canut on the side.

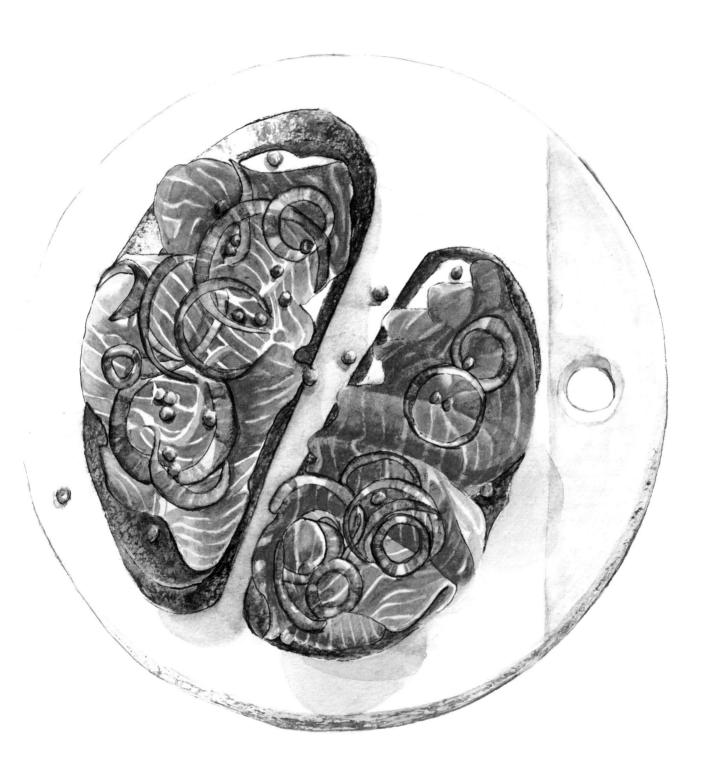

GINGER GARLIC CHICKEN
AND MINT CHUTNEY
WITH CRISPY SHALLOTS AND TAHINI DRIZZLE

Walk through the Porte St. Denis on Rue du Faubourg St. Denis and you will see all sorts of Middle Eastern shops—butchers, four-euro soup shops, and grocers (our stop for harissa, tahini, and their addictively good halvas). Off the street sits Passage Brady, where we would often stop to stock up on Indian spices, massive bunches of cilantro and mint, and the meat tenderizing powder we'd only find there. This powder is basically a mixture of salt, wheat, and pepsin enzyme, which is extracted from papayas and helps tenderize meat. In Indian cuisine, using a paste of raw papaya is quite common and you could use it in this recipe, if you can find it. Otherwise, the powder does the job just fine.

PREP TIME 1 hour   COOK TIME 30 minutes   MAKES 4 tartines

4 sliced of bread, toasted

3 vine-ripened tomatoes, cut into ½-inch (12mm) cubes

Fresh cilantro with tender stems

Ginger Garlic Chicken

2 boneless chicken thighs

½ teaspoon sea salt

1 teaspoon papaya tenderizer

3 tablespoons yogurt

1 inch (2.5cm) piece of ginger, grated

4 garlic cloves, germ removed and minced

1 teaspoon freshly ground black pepper

½ teaspoon cumin seeds, toasted and ground

½ teaspoon coriander seeds, toasted and ground

¼ teaspoon Indian red chili powder or cayenne pepper

Ghee or clarified butter for cooking

2 green chilies, chopped (as per taste)

1 tablespoon fresh mint, chopped

Crispy Shallots

1 cup (240ml) grapeseed oil

2 shallots, thinly sliced

Mint Chutney

1 bunch (30g) mint leaves

1 bunch (30g) cilantro leaves

1 tablespoon tamarind paste (or ½ lemon)

¼ teaspoon cumin seeds, toasted and ground

½ teaspoon sea salt

Tahini Drizzle

3 tablespoons (45ml) tahini

½ lemon

½ teaspoon sea salt

½ teaspoon cumin seeds, toasted and ground

3 tablespoons (45ml) water

1 tablespoon cilantro, finely chopped

Ginger Garlic Chicken

Cut the chicken into 1-inch (2.5cm) cubes and place them in a bowl with the salt and papaya tenderizer. Coat the chicken well and refrigerate it for an hour. After an hour, rinse the chicken with cold water and drain it. Put the chicken in a clean bowl and add the rest of the ingredients, except the ghee, green chilies, and mint. Coat the chicken well and let it marinate for at least another hour or overnight in the refrigerator.

Heat a pan and add the ghee or clarified butter, then add the green chilies and cook until fragrant, about 1 minute. Next, add the chicken and its marinade to the pan and cook until the meat is not pink in the middle. Take the pan off the heat and toss the chicken mixture in a bowl with the fresh mint. Keep warm.

Crispy Shallots

Heat a heavy-bottomed saucepan over medium-high heat and add the oil. Once the oil is hot, add the sliced shallots and cook until they turn dark golden brown. Keep stirring to keep the shallots from burning in spots near the edge of the pan. Drain the fried shallots on a paper towel.

Mint Chutney

Blend all the ingredients together. Add a tablespoon of water to help loosen it up if necessary.

Tahini Drizzle

In a bowl, whisk together the tahini, lemon, salt, cumin, and water until smooth and shiny. If it is still too thick, add 1 tablespoon of water at a time. Check for seasoning. Once it is thin enough to drizzle, stir in the chopped cilantro.

Assemble

Smear the mint chutney on toasted bread, and then begin layering with the chicken, chopped tomatoes, and fried shallots. Finish with tahini drizzle and sprinkle with cilantro leaves.

ZA'ATAR CHICKEN
AND TURKISH SALAD

WITH HARISSA WALNUT BUTTER AND CUMIN-CILANTRO YOGURT SAUCE

U rfa biber pepper flakes—also known as isot—have a lasting, savory spice and deep smokiness that are reminiscent of chipotle peppers (which can be used as a substitute). Once you have tried some, you will have to restrain yourself from putting them in everything. This recipe is for a whole roasted chicken, which means you will have plenty of leftovers for extra tartines.

PREP TIME 30 minutes   COOK TIME 1 hour 15 minutes   MAKES 4 tartines

4 slices bread, toasted

Fresh cilantro for garnish

Sea salt and freshly ground black pepper

Spice Mix

1½ teaspoons cumin seeds

1 teaspoon black peppercorns

½ teaspoon coriander seeds

Za'atar Chicken

4 garlic cloves, germ removed, minced and mashed to a paste

2 teaspoons sumac

¼ teaspoon ground clove

2 teaspoons smoked sweet paprika

2 tablespoons za'atar

4 tablespoons (60ml) extra-virgin olive oil

3 tablespoons (45ml) lemon juice

1 teaspoon lemon zest

1½ teaspoons sea salt

1 whole free range chicken

Cumin-Cilantro Yogurt Sauce

1 garlic clove, germ removed, minced, and mashed to a paste

1 teaspoon fresh lemon juice

1 tablespoon best-quality extra-virgin olive oil

1½ cups (350g) full-fat Greek yogurt, strained

2 tablespoons fresh cilantro leaves, chopped

Turkish Salad

2 tablespoons fresh lemon juice

¼ cup (60ml) best-quality extra-virgin olive oil

1½ teaspoons sumac

½ teaspoon isot or crumbled dried chipotle peppers

2 tablespoons flat-leaf parsley, chopped

2 tablespoons fresh mint, chopped

3 tablespoons fresh dill, chopped

1 pound (450g) cherry tomatoes, halved

1 large cucumber, cut into ½-inch (12mm) cubes

1 yellow pepper, cut into ¼-inch (6mm) cubes

½ red onion, thinly sliced

¼ cup (20g) Kalamata olives, pitted and quartered

Harissa Walnut Butter

1 cup (225g) of Harissa (page 191)

½ cup (50g) toasted walnuts, coarsely chopped

Spice Mix

In a small skillet set over medium heat, toast the cumin seeds, black peppercorn, and coriander seeds until fragrant. Cool slightly and grind to a powder in a mortar and pestle or with a rolling pin. Set aside and divide into three equal portions.

Za'taar Chicken

Combine the garlic, a teaspoon of the spice mix, the sumac, clove, smoked sweet paprika, za'taar, olive oil, lemon juice, lemon zest, and salt. Pat the chicken dry with a paper towel and then rub the mixture over the entire surface of the chicken, as well as under the skin and in the cavity.

Coat the bottom of a Dutch oven (or other large cast iron pot) with olive oil and place the chicken in it.

Put the Dutch oven in a cold oven, then turn the heat up to 450°F (225°C), and cook for 1 hour. For this recipe we are not using the skin, so we don't want it browned. In case you are making a roast to serve it whole, uncover the chicken during the last 15 to 20 minutes to brown the skin.

To check for doneness, you can also tilt the chicken with the help of a roasting fork and check the color of the juices. If they are bloody, the chicken isn't cooked yet. You can also cut into the thickest part of the thigh joint to see if the flesh closest to the bone is still translucent and pink, in which case the chicken is not done. If it isn't, continue roasting for another 10 minutes before you check again. Remove from the oven, tent with foil, and let sit for 10 minutes before carving. Once rested, carve the meat to pull apart into bite-size pieces. Keep warm.

Cumin-Cilantro Yogurt Sauce

Combine the garlic, a teaspoon of the spice mix, lemon juice, and olive oil in a mixing bowl. Whisk until well combined and then stir in the Greek yogurt. Season to taste with salt and pepper, and finish by stirring in fresh cilantro.

Turkish Salad

Make lemon vinaigrette by combining the lemon juice and salt. Whisk until the salt has dissolved and then slowly drizzle in the olive oil, whisking all the while, until thickened. Add the sumac, isot, and fresh herbs.

Combine the remaining ingredients in a large mixing bowl and toss together. Drizzle with the lemon vinaigrette and let sit at room temperature for about 15 minutes before serving.

Harissa Walnut Butter

Place the harissa and half the walnuts in a blender or food processor with a glug of olive oil. Add additional olive oil and cold water (a tablespoon at a time) if required to help bring it all together. Once it's reached a spreadable consistency, remove from the blender or food processor and gently stir in the remaining chopped walnuts. Store in the refrigerator up to a week.

Assemble

Smear a thin layer of Harissa Walnut Butter on the bread and then place small handful of shredded Za'taar Chicken over the top. Spoon over the Turkish Salad so that it fits into the spaces between the chicken. Drizzle with the Cumin-Cilantro Yogurt Sauce, top with fresh cilantro leaves and serve.

ROASTED CHICKEN, BACON, TOMATOES, AND AVOCADO

WITH MAYONNAISE AND BABY GEM LETTUCE

This tartine is so simple, yet such a crowd pleaser—but then again who doesn't love the coming together of smoky bacon and creamy avocado? Extra mayonnaise helps make it even richer.

And if you find yourself in Paris on a Sunday morning, pop downstairs to your local butcher for their *poulet rôti*. There is something incredibly satisfying about buying a rotisserie chicken with a generous helping of baby potatoes that have been cooked in the chicken fat drippings. Toss a green salad to complete your lovely Sunday lunch. And when you have some leftover chicken, make this tartine the next day.

PREP TIME 15 minutes   COOK TIME 15 minutes   MAKES 4 tartines

4 slices of bread, toasted

4 slices of smoked bacon

2 Cold-Oven Chicken breasts (page 20)

4 tablespoons Classic Mayonnaise (page 187)

2 vine-ripened tomatoes, sliced

Extra-virgin olive oil

2 avocados, sliced

1 lime, juiced

Crispy lettuce (2 heads of baby gem lettuce or 1 head of romaine)

Sea salt and freshly ground black pepper

Lemon Vinaigrette

1 tablespoon lemon juice

3 tablespoons best-quality extra-virgin olive oil

Crispy Bacon

Heat a heavy pan, preferably cast iron, over medium heat. Add the bacon and cook on both sides until crispy. Drain excess fat on a paper towel.

Lemon Vinaigrette

Stir the lemon juice with salt and pepper to taste, then whisk in the olive oil until thickened.

Assemble

Shred the chicken and then toss it with the mayonnaise. Set aside. Place the sliced tomatoes on the toasted bread, drizzle with olive oil, and season with salt and pepper. Next, place the avocado slices on top. Squeeze the lime over the avocado and sprinkle with plenty of salt. Layer the chicken and scatter the bacon bits on top. Cut the lettuce into slim wedges and toss together with the vinaigrette before placing on top of the tartine.

TURKEY AND ENGLISH CHEDDAR
WITH PUMPKIN SEEDS AND TARRAGON AÏOLI

For a quintessentially French experience, Rue Cler is the perfect place to wander because it isn't packed with as many tourists as the bustling Rue Montorgueil. This cobblestone street, minutes away from the Eiffel Tower, also happens to be one of the few places in Paris where you can find fresh cranberries around Thanksgiving and Christmas—which makes us wonder if Julia Child, who lived in the neighborhood, had anything to do with this. Needless to say, this tartine is inspired by the holidays and is the perfect way to get the most out of any leftovers.

PREP TIME 20 minutes   COOK TIME 45 minutes   MAKES 4 tartines

4 slices of bread, toasted

¾ cup Tarragon Aïoli (page 196)

8 thin slices of oven-roasted turkey, from the deli or holiday leftovers

1½ cups (150g) sharp white cheddar cheese, shaved

A handful of radish or red beet microgreens

Sea salt and freshly ground black pepper

Cinnamon-Port Cranberry Sauce

1 12-ounce (340g) package fresh cranberries

¾ cup (180g) water

¾ cup (150g) sugar

1 orange, zested and juiced

1 tablespoon ruby red or tawny port

1 cinnamon stick

¼ teaspoon sea salt

Spiced Pumpkin Seeds

1 cup (130g) pumpkin seeds

1 teaspoon extra-virgin olive oil

¼ teaspoon cumin seeds, toasted and ground

½ teaspoon smoked sweet paprika

½ teaspoon chipotle pepper or "isot" (see page 92 for explanation)

¼ teaspoon ground cinnamon

2 teaspoons light brown sugar

Cinnamon-Port Cranberry Sauce

Combine all ingredients in a small saucepan and place over medium-high heat. Bring the liquid to a boil and then reduce heat. Simmer until cranberries burst and soften. Skim off any foam that accumulates on the top. Continue to simmer until the mixture is slightly reduced and thickened, at least 20 minutes. Remove from the heat and discard the cinnamon stick before serving.

Spiced Pumpkin Seeds

Preheat the oven to 350°F (175°C). Combine the shelled pumpkin seeds with the olive oil, ground cumin, paprika, chipotle pepper, ground cinnamon, and brown sugar. Spread the mixture in an even single layer over a baking sheet lined with parchment paper. Bake until the seeds are golden brown and crispy, 15 to 20 minutes. Remove them from the oven and spread out the seeds with a fork so that they don't clump together.

Assemble

Preheat broiler to high, 475°F (245°C). Spread the aïoli over the warm toasted bread and top with two folded slices of turkey. Spoon over a couple dollops of the cranberry sauce and top with shaved sharp white cheddar cheese. Place the tartine directly under the broiler. Cook until the cheese bubbles and starts to blister. Remove the tartine from the oven, sprinkle it with spiced pumpkin seeds, and garnish with microgreens.

TURKEY, AVOCADO, AND MISO-GLAZED EGGPLANT

WITH CASHEW-HONEY GOAT CHEESE AND SEARED ROMAINE

Rue Saint-Anne, a small street nestled amid the iconic Haussmannian buildings of Paris's expansive avenues and just blocks from Opéra Garnier, is populated with Japanese restaurants that are packed with locals. We would always combine a restaurant visit with a bit of shopping down the street at Juji-ya, a Japanese grocery store, or a Korean one-stop shop nearby, where we'd stock up on miso, seaweed to sprinkle on rice, and Korean red chili to make kimchi at home.

PREP TIME 15 minutes   COOK TIME 30 minutes   MAKES 4 tartines

4 slices bread, toasted

4 slices smoked turkey

Sea salt and freshly ground black pepper

Cashew-Honey Goat Cheese

¾ cup (175g) fresh goat cheese, room temperature

½ cup (62g) cream cheese, room temperature

⅓ cup (50g) cashews, toasted and roughly chopped

4 cloves of Garlic Confit (page 190), mashed

1 teaspoon lemon juice

1 teaspoon fresh thyme leaves, chopped

1 teaspoon honey

Lemon Vinaigrette

1 tablespoon lemon juice

3 tablespoons (45ml) best-quality extra-virgin olive oil

Miso-Glazed Eggplant

1 inch (2.5cm) piece of ginger, peeled and grated

1 tablespoon mirin

1 tablespoon sake

2 teaspoons brown sugar

2 tablespoons miso

1 teaspoon soy sauce

1 teaspoon sesame oil

2 tablespoons extra-virgin olive oil

2 medium-size eggplants, cut diagonally into ¼-inch (6mm) slices

Seared Romaine

1 head baby Romaine lettuce

1 tablespoon grapeseed oil

1 lemon, zest only

1 tablespoon Parmigiano Reggiano, grated

Cashew-Honey Goat Cheese

Whip together the goat cheese and cream cheese. Once aerated and fluffy, add in remaining ingredients. Season with salt, pepper, and additional lemon juice as necessary.

Lemon Vinaigrette

Slowly add the olive oil into the lemon juice in a steady drizzle until mixture thickens. Season to taste with salt and pepper.

Miso-Glazed Eggplant

Grate the ginger using a fine grater or Microplane. Squeeze the grated ginger pulp to to extract all of the juice and then discard the fibrous pulp. Heat the mirin and the sake in a small saucepan over high heat. Once the liquid comes to a boil, reduce heat to low and simmer. Whisk in the brown sugar, miso, soy sauce, and ginger juice until well combined and the sugar has dissolved. Remove from heat and stir in the sesame oil.

In a large, ovenproof skillet, heat the olive oil over a medium flame. Sear the eggplants on both sides, working in batches if necessary. Once all the eggplant slices have been cooked, arrange them in the same skillet or on a baking sheet lined with parchment paper if your skillet isn't quite big enough.

Turn on your oven broiler to high, about 475°F (245°C) and allow to preheat. Brush the eggplants with a thin layer of the miso glaze. Place the skillet directly under the broiler. Cook until the glaze begins to bubble and brown, about 3 to 5 minutes. Make sure to keep an eye on it because the sugars in the glaze can caramelize and burn very quickly.

Seared Romaine

Cut the lettuce in half through the hard core at the base, then cut it into slim wedges, using the core as an anchor for the leaves. Heat a pan on high heat. When it's very hot, add the grapeseed oil. Sear the wedges for a minute on each side so that they are lightly charred. Pull off the heat and season with salt and pepper. Zest the lemon directly over the lettuce and sprinkle with Parmigiano Reggiano. Use immediately.

Assemble

Smear the Cashew-Honey Goat Cheese spread on the toasted bread. Lay a turkey slice over the spread and top with the glazed eggplant. Add another dollop of Cashew-Honey Goat Cheese. Lay a wedge of seared Romaine on top and spread a spoonful of Lemon Vinaigrette over the top so that it seeps between the lettuce leaves.

PROSCIUTTO AND BUFFALO MOZZARELLA

WITH ARUGULA AND RED PEPPER MAYONNAISE

This tartine is a really simple one, but it means that you must get your hands on the silkiest Prosciutto di Parma and the freshest, creamiest buffalo mozzarella you can find. For the dressing, we like to use Banyuls vinegar, which is made from a dessert wine of the same name, and has a mellower flavor than the typical red wine vinegar. Sherry vinegar is a good substitute.

PREP TIME 15 minutes   COOK TIME 5 minutes   MAKES 4 tartines

4 slices of bread, toasted

4 slices of Prosciutto

9 ounces (250g) buffalo mozzarella, cut into thick slices

4 whole Roasted Peppers (page 194), cut into medium slices

A handful of arugula

Sea salt and freshly ground black pepper

Roasted Red Pepper Mayonnaise

½ cup Classic Mayonnaise (page 187)

2 tablespoons Roasted Peppers (page 194), drained and chopped

Basil and Banyuls Dressing

1 tablespoon Banyuls vinegar or sherry vinegar

3 tablespoons best-quality extra-virgin olive oil

4–6 fresh basil leaves

Roasted Red Pepper Mayonnaise

Cut a piece of a roasted pepper into tiny cubes, then stir them into the mayonnaise.

Basil and Banyuls Dressing

Whisk together the vinegar with salt and pepper to taste, then drizzle in the olive oil and whisk until thickened. Stack the basil leaves together, gently folding them over the center spine and cut them into very thin slices. Stir the basil into the dressing.

Assemble

Spread a layer of the Roasted Red Pepper Mayonnaise on the toasted bread and then layer the tartine, first with a slice of Prosciutto, followed by the mozzarella and roasted red peppers. Finally, toss the arugula in the Basil and Banyuls Dressing and gently place it on top.

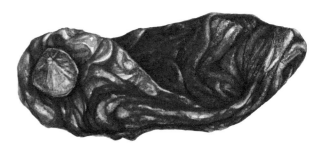

HERB-ROASTED HAM, EGGPLANT, AND TOMATO CONFIT
WITH ALMOND PARSLEY PESTO AND COMTÉ

This is just the kind of sandwich we like to take to a park for a game of *pétanque*. The almond parsley pesto used in this recipe is so versatile, we make large batches and then use it with everything—on sandwiches and pasta, alongside chestnut squash, or on its own with a good crusty bread.

PREP TIME 15 minutes   COOK TIME 15 minutes   MAKES 4 tartines

4 sliced of bread, toasted

4 tablespoons almond parsley pesto
(Follow the recipe for Pistachio Parsley Pesto on page 193, using almonds instead.)

4 slices herb-roasted ham

6–7 pieces of Tomato Confit (page 197) or sun-dried tomatoes as substitute, cut into strips

A handful of mixed young greens (arugula, chard, red beet, mustard)

4 ounces (112g) aged Comté (18 months), shaved into thin slices

Sea salt and freshly ground black pepper

Garlic Eggplant

1 medium eggplant

1 teaspoon sea salt

1 teaspoon dried oregano

1 clove of garlic, germ removed and minced

¼ cup (60ml) extra-virgin olive oil

½ teaspoon freshly ground black pepper

Lemon Vinaigrette

1 tablespoon lemon juice

3 tablespoons best-quality extra-virgin olive oil

Garlic Eggplant

Slice the eggplant into vertical strips about ¼-inch (6mm) thick. Place the strips in a large bowl and salt them lightly. Set the bowl aside for 10 minutes. Drain off any water that has collected in the bottom of the bowl, and then toss the eggplant with the oregano, garlic, olive oil, and pepper to coat. Place a pan over medium heat and cook the eggplant strips on both sides. To get a nice sear, avoid turning the strips frequently—let them sit in one place for 3 to 5 minutes before flipping them. Once the eggplant is well browned and softened, season to taste.

Lemon Vinaigrette

Make the vinaigrette by whisking the lemon juice with salt and pepper to taste in a small bowl and then drizzle in the olive oil.

Assemble

Spread the toasted bread with the almond and parsley pesto. Then add a layer of herb-roasted ham, eggplant, and tomato confit. Next, toss the greens with the Comté and coat with the lemon dressing. Pile the dressed greens and cheese on the tartine.

SPECK, ROASTED FIGS, GOAT CHEESE,
AND PINE NUTS WITH ARUGULA

Roasted figs were all the rage at the Breton restaurant in Paris where Shaheen worked. To prepare them, a cross was cut into the top of three figs, which were then placed in a small copper dish, drizzled with honey, and roasted until the juices bubbled and the figs opened up like flowers. They were served piping hot from the oven with a delicate scoop of vanilla ice cream. With that inspiration in mind, we set out to make something savory— roasted figs with black pepper (or cumin if you enjoy its earthiness), fresh goat cheese, peppery arugula, and Speck together on a tartine.

PREP TIME 15 minutes   COOK TIME 20 minutes   MAKES 4 tartines

4 slices of bread, toasted

4 tablespoons extra-virgin olive oil

½ pound (225g) fresh goat cheese

8 slices of Speck or a good smoked, dry-cured ham

A big handful of arugula

¼ cup (35g) pine nuts, toasted

Sea salt and freshly ground black pepper

Honey Roasted Figs

½ pound (225g) fresh and perfectly ripe figs, quartered

4 teaspoons extra-virgin olive oil

3 tablespoons honey

½ teaspoon coarse sea salt

¼ teaspoon freshly ground black pepper

4 sprigs fresh thyme

Walnut Oil Vinaigrette

1 tablespoon white balsamic vinegar

1 tablespoon walnut oil

1 tablespoon extra-virgin olive oil

Honey Roasted Figs

Preheat the oven to 400°F (200°C). Line a small baking sheet with parchment paper and arrange the figs, flesh side up, so that they're close together but not touching. Drizzle with olive oil, honey, and a pinch each of salt and black pepper. Scatter the thyme in the pan. Bake until the figs have begun to brown and caramelize, 10 to 15 minutes.

Walnut Oil Vinaigrette

Whisk a pinch of salt into the vinegar until it completely dissolves. Drizzle in the walnut and olive oils, whisking vigorously, until the vinaigrette thickens. Season to taste with freshly ground black pepper and additional salt as necessary.

Assemble

Brush each slice of toasted bread with a tablespoon of extra-virgin olive oil, and then smear the bread with fresh goat cheese. Arrange the roasted figs evenly across the tartines, then lay a slice of Speck on the figs, pinching it in spots so that the figs are visible. Just before serving, toss the arugula in the Walnut Oil Vinaigrette and arrange it gently on top of the Speck. Scatter toasted pine nuts over the greens and season with salt and pepper.

SMOKED HAM, BRIE, AND ONION JAM
WITH BUTTERY ALMONDS AND GARLIC ZUCCHINI

We love how zucchini, almonds, and thyme work together in this tartine. The butter-fried almonds alone are incredibly addictive, so we always make a bit more to snack on while we get the rest of the sandwich ready.

The onion jam is not something you can whip up on a whim. It takes a bit of planning and a lot of onions to make it worthwhile—so you can have plenty to jar and use for weeks. It is important that you use a heavy-bottomed pan to cook the onions because you don't want them to stick or burn prematurely. For a full flavor, you want them to cook gently and caramelize evenly.

We like to place fairly thick slices of a perfectly ripe Brie de Meaux—with it's rich, golden color and contrasting white bloom—on the tartines. If you have the good fortune of finding some Rocamadour, by all means use it! This utterly creamy goat cheese, with flavors of artichokes and hazelnuts, is unparalleled.

PREP TIME 20 minutes   COOK TIME 1 hour 15 minutes   MAKES 4 tartines

4 slices of bread, toasted

8 ounces (225g) Brie, rind removed and cut into slices

4 slices dry-cured ham like Bayonne or Serrano

A handful of arugula

Sea salt and freshly ground black pepper

Onion Jam

12–15 cloves of Garlic Confit (page 190)

2 pounds (900g) onions

2 tablespoons extra-virgin olive oil

4 tablespoons brown sugar

½ cup (120ml) water

4 tablespoons balsamic vinegar

Buttery Almonds

1 tablespoon butter

3 sprigs fresh thyme

¼ cup (35g) almonds, coarsely chopped

Garlic Zucchini

1 tablespoon extra-virgin olive oil

1 clove of garlic, germ removed and minced

1 zucchini, cut on a diagonal into ¼-inch (6mm) thick slices

1 teaspoon dried oregano

Hazelnut and Honey Vinaigrette

1½ tablespoons honey vinegar (or 1 tablespoon white wine vinegar with ½ teaspoon honey)

¼ teaspoon sea salt

2 tablespoons hazelnut oil

1 tablespoon extra-virgin olive oil

Onion Jam

Peel the garlic confit and mash together with a fork. Coarsely chop the onions into chunks. Chopping them too finely will make them mushy instead of giving them a chunky, spreadable texture.

In a saucepan over medium heat, add the olive oil and stir in the onions. Reduce the heat to low, and cover for 10 minutes for the onions to sweat.

Uncover the pan, stir in the sugar and continue to cook for 20 to 30 minutes until the onions are golden. Add ¼ cup water, if the onions are drying out too quickly before they're fully caramelized. Cover the pan and continue to cook the onions until they are dark brown, an additional 20 to 30 minutes. Add the balsamic vinegar, mashed garlic confit, and salt. Continue to cook, uncovered, until the water has evaporated, about 10 minutes. Transfer the onion jam to a container after it has cooled. Keep it refrigerated up to 1 month.

Buttery Almonds

Place a pan over medium heat, add the butter, and let it sizzle. Add the thyme, followed by the chopped almonds, and cook for 4 to 5 minutes until the almonds are golden brown. Stir constantly to prevent them from burning. Season with salt and coarsely ground pepper.

Garlic Zucchini

Place a pan with olive oil over medium heat, then add the minced garlic. Stir in the zucchini. Cook the zucchini until it has softened and has a few charred spots. Finally, crumble the dried oregano into the pan, to coat the zucchini. Cook for another minute before taking the pan off the heat. Salt to taste.

Hazelnut and Honey Vinaigrette

In a bowl, whisk together the honey vinegar and salt until the salt has dissolved. Slowly drizzle in the oils, whisking all the while, until thickened. Add freshly ground black pepper and additional salt to taste.

Assemble

Spread the Onion Jam on the toasted bread. Next, top it with slices of Brie, smoked ham, and zucchini. Finally, toss the arugula with the Hazelnut and Honey Vinaigrette and place it gently on top. Scatter the tartine with the buttery thyme almonds and serve.

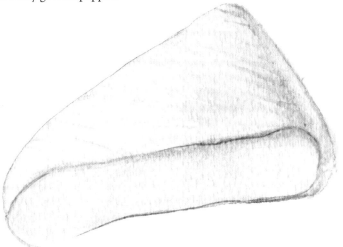

PORCHETTA

WITH CARAMELIZED APPLE AND FENNEL SAUCE

This recipe for porchetta makes a lot—it's only fair to scale up when making pork cooked over 5 hours to moist, fork-tender perfection. If you can't find fennel pollen, you could substitute with toasted and ground fennel seeds. When we find it, we really like using a fresh, full-fat cream cheese such as Robiola Ossela. It's so versatile and works beautifully dolloped on roasted vegetables or smeared on toast with a touch of honey.

PREP TIME 30 minutes   COOK TIME 5 hours   MAKES 4 tartines + extra porchetta

4 slices of bread, toasted

2 tablespoons (30ml) cup extra-virgin olive oil

2 teaspoons fresh parsley, chopped

2 teaspoons fresh oregano, chopped

Zest of 1 lemon

8 ounces (225g) fresh cream cheese

A big handful of arugula

Sea salt and freshly ground black pepper

Porchetta

1 boneless pork shoulder with skin on (about 3.5 pounds/1.5kg)

15 fresh sage leaves

3 sprigs fresh thyme

3 sprigs fresh rosemary

4 garlic cloves, germ removed and minced

1 tablespoons fennel pollen

2 tablespoons extra-virgin olive oil

½ cup (120ml) white wine

Caramelized Apple and Fennel Sauce

3 tablespoons (45g) sugar

1½ tablespoons (20g) butter

3 Granny Smith apples, peeled and chopped

½ teaspoon fennel seeds, toasted and ground

Hazelnut Oil Vinaigrette

1 teaspoon red wine vinegar

3 tablespoon hazelnuts oil

Porchetta

Preheat the oven to 450°F (225°C).

With a sharp knife, cut through the pork skin in a crisscross pattern.

In a food processor, pulse the sage, thyme, rosemary, and garlic together (you could finely chop them, too). Place the mixture in a small bowl and stir together with the fennel pollen, salt, pepper, and olive oil.

Lay the pork with the skin side on a chopping board and rub half of the herb mix on the fleshy side. Roll the pork over itself and tie it tightly with kitchen twine. Rub the remaining herb mix on the skin side.

Place the pork in a roasting pan with the skin side up and roast for 30 minutes. Remove the pan from the oven and pour in the white wine. Give the roasting pan a scraping to dislodge the browned bits. Use a spoon to baste the pork with the liquid. Reduce the temperature to 250°F (125°C). Put the pan back into the oven and roast the pork for another 4 hours, while you continue to baste every 30 to 40 minutes.

Rest for 15 minutes before carving 2 to 3 thin slices per tartine. If you don't need the pork immediately, it's much easier to carve into neat slices when cooled.

Caramelized Apple and Fennel Sauce

Heat the sugar in a heavy-bottomed pan and cook over medium heat until caramelized. Stir it from time to time and stay alert—the sugar can burn quickly because it is such a small quantity. Once it's a deep amber liquid, add the butter and stir to combine. It will froth up, so be careful.

Next, add the apples and cook until softened.

Once the apples are softened, add the ground fennel seeds, stir, and cook, covered, for another minute or so.

Purée the mixture in a food processor or with an immersion blender.

Hazelnut Oil Vinaigrette

Drizzle the hazelnut oil into the vinegar and whisk until thickened. Season to taste with salt and pepper.

Assemble

Combine the olive oil with the chopped herbs and lemon zest. Season to taste with salt and pepper and then toss the porchetta slices to coat in the mixture. Spread the cream cheese on the toasted bread and then top with a thin layer of the apple and fennel sauce. Place slices of the Porchetta on top. Toss the arugula in the vinaigrette and pile it on the Porchetta.

LARDO DI COLONNATA

WITH BASIL PESTO

Lardo di Colonnata is the creamy, melting, tender version of pork fat cured between layers of salt, herbs, and garlic. You can buy lardo in blocks or thinly sliced like ham. Few things get better than paper-thin shavings of lardo on toast smeared with this zesty pesto.

PREP TIME 5 minutes   MAKES 4 tartines

4 slices of thickly cut sourdough bread, toasted

4 tablespoons Basil Pesto (page 186)

8 slices of Lardo di Colonnata

Freshly ground black pepper

Assemble

Spread the pesto on the toasted slices of bread. Lay two slices of lardo on each slice. Sprinkle with freshly ground black pepper and serve.

BRESAOLA
AND MARINATED ZUCCHINI
WITH CRUNCHY ALMOND BROWN BUTTER

In this tartine, the flavor of bresaola—an Italian dry-cured beef—is accentuated by the addition of citrus, herbs, and zucchini slices that have been marinated in lemon and garlic. The longer you leave the mix in the refrigerator, the more tender and mild it becomes.

PREP TIME 30 minutes active, 2 hours rest   COOK TIME 15 minutes   MAKES 4 tartines

4 slices of bread, toasted

8 very thin slices of Bresaola (or other dry-cured beef)

1 tablespoon fresh basil leaves, rolled up and thinly sliced

½ cup (50g) Parmigiano Reggiano, shaved

2 tablespoons Dukkah (page 188) + extra for garnish

Sea salt and freshly ground black pepper

Marinated Zucchini

1 small garlic clove, germ removed and minced

Zest of 1 lemon

2 tablespoons lemon juice

2 tablespoons extra-virgin olive oil

1 pound (450g) green and yellow zucchini, sliced thinly on the diagonal using a mandoline

Crunchy Almond Brown Butter

2 tablespoons salted butter

3 tablespoons crunchy almond butter

1 teaspoon honey

½ teaspoon lemon zest

1 tablespoon lemon juice

Marinated Zucchini

Combine the garlic, lemon zest, lemon juice, olive oil, salt, and pepper to taste, in a medium mixing bowl. Add the shaved zucchini and toss to coat. Refrigerate for about 2 hours before using.

Crunchy Almond Brown Butter

Place the salted butter in a small saucepan over medium heat. Let the butter melt, come to a boil, foam, and then settle to form brown butter. This will take a few minutes and can burn very quickly, so be sure to keep your eye on the stove. Rather than stir, swirl the pan around to check the status of the browning.

Once you detect a distinctly nutty scent, transfer to a shallow bowl and refrigerate until firm.

Combine the brown butter with the almond butter. Add the honey, lemon zest, and lemon juice. Season the butter with additional honey or salt as desired.

Assemble

Remove the zucchini from the refrigerator and toss it with the basil, Parmigiano Reggiano, and Dukkah (page 188).

Smear one side of each slice of bread with the Crunchy Almond Brown Butter. Gently fold two slices of Bresaola onto the bread and top with a neat handful of the zucchini mixture.

MEATBALLS in AMALFITANA SAUCE
with ROASTED PEPPER AND GRUYÈRE

These meatballs were among the most popular items on our menu. Although we served them stuffed in a baguette to go, you can make them at home and serve the meatballs in individual gratin dishes. This way, you can pop the finished dish under the broiler until the Gruyère melts and the sauce bubbles. This recipes makes enough to feed an army and is the perfect excuse to have friends over.

PREP TIME 45 minutes   COOK TIME 2 hours   MAKES 4 tartines + extra meatballs

4 slices of bread, thickly cut

1 large clove of garlic, germ removed

2 whole Roasted Peppers (page 194) cut into 1-inch (2.5cm) pieces

4 ounces (115g) Gruyère, shaved

A handful of arugula

Extra-virgin olive oil

Sea salt and freshly ground black pepper

Amalfitana Sauce

3 tablespoons extra-virgin olive oil

1 small red bell pepper (seeds and ribs removed), chopped

3 garlic cloves, germ removed and minced

5–6 pieces Tomato Confit (page 197) or sun-dried tomatoes, chopped

1 tablespoon 'Nduja or ½ hot red pepper (like Serrano), minced

3½ pounds (1.6kg) canned whole San Marzano tomatoes

1 small bunch (10–15g) basil leaves

Meatballs

2 medium onions, finely chopped

6 cloves of garlic, germ removed, peeled and minced

3 ounces (85g) day-old bread, crust removed and cut into 1-inch (2.5cm) cubes

1 cup (240ml) whole milk

½ cup (50g) Parmigiano-Reggiano, finely grated

2 tablespoons flat-leaf parsley, finely chopped

2½ teaspoons fresh oregano, finely chopped

Zest of ½ lemon

2 eggs

½ pound (225g) ground veal

½ pound (225g) ground pork

½ pound (225g) ground beef

Extra-virgin olive oil

Lemon Vinaigrette

Zest of 1 lemon

1 tablespoon lemon juice

3 tablespoons best-quality extra-virgin olive oil

Amalfitana Sauce

Place a saucepan over medium heat. Add the olive oil and, once hot, add the bell pepper. When the cubes have softened and start to brown around the edges, stir in the garlic and cook for an additional minute or two. Add the tomato confit (or sun-dried tomatoes) and hot pepper.

Using your hands, crush the whole tomatoes in their juices and add them to the saucepan, stirring thoroughly until it comes to a rolling boil. Reduce the heat to a gentle simmer and cook, uncovered, allowing the sauce to reduce by one-quarter, about 30 to 40 minutes.

Once the sauce is ready, remove the pan from the heat, tear the basil leaves over the sauce, and stir them in.

Meatballs

Coat the bottom of a medium frying pan with olive oil and set over a medium flame. When the oil is hot, stir in the chopped onions and cook until the edges start to brown. Add the garlic and cook for another minute until fragrant. Set aside to cool.

Place the day-old bread into the whole milk and let it sit until the bread has absorbed as much milk as possible, and is now mushy. Squeeze out the excess milk and place the moistened bread into a large mixing bowl. Add the sautéed onions and garlic, Parmigiano Reggiano, parsley, oregano, lemon zest, and eggs. Stir to combine.

Add all three meats to the rest of the ingredients in the bowl and mix gently. (We like to use disposable latex gloves.) Season with salt and pepper. Test the seasoning by cooking a small meatball.

Keep a bowl of cold water next to you for dipping your hands as you form the meatballs into golf ball–size spheres. Line them up on a baking tray so they are ready to fry in batches.

Preheat the oven to 375°F (185°C).

Place the tomato sauce in a large casserole dish and have it ready, next to the stovetop.

In a nonstick pan, heat a thin layer of olive oil over a medium flame. Once warm, fry the meatballs, leaving enough space between them so that they don't touch one another. Brown the meatballs on all sides and then let them rest briefly on a paper towel–lined dish to soak up the excess oil and then add them to the tomato sauce.

After frying the first two batches of meatballs in one pan, use a clean one for the next batches to prevent any burned meat left in the pan from ruining the flavor of the meatballs.

Once all the meatballs are arranged in the casserole dish, place it in the preheated oven and cook until the sauce bubbles (about 15 to 20 minutes).

Assemble

Make the lemon vinaigrette by whisking together the zest and lemon juice with salt and pepper. Continue to whisk as you drizzle in the olive oil. Toss together with the arugula at the last minute. Brush the bread with olive oil and toast in a hot cast iron skillet. Once toasted on both sides, rub the bread with the cut side of half a large garlic clove. Leave the toast in the pan. Spoon the meatballs and sauce over the toast, followed by the mixed peppers and shaved Gruyère. Place the pan under the broiler long enough for the cheese to melt over the meatballs. Finally, top with the dressed arugula and serve.

You can also serve the meatballs in gratin dishes with plenty of sauce spooned over the top and sprinkled with Gruyère. Place the dish under the broiler until the cheese is melted and the sauce bubbles. Remove the dish and serve the meatballs over pasta, and the dressed arugula on the side.

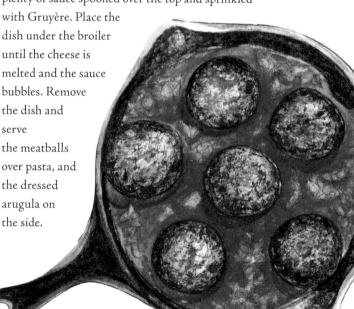

BAVETTE AND TAPENADE
WITH WILTED SWISS CHARD, STILTON, AND RED PEPPER CHIMICHURRI

In France, when you order a steak it is either *bleu* (cold inside), *saignant* (rare, literally means "bleeding"), or *à point* (medium). Cooking steak any longer than that is considered a true injustice to quality meat. Ask for *bien cuit* (well done) and be prepared to be met by a peculiar gaze from your server. We like to cook the meat in this recipe to medium rare. At classical cooking schools they tell you not to season the meat beforehand, because the salt draws the juices out too much and the pepper might burn when it meets the smoking hot pan. We sprinkle meat with freshly ground black pepper right after it comes out of the pan and is resting, but we like to salt the meat before cooking and let it rest for 10–15 minutes, so that the salt can seep through and really bring out the flavor of the meat.

PREP TIME 20 minutes   **COOK TIME** 30 minutes   **MAKES** 4 tartines

4 slices of bread, toasted

1 pound (450g) bavette steak (or flank steak)

1 tablespoon grapeseed oil

3 tablespoons butter

Flaky sea salt, like Maldon or fleur de sel

2 ounces (60g) Pecorino Romano, shaved

Sea salt and coarsely ground black pepper

Anchovy Mayonnaise

1 anchovy filet, finely chopped

3 tablespoons Classic Mayonnaise (page 187)

Wilted Swiss Chard

1 tablespoon extra-virgin olive oil

1 clove of garlic, germ removed and minced

1 bunch Swiss chard, stalk and leaf separated

1 tablespoon capers

Jalapeño and Roasted Red Pepper Chimichurri

1 jalapeño pepper

1 clove of garlic, germ removed and minced

1 tablespoon fresh oregano, finely chopped

A handful of flat-leaf parsley, finely chopped

½ Roasted Pepper (page 194), chopped into small cubes

1 tablespoon Banyuls vinegar (or red wine vinegar)

2 tablespoons best-quality extra-virgin olive oil

Anchovy Mayonnaise

Mash the anchovy to a paste with a mortar and pestle. Stir into the mayonnaise.

Wilted Swiss Chard

Add the olive oil to a large pan over medium heat. Add the garlic and cook until fragrant. Stir in the chopped stems of the Swiss chard and cook for 2–3 minutes until softened, followed by the torn leaves. Cook until the leaves are wilted. (If the Swiss chard seems too dry, add a couple of tablespoons of water and cover briefly to sweat.) Remove from the heat, drain off any excess liquid, and then toss to coat in the mayonnaise. Stir in the capers and season with salt and freshly ground black pepper.

Jalapeño and Roasted Red Pepper Chimichurri

Char the jalapeño on all sides over an open flame on the stove top and then wrap it in foil for 10 minutes and set aside. Peel and discard the stem once cool. Don't remove the seeds if you like it hot. Put the jalapeño and garlic in a mortar and pound together. Stir in the oregano, parsley, roasted red pepper, vinegar, and the remaining olive oil. Season to taste.

Bavette Steak

Preheat the oven to 250°F (120°C). Rub the bavette (or flank steak) with the oil and half a teaspoon of salt, and set it aside for 10 minutes. Heat a cast iron pan until it begins to smoke. Place the steak in the pan and cook it for a minute on each side to give it a good sear. Add the butter, tilt the pan, and keep spooning the foamy butter over the steak. Then put the pan into the oven and cook for 10–15 minutes, depending on the thickness, until the internal temperature reads 130°F (55°C). Remove the pan and let it rest for 10 minutes before carving it into medium slices.

Assemble

Spread the chimichurri over the toasted bread. Then add a layer of the wilted chard followed by the steak slices. Sprinkle with flaky sea salt and coarsely ground black pepper. Top with shaved Pecorino Romano. Serve with a simple arugula salad on the side.

BRILLAT-SAVARIN, HONEY, PISTACHIO, AND PEAR

Few things are as satisfying to us as the perfect balance of sweet and savory. This simple tartine brings together Brillat-Savarin—a luscious triple-cream bloomed-rind cheese, named after France's most renowned gastronome—with caramelized pears and toasted pistachios. If you can't find Brillat-Savarin, Sant'André or Boursault will do just as nicely.

PREP TIME 10 minutes   COOK TIME 15 minutes   MAKES 4 tartines

4 slices of bread, toasted

2 tablespoons walnut oil

4 tablespoons honey

1 7-ounce (200g) wheel of Brillat-Savarin

2 tablespoons salted pistachios, chopped coarsely

Sea salt and freshly ground black pepper

Rosemary Caramelized Pears

2 tablespoons sugar

1 tablespoon butter

3 sprigs fresh rosemary

2 pears, peeled, cored and chopped into ½-inch (12mm) pieces

Rosemary Caramelized Pears

Add the sugar to a heavy-bottomed saucepan set over medium heat. As the sugar heats, it will melt and turn into a liquid. It will then change color to light golden and finally a deep amber. Take the pan off the heat and stir in the butter. It will sizzle and foam at this point, and some of the sugar may harden in places. Continue to stir until the foaming subsides. Stir in the rosemary. Finally, add the pears and stir to coat with the caramel. The pears will begin to sweat and, depending on the kind you're using, they can get quite watery. Turn the heat up and reduce the liquid until the caramel forms a shiny glaze on the pears.

Assemble

Drizzle the toasted bread with walnut oil. Next, smear on a thin layer of honey. Place slices of Brillat-Savarin on top, and then spoon over the caramelized pears and their juices. Scatter the chopped pistachios over the top. Finish with salt and freshly ground black pepper and serve.

GRILLED CHEESE

While it isn't a tartine, we couldn't resist slipping in a recipe for a grilled sandwich oozing with the buttery flavor of Gruyère and reminiscent of a classic French onion soup with oodles of caramelized onions.

PREP TIME 10 minutes COOK TIME 10 minutes MAKES 4

8 slices Pain de Mie (page 75) or other soft white bread

6 tablespoons (85g) salted butter, softened

12 ounces (340g) Gruyère, shredded or sliced

½ cup Onion Jam (page 104)

2 tablespoons Dijon mustard

Spread butter on one side of each of the slices of bread. On the opposite side of four of those slices, spread about two tablespoons of onion jam and then top with Gruyère. Spread a thin layer of Dijon mustard on the non-buttered side of the other four slices of bread and then place them on top of the cheese, butter-side up.

In a skillet set over medium-low heat, grill the sandwiches for about 5 minutes on each side, until the bread is golden and the cheese is melted.

TIP: To change things up, you can add a mix of Gruyère and your favorite blue cheese. And for some crunch, add some thin slices of tart Granny Smith apples.

DESSERTS

One day, in late autumn, I was walking in St. Germain, on my way to Luxembourg Gardens, when I came upon Gérard Mulot's shop and was distracted by the sight of beautiful, glimmering, classical French pastries. As it happened, a frail elderly lady with perfectly coiffed hair and red lipstick, and a shopping cart in tow, paused in her path as well. We both looked through the shop window—as if just gazing at the pastries was all we needed. Then, we looked at each other and smiled. With childlike excitement in her eyes she said, *"J'aime bien les pâtisseries!"* and I replied, *"Moi aussi!"* Just the exchange of those few words, and we were both on our way. I will never forget that glint in her eyes.

—Shaheen

BAKING BASICS

Desserts are an indulgence, and the coming together of taste and texture is of paramount importance. In this section you'll find a range of recipes, from easy financiers that come together in minutes, to intricate patisserie-style desserts that need a bit of planning.

A few basics before you start baking:

+ Use ingredients at room temperature unless the recipe specifies otherwise.
+ Always take the baking time given in recipes as indicative, not absolute. Check for doneness with your senses: the color, the touch, the smell. The baking time will also change based on the kind of pan you use (cakes bake faster in dark-colored pans compared to light-colored ones), the size of the pan, and the other items you might be baking in the oven at the same time.
+ Always use sifted flour, confectioners' sugar, baking soda, and baking powder. If a recipe calls for multiple such dry ingredients, first whisk, then sift so that they are evenly distributed.

INGREDIENTS

Use the best ingredients you can find, everything else will follow. Never skimp on quality—we would rather you use less of a high-quality ingredient—and enjoy every bit it—than use a lot of an inferior ingredient and enjoy it less.

For chocolate, we use Valrhona. We keep trying out the different grades of chocolate in their line, but our long-time favorites are 70 percent Guanaja and 64 percent Manjari. Belgian Callebaut is good, too, if you can't find Valrhona.

We always use the oily, rich vanilla beans that Shaheen brings back from India. We also especially love the thick, pulpy Madagascar beans that are intensely fragrant and chocolaty. If you'd like, you can make your own vanilla extract by splitting and scraping the seeds from 6 to 8 beans and then infusing them in a small jar of vodka for 3 to 4 months at room temperature, along with the beans. For the recipes in this chapter, we've used vanilla beans, but you can use vanilla extract or vanilla paste just as well. If you buy beans, they are best stored in the freezer. Pull them out 5 minutes before you need to use them and you're good to go!

All the recipes call for unsalted butter, but if your only option is salted butter, then use it and eliminate the salt in the recipe. The only place where we'd urge you to go buy quality French butter is for the Black Sesame Salted Caramel on page 131—otherwise it's just not worth it!

EQUIPMENT

Always use a scale when baking. Measuring with cups can be very imprecise—for example, a cup of flour can measure anywhere between 120g and 150g depending on how tightly packed it is. This can make a huge difference! Because our recipes are very specific in terms of calling for 25g of milk or 8g of a spice mix, trying to measure them in cups or rounding them off to the nearest spoon is nearly impossible. In these recipes, we have given the closest approximation of cup measures but we promise you, when you switch to a scale, your baking will be a lot more consistent.

We like to use solid metal pans for baking—never silicone—especially when we're looking for a good crust and browning. Silicone molds are great for cold preparations—to set mousses, creams, and the like.

Some very handy tools to have in the pastry kitchen are a Microplane zester, small palette knife, lots of silicone spatulas (to help scrape every bit of cake batter), disposable piping bags, piping tips in various sizes, and a set of round pastry cutters.

RASPBERRY AND GERANIUM TART

W e really enjoy infusing our creams with herbs that add an unexpected, delicate perfume to the dessert. At first glance this tart looks like an ordinary raspberry tart, but after one bite you'll know that it is a twist on the classic recipe, made with French crème pâtissière. We start the process of making the pastry cream the night before, by infusing the milk with rose geranium leaves. After we've chilled the pastry cream, we then fold in some whipped cream for a lighter texture.

PREP TIME 15 minutes + 3 hours rest   COOK TIME 50 minutes   SERVES 6–8

1 recipe Sweet Pastry Dough (page 195)

Geranium Pastry Cream
- 1 cup (240g) whole milk
- 3–4 geranium leaves
- 3 egg yolks
- ⅓ cup (67g) superfine sugar
- 2 tablespoons (17g) cornstarch
- ½ cup (120g) whipping cream
- 1 tablespoon (15g) unsalted butter

- ½ recipe Sweet Pastry Dough (page 195)
- ½ pound (225g) raspberries or strawberries

Sweet Pastry Tart

Flour a work surface generously and roll the dough out to a thickness of ⅛ inch (3mm) and a diameter of about 9–10 inches (23–25cm). Line an 8-inch (20cm) tart pan with a removable bottom with the dough. Prick the dough with a fork and trim off any excess dough that may be hanging over the sides of the pan. Chill for 10 minutes in the freezer. Remove the pan from the freezer, line it with parchment paper, and then fill the bottom with pie weights. Bake the tart in a preheated oven at 340°F (170°C) for 20 minutes. Remove the pie weights and paper and bake the tart for an additional 10 to 15 minutes, until golden brown. Cool completely before filling.

Geranium Pastry Cream

In a heavy-bottomed saucepan, bring the milk to a boil with the geranium leaves, then turn off the heat and cover with plastic wrap. Let the geranium leaves steep in the milk overnight in the fridge. The next morning, bring the milk back to a simmer while you prepare the egg yolks.

In a bowl, whisk the egg yolks and sugar together until the mixture lightens in color. Then add the cornstarch and whisk until smooth.

Discard the geranium leaves and pour the hot milk into the bowl over the egg yolk mixture, as you continue to whisk. Add all of the milk, making sure it's evenly mixed. Pour this mixture back into the saucepan and whisk as you cook it over medium heat.

Keep cooking until the mixture thickens and comes to a boil. Don't worry, the yolks will not scramble and separate.

Cook the milk mixture until it has thickened and is smooth and shiny. Pour this Geranium Pastry Cream into a clean bowl and stir in the butter until it has melted into the cream.

Cover the cream with plastic wrap, making sure it touches the surface.

Chill thoroughly—at least 2 to 3 hours—before proceeding.

Once chilled, pass the cream through a fine sieve, pushing it through with a plastic scraper to make sure it is free of lumps.

In another bowl, whip the cream to soft peaks.

Fold the whipped cream into the pastry cream gently to lighten its texture and color.

Spread the vanilla pastry cream into the cooled tart shell and place the raspberries in concentric circles, starting from the outside. Serve.

RYE, CHOCOLATE, AND SEA SALT COOKIES

On a recent trip to Stockholm, Shaheen discovered these modern Swedish cookies at a lovely little bakery called Bakery and Spice. As soon as she got back home, she rustled up a batch of the cookies from a recipe that was based on the memory of gooey chocolate cookies bound together with crunchy rye and topped with flaky sea salt. The beauty of these cookies lies in their petite size. To make sure the cookies are the same size, you can weigh them before putting them in the oven to bake. Each cookie should weigh 12g, just under a tablespoon. You don't have to weigh the cookies, but it helps achieve beautiful, uniform results.

PREP TIME 15 minutes + 1 hour rest   COOK TIME 10 minutes   MAKES 4 dozen cookies

1½ cups (175g) rye flour

½ teaspoon (3g) baking soda

⅓ cup (30g) cocoa powder

⅓ cup (50g) confectioners' sugar

½ cup + 2 tablespoons (140g) unsalted butter

½ cup + 2 teaspoons (120g) unrefined cane sugar

1 egg

6 ounces (170g) dark chocolate, chopped

Maldon sea salt

Sift together the rye, baking soda, cocoa, and confectioners' sugar.

In another bowl, beat the butter with the cane sugar until smooth. Add the egg and continue to beat until emulsified.

Next, fold in the flour mixture followed by the chopped chocolate. Refrigerate for at least 1 hour.

Preheat oven to 350°F (175°C).

Measure tablespoon-size balls of dough and press them down slightly onto a cookie sheet. Sprinkle with Maldon salt and bake for 9 to 10 minutes.

PISTACHIO AND CHERRY FINANCIERS

Typically, financiers are small cakes made at bakeries using leftover egg whites. In this recipe, we use muffin pans and fill them just halfway, so they look like small, delicate cakes rather than big, bulging muffins. We love them with black cherries, but they're also great with raspberries. You can also swap the almond extract with a vanilla bean or orange or lemon zest, if you like.

PREP TIME 10 minutes   COOK TIME 15 minutes   MAKES 12

SCANT ½ cup (105g) unsalted butter + extra for brushing

A few drops of almond extract

½ cup (50g) ground pistachios

¼ cup (25g) ground almonds

¾ cup + 1½ tablespoons (135g) confectioners' sugar

⅓ cup (45g) all-purpose flour + extra for dusting

3 egg whites

½ cup (50g) pistachios, chopped

Preheat the oven to 350°F (180°C). Brush the cups in the muffin pan with a thin coat of butter. Let the butter set. If it's too hot, then pop it into the fridge for a few minutes. Dust with flour and tap off the excess.

In a small saucepan, melt the butter and add a few drops of almond extract.

In a bowl, stir together and then sift the pistachios, almonds, sugar, and flour.

In a separate bowl, whisk the egg whites by hand until lightly frothy. Pour the egg whites into the bowl with the nut mixture and incorporate thoroughly. Next, fold in the melted butter and almond extract.

Pipe or spoon the batter into the prepared muffin pans and insert a few pitted cherries into each cup. Sprinkle with the chopped pistachios. Bake the financiers for 10 to 15 minutes (depending on size), until a skewer comes out clean.

Cool the pans on a wire rack before serving.

CHOCOLATE AND
PASSION FRUIT TART

Milk chocolate and passion fruit are a match made in heaven, one that we wish we'd discovered sooner. We first experienced the flavor in Pierre Hermé's Mogador macaron, and since then we've made this passion fruit ganache for tarts and truffles.

PREP TIME 10 minutes + a few hours rest   COOK TIME 40 minutes   SERVES 6–8

1 recipe Sweet Pastry Dough (page 195)

Passion Fruit Ganache
- ½ pound (225g) milk chocolate
- ¼ pound (112g) dark chocolate
- ¾ cup (200g) passion fruit purée, strained
- 1 tablespoon (15g) honey
- 4 tablespoons (60g) unsalted butter

Sweet Pastry Tart

Flour a work surface generously and roll the dough out to a thickness of ⅛ inch (3mm) and a diameter of about 9–10 inches (23–25cm). Line a 9-inch (23 cm) tart pan with the dough. Prick the dough with a fork, trim off any excess dough that may be hanging over the sides of the pan, and chill for 10 minutes in the freezer. Line the inside of the tart pan with parchment paper and fill with pie weights. Bake the tart in a preheated oven at 340°F (170°C) for 20 minutes. Remove the pie weights and parchment paper and bake the tart for an additional 10 to 15 minutes, until golden brown. Cool completely before filling.

Passion Fruit Ganache

Partially melt the chocolate in a bowl set over a pan of simmering water, making sure the water does not touch the bowl. Set aside. In a small saucepan, bring the passion fruit purée and honey to a boil. Pour the hot passion fruit purée over the chocolate, a third at a time, stirring between each addition. Once it turns into a smooth, shiny ganache, add the pieces of butter and stir until incorporated.

Assemble

Let the ganache cool slightly (to about 95°F/35°C) and then pour it into the baked tart crust. Refrigerate for a few hours until set.

TIP You can brush the tart with melted chocolate and let it set before filling it with ganache to keep the pastry from turning soft with the filling.

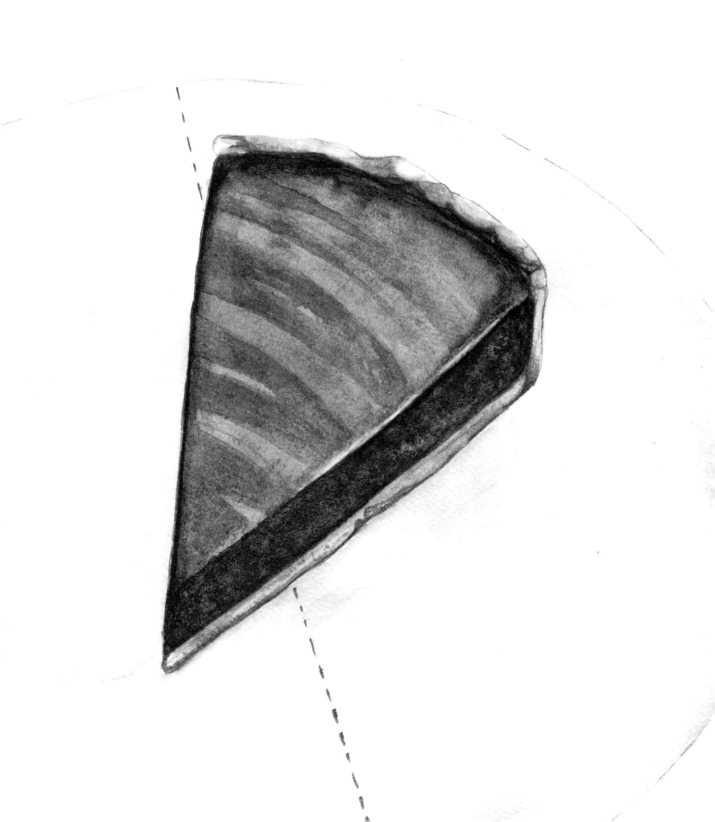

FIG AND HAZELNUT TART

The hazelnut cream in this tart is based on the recipe for classic French almond cream, which is traditionally made with a glug of rum. The cream is then spread on a day-old croissant, topped with sliced almonds, and then baked again to make almond croissants. Here, we use toasted and ground hazelnuts because they pair so beautifully with figs.

PREP TIME 20 minutes   COOK TIME 1 hour 15 minutes   SERVES 6–8

1 recipe Sweet Pastry Dough (page 195)

10 ripe figs

1 tablespoon (15g) granulated sugar

Hazelnut Cream

1 cup (130g) hazelnuts

½ cup + 1 tablespoon (125g) unsalted butter

HEAPING ½ cup (125g) superfine sugar

2 eggs

1 vanilla bean, split, and seeds scraped out

Egg Wash

1 egg yolk

1 teaspoon milk

Roll out the cold tart dough into a 10-inch (25cm) circle over a sheet of parchment paper. Transfer to a baking tray and keep refrigerated until ready to use.

Hazelnut Cream

Toast the hazelnuts in a preheated oven at 300°F (150°C) until they turn a light golden brown, about 15 minutes. Using the palms of your hands, rub the skin off the hazelnuts in batches. Pulse the hazelnuts to a powder in a food processor.

To make the hazelnut cream, beat the butter until soft and then beat in the sugar, eggs, vanilla, and ground hazelnuts. Don't beat the mixture too much—you want it to be smooth, not airy and fluffy from overbeating.

Egg Wash

Using a pastry brush, mix together the egg yolk and milk in a small bowl.

Assemble and Bake

Preheat the oven to 350°F (175°C). Spread the hazelnut cream generously onto the dough, leaving a perimeter of about two fingers' width around the outer edge of the dough. Slice the figs and fan them out in concentric circles over the hazelnut cream—starting from the outside in. Fold the edges over the figs and brush with the egg wash. Give it a generous sprinkling of sugar.

Put the tart into the oven and bake for about 45 to 50 minutes, until the hazelnut cream is golden brown and puffed up. Cool completely before slicing.

RYE AND MOLASSES CAKE
WITH FRESH PEARS

The rye lends a brilliant nuttiness to this cake, and the sticky molasses keeps it wonderfully moist for days. You can substitute the almonds with another nut—walnuts or hazelnuts, if you like; and make sure you use ripe, flavorful pears.

PREP TIME 15 minutes   COOK TIME 45 minutes   SERVES 6–8

1 cup + 2 tablespoons (145g) rye flour

1 cup (100g) ground almonds

1 teaspoon (5g) baking powder

SCANT 1 cup (200g) unsalted butter

½ cup (100g) light brown sugar

½ cup (100g) dark brown sugar

4 eggs

¼ cup (80g) molasses

2 pears, thinly sliced

Preheat the oven to 350°F (175°C). Brush a loaf or Bundt pan with melted butter and dust with flour.

In a bowl, whisk together the rye flour, ground almonds, and baking powder.

In another bowl, beat the butter and the sugars together until light in color. Next, beat in the eggs, one at a time, followed by the molasses. Continue to beat the mixture until it is evenly mixed. (It may look like it has split, but don't worry, it will come together eventually.)

Fold the dry ingredients into the wet mixture in the bowl and mix until it forms a smooth batter.

Pour the batter into the prepared pan and top with the pear slices.

Bake the cake for 35 to 45 minutes, until a skewer comes out clean, and then turn it out on a wire rack to cool.

Serve warm with lightly whipped cream on the side.

APRICOT AND ROSEMARY TARTE TATIN
WITH HONEY CREAM

A copper tarte tatin mold would be a dream for this one, but until we find one at a *vide grenier* (one of the charming flea markets dotted across France), we're going to be baking this tarte tatin in a cast iron pan, which does a wonderful job because you can pop it from the stove top to the oven with ease. The only thing to be careful about is watching the caramel closely because it's hard to tell when it's turning the right color in a black pan.

PREP TIME 15 minutes + 20 minutes rest   COOK TIME 45 minutes   SERVES 6–8

1 recipe Sweet Pastry Dough (page 195)

Apricot and Rosemary Tarte Tatin
12 apricots

¾ cup (150g) superfine sugar, divided

¼ cup (55g) unsalted butter

2–3 sprigs fresh rosemary

Honey Cream
¾ cup (180g) whipping cream

1 heaped tablespoon (25g) honey

1 vanilla bean, split, and seeds scraped out

Apricot and Rosemary Tarte Tatin
Preheat the oven to 380°F (190°C).

Cut the apricots into half and remove the pits.

In a cast iron pan set over medium heat, add half the sugar and cook until it melts and turns golden. Then add the remaining sugar and cook until a dark caramel forms. If you are using a dark pan and can't tell from the color if the caramel is forming, it should look very fluid and also bubble up around the edges of the pan, about 350°–360°F (175°–180°C). At this point, pull it off the heat and add the butter. Stir until combined. Be careful as the butter will foam and may splatter. Next, add the rosemary and then the apricots, skin side down, to the pan.

Sweet Pastry Tart
On a sheet of parchment paper, roll out the dough to a diameter that is slightly larger than the cast iron pan you are using. For example, a 10–12-inch (25–30cm) circle of dough is average for a 9-inch (23cm) cast iron skillet.

Prick the rolled dough with a fork and then transfer the dough on the parchment paper to the refrigerator for 15 minutes to chill. Remove the dough and place it over the apricots, tucking in the edges between the pan and the apricots. Bake in the oven for 35 to 40 minutes, until the dough is golden brown.

Remove from the oven and let cool for 5 to 10 minutes to allow the caramel to thicken slightly.

Place a plate over the pan and invert the tarte tatin onto the plate. If the caramel has hardened, you may need to use a knife to dislodge the tart from the pan. Discard the rosemary sprigs.

Honey Cream
Combine the whipping cream, honey, and vanilla bean seeds, and whisk until soft peaks form.

Serve the tarte tatin warm with the lightly whipped honey cream.

TONKA BROWN BUTTER MADELEINES

You can use this honey madeleine recipe as a vehicle for many, many flavors. We are currently fixated on tonka beans. These are dark, wrinkled seeds from Cumaru trees that grow in South America. The beans can be grated, much like nutmeg, and lend complex vanilla, sour cherry, and licorice flavors to recipes. And because the flavor is so strong, you only need to use a third of a bean in this recipe to perfume your madeleines. Instead of tonka, you can use vanilla, citrus zest, or almond extract.

PREP TIME 15 minutes   COOK TIME 20 minutes   MAKES 12 large or 24 mini madeleines

½ cup + 2 teaspoons (120g) unsalted butter

2 teaspoons (15g) wild forest honey

⅓ tonka bean, grated

¾ cup + 2 teaspoons (100g) all-purpose flour

SCANT 1 teaspoon (4g) baking powder

1½ (70g) eggs

1 tablespoon + 2 teaspoons (25g) whole milk

⅓ cup (65g) superfine sugar

Place the madeleine pan in the fridge.

Brown the butter in a heavy-bottomed saucepan over low heat. At first the butter will melt, then sizzle, and once all the moisture is evaporated, the milk solids in the butter will begin to caramelize, turning light golden. You will need to keep stirring the butter to check the color at the bottom of the pan, because on the surface, the butter will still look light and intensely foamy. Remove from the burner or it will continue to brown in the residual heat. For this recipe, use both the butter and the browned bits. If the milk solids turn black, simply strain the butter—and you can still use it. Measure ⅓ cup + 1 tablespoon (90g) of browned butter for the recipe.

Pour the warm browned butter into a bowl. Add the honey and grated tonka bean and stir to combine.

Sift the flour and baking powder together in another bowl.

In a third bowl, whisk together the eggs, milk, and sugar.

Add the dry ingredients to the egg mixture and fold gently until well combined. Next, stir in the browned butter. Mix until just combined. Transfer the mixture to a piping bag and let it chill in the fridge for at least 2 hours or, ideally, overnight.

Preheat the oven to 425°F (210°C). Remove the madeleine pan from the fridge and brush evenly with melted butter. Let the butter firm up and dust with flour. Tap off the excess. Pipe the mixture into the pan and bake for 7 minutes until the "hump" appears. Lower the oven temperature to 180°C, rotate the pan, and bake the madeleines for another 4 to 6 minutes.

CHOCOLATE BROWNIE COOKIES
with BLACK SESAME SALTED CARAMEL

A cookie on its own is nice, but when you sandwich two cookies with caramel—and in this recipe, it's caramel with toasted black sesame seeds—you get a dessert that can stand on its own (although a scoop of vanilla ice cream on the side doesn't hurt). We like to have a pot of caramel in the fridge to uplift desserts and ice creams. Just make sure to pull it out of the fridge 15 to 20 minutes beforehand so that it's fluid enough to drizzle.

PREP TIME 15 minutes + overnight rest   COOK TIME 10 minutes

MAKES about 20 cookies to make 10 caramel sandwiches

½ pound (225g) dark chocolate

½ cup (60g) all-purpose flour

⅓ cup + 1 tablespoon (40g) cocoa

1½ teaspoons (8g) baking powder

SCANT ½ cup (100g) unsalted butter

1 cup (200g) superfine sugar

2 eggs

¼ cup (60g) whole milk

Melt the chocolate in a heatproof bowl set over a pan of simmering water, making sure the water does not touch the bowl.

Stir together and then sift the flour, cocoa, and baking powder into a bowl.

In a large bowl, beat the butter with an electric beater until creamy. Add the sugar gradually until incorporated. Next, add the eggs, one at a time. Then beat in the chocolate until well incorporated.

Turn the speed down and add the milk, making sure to do so slowly to avoid splattering.

Finally, fold the flour mixture into the wet ingredients by hand with a spatula until well combined and no traces of dry ingredients can be seen. Cover the bowl with plastic wrap and chill the dough for at least 2 hours.

Preheat the oven to 350°F (175°C). Line a baking sheet with parchment paper.

Using an ice cream scoop or just your hands, work the dough into even-size balls (about ⅓ cup/40–50g). Leave about 1½-inches (4cm) space between them on the baking sheet.

Bake the cookies for 10 minutes and then turn off the oven. Let the cookies rest in the hot oven for exactly 2 minutes more before removing them from the oven. Because the cookies will still be very delicate, let them continue to rest on the baking sheet until they get firmer. At that point, transfer them to a cooling rack. Once they are cool, sandwich the cookies with sesame caramel.

BLACK SESAME SALTED CARAMEL

Make a caramel once, and you will never ever buy it again. It is incredibly easy to make, as long as you are vigilant about a few key steps. Measure all of the ingredients and have them ready before you turn the heat on, because once the sugar starts to turn a nice dark caramel color it can burn very quickly and even set off your smoke alarm.

To make the caramel, we use a heavy-bottomed saucepan for even heat distribution—to avoid burning the sugar in spots. Using a light-colored pan—a white enamel or stainless steel pan—makes it easy to keep an eye on the color of the caramel. You can also use a digital candy thermometer, but it's actually easier to gauge where you are in the process by simply observing the changing color of the sugar. Always take the pan off the heat before adding the butter and cream, because the caramel may spill over and the goop will get everywhere. And, finally, keep the cream warm so that when you add it to the caramel it doesn't seize and solidify the caramel.

PREP TIME 5 minutes   COOK TIME 10 minutes   MAKES 1½ cups

½ cup (120g) whipping cream

1 cup (200g) superfine sugar, divided

6 tablespoons + 1 teaspoon (90g) unsalted butter (the best you can get your hands on)

1 teaspoon Maldon Sea Salt or Fleur de Sel

1 teaspoon ground almonds

2 tablespoons black sesame seeds, toasted

In a small pan, warm the cream.

In a thick-bottomed pan add half of the sugar and cook until it melts. Add the remaining half of the sugar. Don't be afraid to give it a gentle stir if you notice the color at the edges or in some spots changing more quickly than the rest.

Once the sugar has reached a deep brown color, take the pan off the heat and add the cream one-third at a time, stirring gently between additions. It will foam up, so make sure you're using a pan with high sides. Put the pan back on the heat and stir until all of the cream has combined with the caramelized sugar.

Next, take the pan off the heat and stir in all of the butter, whisking it in until the caramel sauce is smooth and shiny.

With the pan off the heat, stir in half of the salt and all of the ground almonds. Let the sauce cool completely. Stir in the remaining salt and the toasted black sesame seeds.

Store in the refrigerator up to 3 weeks.

NOTE Because caramel is made up of such simple ingredients, make sure to buy the best-quality ingredients. In France, we use Bordier butter but overseas Lescure or Échiré does the job beautifully. For the salt, it's either Maldon or Fleur de Sel. We have a special affinity for the English salt (Maldon) because its flaky crystals don't dissolve as easily and surprise with an unexpected crunch of salt.

VANILLA MILK CAKE

WITH TUBEROSE GANACHE

This milk cake is essentially a pound cake that is moistened with hot milk to give it an extra soft, tight crumb. Even if the cake has been sitting around for a while, you can still toast a couple of slices to make a peanut butter and banana sandwich. As for the tuberose ganache, the recipe came about when we were talking about using fresh flowers and herbs to infuse our cream and were inspired by a vase of tropical tuberoses in Jennie's studio in Bogota.

PREP TIME 20 minutes + 24 hours rest   COOK TIME 1 hour   MAKES 1 large loaf

Tuberose Ganache

Petals of 5 tuberose flowers

½ cup + 1 tablespoon (140g) whipping cream

3.5 ounces (100g) dark chocolate, finely chopped

1 tablespoon (15g) unsalted butter

Vanilla Milk Cake

½ cup (120g) whole milk

1 vanilla bean

¾ cup + 2 tablespoons (200g) unsalted butter + more for brushing and finishing

1 cup (200g) superfine sugar

1 teaspoon (5g) fine sea salt

4 eggs

2 cups + 1 tablespoon (250g) all-purpose flour

1 teaspoon (5g) baking powder

Tuberose Ganache

Start a day ahead of baking the cake.

Rinse the tuberose petals under cold water and lay them on a paper towel to dry.

Bring the whipping cream to a boil in a small saucepan. Reduce the heat to a simmer. Add the tuberose flower petals and simmer the cream for 3 to 5 minutes. Remove the pan from the heat, and let the cream and tuberose petal-mixture cool in the refrigerator overnight.

Strain the cream and discard the tuberose petals. Make sure that you have 100g (you can add more regular cream if necessary).

In a bowl set over simmering water, partially melt the chocolate. In a small saucepan, bring the cream to a boil once again and then pour it directly over the chocolate, a third at a time, stirring between additions. Stir in the butter until it has completely blended into the ganache.

Vanilla Milk Cake

Preheat the oven to 340°F (170°C). Brush a large 9 × 5 × 3-inch (28 × 13 × 8cm) loaf pan with butter and line it with parchment paper.

Pour the milk into a saucepan. Split and scrape the seeds out of the vanilla bean and add them to the saucepan. Bring the milk to a simmer, and then turn off the heat to let the milk infuse with the vanilla while you to proceed to the next steps.

In a bowl, beat the butter and sugar together until light and creamy. Add the sea salt. Add the eggs, one at a time, and keep beating them into the butter mixture until they are well incorporated and the mixture is fluffy.

In another bowl, whisk the flour and baking powder together and then sift it.

Using a spatula, fold the flour and baking powder mixture into the egg mixture, alternating with the vanilla milk. Begin and end with the flour.

Pour the batter into the prepared cake pan and smooth the top. Bake the cake for 35 to 40 minutes. It is ready when a skewer inserted in the center comes out clean.

Let cool, then serve the cake with the tuberose ganache on the side.

PISTACHIO AND VANILLA LOAF

This cake is one of our favorites from the recipes Shaheen teaches in her baking classes. It is rich with pistachios and almonds, and there is very little flour, just enough to add structure and absorb the butter and nut oils. It takes a long time for the cake to bake, but the wait is totally worth it. In addition to flavoring the cake with vanilla, we like to add the zest of grapefruit or lemon or sometimes a few drops of almond extract, to give the cake a lovely scent.

PREP TIME 10 minutes   COOK TIME 50 minutes   MAKES 1 large loaf

1 cup + 2 tablespoon (120g) ground pistachios

1 cup (100g) ground almonds

¾ cup + 1 tablespoon (100g) all-purpose flour, sifted

½ teaspoon (3g) salt

1 cup + 2 tablespoons (250g) unsalted butter

1 cup + 2 tablespoons (225g) superfine sugar

4 eggs

1 vanilla bean

Preheat the oven to 340°F (170°C). Grease and line a large 9 × 5 × 3-inch (28 × 13 × 8cm) loaf pan with parchment paper.

In a bowl, whisk together the ground pistachios and almonds, flour, and salt.

In another bowl, beat the butter and sugar with a hand mixer or stand mixer until light and fluffy. Gradually beat the eggs into the mixture until incorporated.

Split and scrape the seeds out of the vanilla bean, then stir the seeds into the mixture. You can put the used bean in a jar of sugar to perfume it.

Next, fold the ground nuts and flour into the egg mixture with a spatula.

Pour the batter into the prepared pan and bake for 50 to 60 minutes, testing for doneness with a skewer. If it comes out clean, the cake is done.

Remove the cake from the oven and leave it in the pan for 10 to 15 minutes before turning it out onto a wire rack. Allow the cake to cool completely before slicing.

CHOCOLATE MOUSSE
with CARAMELIZED PECANS

A classic chocolate mousse always reminds us of our once-favorite bistro in the Marais, Chez Janou. When you order a chocolate mousse there, you are brought a bowl, large enough to fit a football, filled with mousse, and you can eat to your heart's content. Whenever we make this mousse we hope to bring the same joy to our guests as that bowl did for us. Our version is sweetened with maple syrup for its delicate flavor and topped with caramelized pecans for textural contrast. Whatever you do, use the best-quality chocolate you can buy.

PREP TIME 20 minutes + 4 hours rest   COOK TIME 15 minutes   MAKES 6 servings

Chocolate Mousse
- 10.5 ounces (300g) dark chocolate
- 6 tablespoons (85g) unsalted butter
- 2 egg yolks
- 7 egg whites
- 2½ tablespoons (50g) maple syrup

Caramelized Pecans
- ¾ cup (75g) pecans
- ¼ cup (50g) superfine sugar

Chocolate Mousse
Melt the chocolate and butter together in a bowl set in a pan over simmering water, making sure the water does not touch the bowl.

Next, whisk in the egg yolks into the chocolate mixture. If you're worried about cooking the egg yolks, pour the chocolate mixture over the yolks a little at a time as you whisk.

In another bowl, add the egg whites and maple syrup and whisk to soft peaks.

Fold the whites into the chocolate mixture a third at a time, until they're completely incorporated and the mixture is homogeneous.

Pour the mousse into a bowl or ramekins to make individual portions. Refrigerate the mousse for at least 3 to 4 hours, preferably overnight.

Remove the mousse from the fridge 20 minutes before serving for best taste.

Sprinkle the caramelized pecans over the mousse right at the last minute.

Caramelized Pecans
Chop the pecans into small pieces, and then use a wide mesh sieve to get rid of the pecan "dust."

In a saucepan, mix together the sugar and chopped pecans and cook over medium heat until the sugar caramelizes and coats the pecans. Refer to notes on caramelization on page 131.

Lay the caramelized pecans on parchment paper and, using a fork, separate the pieces of pecans while they're still warm.

Once cooled, break the pecans into pieces and store them at room temperature in an airtight container.

SUPER-MOIST CHOCOLATE LOAF
WITH GIANDUJA GANACHE

This chocolate loaf is incredibly soft, thanks to the clever use of the light texture and neutral flavor of grapeseed oil. Unlike butter, the oil doesn't firm up in the fridge, so the cake remains pillowy soft. We like to bake it in a loaf pan and then top it with generous mounds of Gianduja ganache and caramelized hazelnuts. You can also bake it in a round cake pan and use it for a layer cake. We suggest that you use grapeseed oil, but if you can't find it, use sunflower oil or any other neutral-flavored oil.

PREP TIME 20 minutes + 2 hours rest   COOK TIME 1½ hours   MAKES 1 large loaf

Chocolate Loaf

- 1⅓ cups (160g) all-purpose flour
- ½ cup + 2 tablespoons (60g) cocoa powder
- 1 teaspoon (5g) baking powder
- 2 eggs
- 1¼ cups (250g) superfine sugar
- ¼ cup (50g) grapeseed oil
- SCANT ½ cup (100g) heavy whipping cream
- ¾ cup (180g) whole milk

Gianduja Ganache

- 1 cup (130g) hazelnuts, toasted
- ¾ cup (120g) confectioners' sugar
- 4 ounces (112g) dark chocolate
- 1 cup (240g) whipping cream

Caramelized Hazelnuts

- ½ cup (65g) hazelnuts
- ¼ cup (50g) superfine sugar

Chocolate Loaf

Preheat oven to 320°F (160°C). Brush a large loaf pan with butter and line it with parchment paper.

Sift together the flour, cocoa, and baking powder.

In a bowl, beat the eggs with the sugar until lighter in color. If using a stand mixer, use the whisk attachment.

Pour the oil into the bowl while continuing to beat the egg mixture.

Once all the oil is incorporated, reduce the speed and pour in the cream and milk.

Continue using the beaters on low speed and mix in the flour mixture until it is combined. Then with a spatula, scrape the sides of the bowl to incorporate any unmixed flour.

Pour the batter into the prepared pan and bake for 50 to 60 minutes, until a skewer comes out clean.

Gianduja Ganache

Toast the hazelnuts in a 300°F (150°C) oven until they are fragrant and light golden brown, about 15 minutes. If they have skins, rub them off between your palms.

Transfer the hazelnuts to a food processor and grind them into a paste. The hazelnuts turn to a paste quickly when they're warm. First, they're reduced to a powder, which clumps up and then finally transforms into a fluid paste. At this stage, add the confectioners' sugar and continue to pulse the mixture until it forms a smooth paste.

Transfer the hazelnut paste to a bowl and add the chocolate.

In a saucepan, bring the cream to a boil and pour it over the chocolate-hazelnut mixture. Stir until all the chocolate has melted and it forms a thick, shiny ganache.

Scrape down the sides of the bowl and cover it with plastic wrap, making sure it touches the surface of the ganache. Refrigerate for about 2 hours. Beat the ganache with electric beaters to give it a smooth and spreadable consistency. To prevent the cream from turning into butter, be careful not to overbeat it. Use up any leftover ganache by spreading it on toast.

Caramelized Hazelnuts

Toast the hazelnuts in a preheated oven set at 300°F (150°C) for 15 minutes until they're golden and fragrant. If they have skins, rub them off between your palms. It's okay to leave a bit of the skin on the nuts, but you want to avoid any loose pieces of papery skin.

Add the sugar to a heavy-bottomed saucepan and cook it over medium heat. The sugar will begin to melt and then turn light golden. Stir it so it is evenly colored and continue to cook until the sugar is deep golden and the edges show signs of bubbling. Refer to notes on caramelization on page 131. Add the toasted hazelnuts at this point and stir to coat the nuts in the caramel. Continue to cook for another minute; then turn the nuts out onto a silicone baking mat and let them cool. You can use two forks to separate the nuts while the caramel is still soft. When they're completely cool, store them in an airtight container.

Assemble

With the help of a small offset spatula, spread a thick layer of the ganache on top of the loaf cake. Top it with the caramelized hazelnuts and serve.

CHOCOLATE AND HAZELNUT BUTTER CAKES

These are the most luscious little chocolate cakes you will ever eat. They are enriched with toasted hazelnut butter, which you can either buy or make from scratch. If you make the hazelnut butter yourself, we recommend that you make a little extra, just so you can slather it on toast with some honey and sea salt. These cakes are also extremely delicate, so it really helps to use silicone molds. In general, we're averse to using silicone because it leaves a shiny unevenly browned crust on baked goods. In this case however, our goal is to simply set the cakes rather than brown them, so silicone does the job well and makes unmolding a dream.

PREP TIME 20 minutes   COOK TIME 30 minutes   MAKES 6–8 individual cakes

1½ cups (200g) hazelnuts

2 tablespoons (20g) cacao nibs

½ cup + 3 tablespoons (150g) unsalted butter, + more for greasing the molds

SCANT ¼ cup (25g) cocoa powder + more for dusting the molds

½ cup (60g) all-purpose flour

Pinch of salt

6 ounces (165g) 70 percent dark chocolate, in pieces

3 eggs

1 cup (200g) superfine sugar

Hazelnut Butter

Preheat oven to 350°F (175°C).

Lay the hazelnuts on a baking sheet and toast them in the oven for 15 to 17 minutes until they're evenly toasted and golden brown. Transfer all but 1 tablespoon of the hazelnuts to a food processor and grind them to a paste. The hazelnuts turn to a paste quickly when they're warm. First, they're reduced to a powder, which clumps up and then finally transforms into a smooth hazelnut butter. You could skip this step and use pure hazelnut butter instead.

Cake

Brush silicone molds with a little melted butter and dust with cocoa powder. Sprinkle the bottom of each mold with the remaining tablespoon of hazelnuts, chopped, and cacao nibs. Sift together the cocoa, flour, and salt. Melt the chocolate and butter in a heatproof bowl set over a pan of simmering water. Once melted, remove it from the heat and let cool.

Using a whisk attachment on a stand mixer or electric beaters, whisk the eggs and sugar together until pale and frothy, about 5 minutes. Stir a little of this mixture into the hazelnut butter to loosen it, then stir the hazelnut butter back into the remaining egg mixture. Stir the cooled chocolate mixture into the egg mixture. Fold in the flour and cocoa mixture.

Pour the batter into the prepared molds and transfer them to a baking sheet. Place in the oven and bake 8 minutes for small molds, a little longer for larger molds. The top should have crusted and feel soft and moist to the touch; a skewer or toothpick inserted in the middle should *not* come out clean but rather with moist crumbs attached to it.

Cool the cakes for 10 minutes or more before unmolding them. Serve with soft whipped cream or vanilla ice cream.

CARAMELIZED NUT TARTELETTES

Rue des Martyrs in Montmartre is packed with food shops and local charm. Arjun, Shaheen's husband, would often pick up pastries from Sébastien Gaudard Pâtisserie, a particularly charming shop on this street. The caramelized nut tart was one of our favorites, which inspired us to create a version of our own. Liquid gold caramel is a thing of beauty—here, this cream caramel is used to enrobe the toasted nuts and then is spooned into a baked tart shell. Make sure to let the caramel cool before spooning it into the baked tarts so that it firms up and holds instead of dripping over the sides.

PREP TIME 15 minutes COOK TIME 45 minutes SERVES 8–10

1 recipe Sweet Pastry Dough (page 195)

Caramelized Nuts
1¼ cups (160g) mixed nuts (almonds, hazelnuts, pecans)

SCANT ½ cup (110g) whipping cream

Pinch of sea salt

¾ cup (160g) superfine sugar

1 teaspoon ground almonds

Tart Base
Roll out the sweet pastry dough to a thickness of ⅛ inch (3mm). Use a pastry cutter to fit the dough into mini tart pans, about 3 inches (7.5cm) in diameter. Prick the dough with a fork and bake the tart shells for 10 to 15 minutes with pie weights. Then remove the weights, and continue to bake for another 5 to 7 minutes until golden brown. Cool completely before filling.

Caramelized Nuts
Preheat the oven to 300°F (150°C). Toast the different nuts on separate baking trays until they're light golden and fragrant. The timing will vary based on the size of the nut and its oil content—anywhere between 8 to 15 minutes. Rub the skins off the hazelnuts when they loosen—don't worry about getting all of them off.

Warm the cream with a pinch of sea salt.

To make the caramel, add the sugar to a heavy saucepan in 2 to 3 batches, until it turns dark amber and becomes gently frothy around the edges of the pan. The temperature of the caramel should register about 350°F (180°C) on a digital candy thermometer. Refer to notes on caramelization on page 131.

Turn off the heat, and pour the warm cream over the caramel in batches or it will froth up too vigorously and overflow. Stir until smooth.

Stir the ground almonds into the caramel sauce—this firms up the sauce and helps it hold its shape. Let the mixture cool for 10 to 15 minutes. Finally, stir in the toasted nuts and coat thoroughly. The caramel will firm up considerably as it cools.

Assemble
Once it's just warm to the touch, spoon the caramel-and-nut mix into each baked mini tart shell. It will spread slightly, so don't overfill the shells. Serve immediately.

ORANGE FENNEL COOKIES

Inspired by a recipe from Jennie's Great Grandma Holman, these cookies have a rich pillowy texture and the aroma of freshly baked biscotti. The glaze intensifies the orange flavor of the cookies and keeps them fresh for a couple of days, if they last that long.

PREP TIME 15 minutes   COOK TIME 30 minutes   MAKES 4 dozen small cookies

2¾ cups (330g) all-purpose flour

½ teaspoon fine sea salt

2 teaspoons whole fennel seeds, toasted and ground (about 1½ teaspoons ground)

1 cup (225g) unsalted butter

⅓ cup (75g) light brown sugar

½ cup + 1 tablespoon (115g) superfine sugar

1 egg

1 vanilla bean, split, and seeds scraped out

¼ cup (60g) freshly squeezed orange juice

1 teaspoon (5g) baking soda

Orange Glaze

1¼ cups (155g) sifted confectioners' sugar

2 tablespoons (30g) freshly squeezed orange juice

1 tablespoon (15g) unsalted butter, melted

Zest of ½ orange

Preheat the oven to 375°F (190°C).

In a large bowl, mix together the all-purpose flour, salt, and ground fennel seeds.

In another large bowl, using an electric beater, beat the butter together with both the sugars until it lightens in color. Then mix in the egg and vanilla seeds until it looks light and fluffy.

In a small bowl, whisk the orange juice into the baking soda little by little until it foams a bit; then beat it into the wet mixture. Next, gently fold in the dry ingredients a third at a time.

Roll the dough into tablespoon-size balls and place them evenly on a baking sheet lined with parchment paper. (We like to keep a bowl of cold water next to us for coating our hands to easily form the balls.) The cookies don't spread very much, so it's okay to leave one inch (2.5cm) between each ball.

Bake for 8 to 10 minutes, until the bottoms of the cookies are golden brown and the tops are firm but not hardened. Transfer to a cooling rack.

Orange Glaze

Combine the glaze ingredients in a small bowl. While the cookies are still warm, hold them upside down and dip the tops into the orange glaze to give them a thin coating. Place the cookies right side up on a cooling rack and let them set. Once they are completely cool, you can store them in an airtight container for up to a week.

ALMOND, ORANGE, AND OLIVE OIL CAKE
WITH CHOCOLATE GANACHE

The most crucial step in this recipe is to let the syrup cool down and apply it to the cake while it is still warm (but *not* when it is hot out of the oven): Simply brush the cooled syrup all over the cake and let it soak in. This will give it a soft-textured crust and crumb. The cake only needs a couple of delicate brushings—If you use all of the syrup, it will get soggy. Remember, never brush hot syrup on a hot cake or the crust will disintegrate.

PREP TIME 15 minutes   COOK TIME 40 minutes   MAKES 1 large loaf

Cake
- 2⅓ cups (240g) ground almonds
- SCANT 1 cup (110g) all-purpose flour
- ½ teaspoon (3g) baking powder
- ¾ cup + 1 tablespoon (190g) unsalted butter, soft
- SCANT 2 cups (170g) confectioners' sugar
- 2 egg yolks
- 1 egg
- 2 tablespoons (30g) whole milk
- 2 tablespoons (30g) extra-virgin olive oil
- Zest of 1 orange
- 4 egg whites
- ¼ cup (50g) superfine sugar

Soaking Syrup
- 3 tablespoons (45g) sugar
- 3 tablespoons (45g) water
- 3 tablespoons (45g) orange juice

Ganache
- 4.2 ounces (120g) dark chocolate
- ½ cup (120g) whipping cream

Cake
Preheat the oven to 350°F (170°C). Prepare a loaf pan by brushing it with butter and then lining it with parchment paper.

In one bowl, combine the ground almonds, flour, and baking powder. In another bowl, beat the softened butter and confectioners' sugar until you obtain a homogeneous texture. Whisk in the egg yolks, whole egg, milk, olive oil, and orange zest. Once the mixture is smooth, fold in the dry ingredients.

In a third bowl, beat the egg whites and sugar into firm peaks. Next, fold the egg whites into the almond batter. Pour the cake mix into the prepared pan and bake for 25 to 35 minutes, until a skewer comes out clean. Cool on a wire rack.

Soaking Syrup
Add the sugar and water to a saucepan and bring to a boil. Take the pan off the heat and add the orange juice. Let the mixture cool down.

Ganache
Partially melt the dark chocolate in a bowl set over a pan of simmering water, making sure the water does not touch the bowl. In a small saucepan, bring the cream to a boil. Pour it over the chocolate, a third at a time, and stir until the mixture forms a smooth, shiny ganache.

Assemble
When the cake comes out of the oven and has cooled to the touch, brush the cake with the soaking syrup. Finally, spoon the ganache over the cake before serving.

BANANA, GINGER, AND CHOCOLATE CAKE

We like to make this cake in a loaf pan, so it stays moist for days as we slice sliver after sliver of the cake. Or, if we're having company and know it's going to go down fast, we make tiny individual cakes in oval molds for a delicate appearance. You can also use a muffin pan and fill it only halfway to get dainty little cakes—just be sure to reduce the baking time to about 15 minutes. If you want the cake to have a strong banana flavor, use an overripe and mushy banana, For a milder flavor, use a perfectly ripe banana or one that has just a few brown spots.

PREP TIME 15 minutes   COOK TIME 30 minutes   SERVES 6–8

- 3 tablespoons (45g) unsalted butter, melted + more for greasing the pan
- 1 cup (120g) all-purpose flour
- ⅓ cup + 2 teaspoons (75g) superfine sugar
- ½ teaspoon (3g) baking soda
- ½ teaspoon (3g) fine sea salt
- 3 ounces (85g) chocolate, cut into chunks
- 1.5 ounces (40g) Ginger Confit, chopped (recipe on facing page)
- 1 vanilla bean
- 1 egg
- 1 banana, mashed
- 1 heaping tablespoon (20g) plain yogurt

Preheat the oven to 350°F (175°C). Brush a muffin pan with some of the melted butter. Let the butter firm up (if you're in a hurry, pop the pan in the freezer for a minute), then dust it with flour, making sure to tap off any excess.

In a large bowl, whisk together the flour, sugar, baking soda, and salt. Add the chocolate chunks and ginger confit.

Split and scrape the vanilla bean. In another bowl, lightly beat the egg and add the mashed banana, yogurt, melted butter, and vanilla seeds and mix well. Pour the banana mixture into the dry ingredients and gently fold it in with a spatula, incorporating all the dry ingredients to form a smooth batter.

Pour the batter into the prepared pan. Bake for 25 to 35 minutes or until a skewer comes out clean. Let the banana cake cool in the pan for 5 minutes before transferring it to a cooling rack.

GINGER CONFIT

PREP TIME 15 minutes   COOK TIME 30–45 minutes   MAKES 1 cup (225g)

½ pound (225g) fresh tender ginger,
   peeled and sliced thinly

2 cups (400g) superfine sugar + more
   for coating the ginger slices

2 cups (480g) water

Add all the ingredients to a saucepan and bring to a boil. Lower the heat to medium and simmer until the temperature reaches 225°F (106°C) on a thermometer, stirring frequently. This should take 30 to 45 minutes, until the ginger slices are floppy and the sugar has thickened considerably.

Drain the ginger mixture while it is still hot, so the syrup will drain through a sieve. If you'd like, you can use the syrup to sweeten lemonade.

Sprinkle the drained slices of ginger with sugar as you toss them in a bowl. Spread the ginger slices on a cooling rack for a few hours or overnight, until they're dry enough not to stick to your fingers.

Alternatively, you can store the ginger in its own syrup for up to one year if you keep it refrigerated. If you've tossed the ginger in sugar, it can be stored at room temperature for a few months in a sealed container.

CITRUS-SCENTED BAKLAVA
WITH WARM SPICES

Making baklava is a labor of love. We hand-chop the nuts instead of using a food processor (this tends to make them oily), and we brush each sheet of phyllo with lots of butter (be *very* generous). The last time we made baklava, in Shaheen's orange kitchen in the 19th arrondissement of Paris, we tripled the recipe and had nuts flying all over the place. We made it for the last picnic with friends at Buttes Chaumont, and whenever we meet them they still talk about this baklava. Make sure you use raw nuts and not roasted and salted ones.

PREP TIME 45 minutes   COOK TIME 1 hour   SERVES 10–12

Soaking Syrup
- 1½ cups (300g) sugar
- ½ cup (120g) water
- 1 unwaxed lemon, halved
- 1 clementine, halved
- 1 orange, halved
- 1 6-inch (15cm) stick of cinnamon
- 1 cup (320g) honey

Baklava
- 3⅓ cups (500g) almonds, finely chopped
- 2 cups (250g) walnuts, finely chopped
- 2 cups (250g) pistachios, finely chopped
- 1¼ cups (250g) superfine sugar
- 1 tablespoon cinnamon
- ¼ teaspoon ground cloves
- ¼ teaspoon ground cardamom
- ½ teaspoon fine sea salt
- 1⅔ cups (375g) unsalted butter, melted and cooled slightly
- 1 package (approx. 400g) phyllo pastry sheets, thawed if frozen

Soaking Syrup
Combine the sugar and water in a saucepan. Squeeze the juice from the lemon, clementine, and orange into the sugar mixture and throw in the fruit halves as well. Add the cinnamon stick. Bring the mixture to a boil over moderate heat until the sugar is dissolved; then simmer 10 minutes. Skim as necessary. Stir in the honey and bring the mixture to a boil. Remove it from the heat and cool to room temperature. Pour the mixture through a sieve into a large bowl and discard the fruit, leaving the cinnamon stick in the strained mixture. Chill until it is completely cold.

NOTE One time we left the fruit halves in, thinking that more of the citrus flavor might be drawn into the syrup. Instead it made it rather strong, so it's best to discard the fruit before cooling the syrup.

Baklava

Preheat oven to 340°F (170°C).

Stir together the chopped almonds, walnuts, pistachios, sugar, cinnamon, cloves, cardamom and salt until well combined. Add 5 tablespoons (about 75g) of the melted butter and stir to coat.

Thoroughly brush a 13 × 9-inch (33 × 23cm) baking dish with melted butter. Cut the phyllo sheets in half along the width and stack them, keeping them covered with a damp kitchen towel. Lay 2 sheets of phyllo in the bottom of the baking dish and brush the top sheet with butter, making sure to brush all the way through the edges to avoid dried and brittle bits once baked. Continue to layer 2 sheets at a time then brush every second sheet with butter, until you have used 12 sheets of phyllo. After brushing the twelfth sheet of phyllo with butter, scatter about 2 cups (200–250g) of the nut mixture evenly over the phyllo.

Repeat this layering process 3 more times, but with 8 sheets in each layer. Finally, top with 12 sheets of phyllo. (You will use 48 sheets of phyllo in all.) Butter the top and refrigerate the dish for 10 to 15 minutes for the butter to firm up.

With a sharp knife, cut the baklava into 16 equal rectangles, then cut each piece in half diagonally to make triangles, making sure to cut all the way through.

Bake the baklava until it is golden, about 1 hour. Remove from the oven and pour the cold syrup in a thin drizzle all over the baklava—the coming together of the the cool syrup hitting the sizzling pan of hot baklava creates a wonderfully delicate hiss. Let the baklava rest at room temperature for at least 6 hours before serving. Store at room temperature.

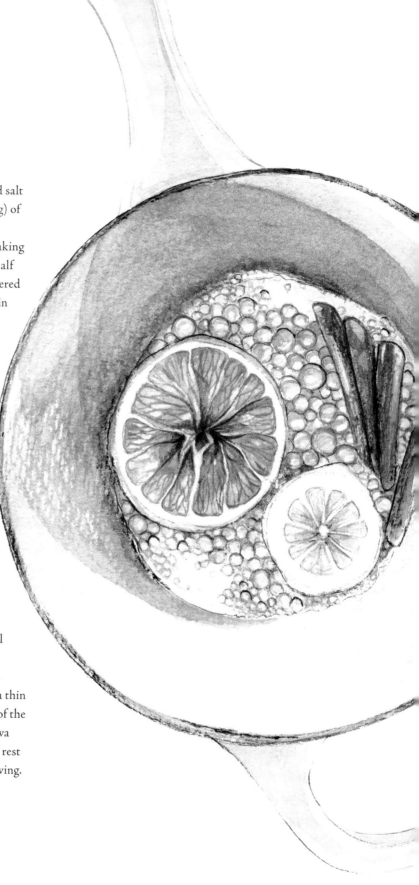

NOISETTE

If there is just one dessert in this book that you have to make, let it be this one. It takes time and a bit of planning, but it's worth the effort. The chewy, hazelnut-based Dacquoise and crunchy layer of praline feuilletine (bits of paper-thin, crispy crêpes), topped with a rich hazelnut ganache and a light, billowy layer of milk chocolate Chantilly—all of which can be enjoyed in a single bite—are a flavor and texture party in the mouth.

Note: You can buy feuilletine online, or if you don't want a large quantity, you can order another French product, Gavottes—crispy, lace crêpes covered in milk chocolate—instead. Just crush the cookies before using them to make Noisette.

PREP TIME 1 hour 15 minutes + overnight rest   COOK TIME 1 hour   SERVES 10

Dacquoise

- SCANT 1 cup (90g) ground hazelnuts
- 1 cup + 2 tablespoons (150g) confectioners' sugar
- 5 egg whites
- ¼ cup + 1 teaspoon (55g) superfine sugar
- A handful of chopped hazelnuts

Praline Paste

- 1½ cups (200g) toasted hazelnuts
- 1 cup (200g) superfine sugar

Hazelnut Paste

- 4 ounces (100g) hazelnuts

Praline Feuilletine

- 2.2 ounces (65g) milk chocolate
- 1 tablespoon + 1 teaspoon (20g) butter
- 3 ounces (85g) hazelnut praline
- 3 ounces (85g) hazelnut paste
- 3 ounces (85g) feuilletine (available in some stores and online)

Praline Ganache

- 3.5 ounces (100g) dark chocolate
- 5.6 ounces (160g) praline paste
- ¾ cup (180g) whipping cream

Milk Chocolate Chantilly

- 7 ounces (200g) milk chocolate
- 1⅔ cups (400g) whipping cream

Caramel Sauce

- ¼ cup (60g) whipping cream
- ½ cup (100g) superfine sugar
- 3 tablespoons (45g) unsalted butter
- Sea salt

Dacquoise

Whisk together the ground hazelnuts and confectioners' sugar in a medium bowl.

In a large bowl, beat the egg whites and add the superfine sugar slowly into the bowl. Whisk until stiff peaks form.

Fold the ground hazelnut and confectioners' sugar mixture into the whites and then transfer it to a pastry bag with a large plain tip.

On a baking sheet lined with parchment paper, pipe a circle of 9-inch (22cm) diameter. Work your way in a spiral from the inside outward. You can also make individual portions and pipe the dacquoise to 2½–3 inches (5–7.5cm) in diameter. You can use the help of cake rings to get perfect circles. Scatter the chopped hazelnuts on the surface. Bake the cake at 360°F (180°C) for 10 to 15 minutes, until a skewer comes out clean.

The cake will rise quite a bit while baking and deflate on cooling. This is normal. Once it has cooled completely, you can proceed with assembling the cake.

Praline Paste

Toast the hazelnuts in at 300°F (150°C), until they are fragrant and light brown, about 15 minutes.

Add all of the sugar to a heavy saucepan placed over medium heat. As the sugar heats up, it will begin to melt and then turn light golden. If you see bits of dry sugar in the pan, stir it lightly with a wooden spoon. Turn the heat down and continue to cook until all of the sugar is dark golden. Add the toasted hazelnuts. Stir them into the caramel for another minute, coating them thoroughly.

Transfer the caramelized hazelnuts to a sheet of parchment paper to cool. Reserve a few for garnish and grind the rest in a food processor. The hazelnuts will grind down to a powder and then to a paste with the consistency of a runny nut butter.

Hazelnut Paste

Toast the hazelnuts in a 300°F (150°C) oven until they are fragrant and light brown, about 15 minutes.

Grind the toasted hazelnuts to a paste in a food processor. Do not be tempted to add oil or anything at all. As you continue to grind, the oils in the hazelnuts are released and it will turn into the nut butter or hazelnut paste to use in this recipe. You can also use store-bought pure hazelnut butter instead.

Praline Feuilletine

In a saucepan over low heat, melt the milk chocolate and butter together and cool completely. Add the praline paste and hazelnut paste, and stir until smooth. Finally, stir in the feuilletine at the last minute before assembly.

Praline Ganache

In a bowl, add the chocolate and praline paste. Heat the cream in a saucepan over medium heat until the cream comes to a simmer. Pour the hot cream over the chocolate and praline mixture and let it rest for half a minute. Then stir the mixture until all the chocolate has melted. Refrigerate the ganache until you are ready to use it. When the ganache is ready for piping, beat it with a wooden spoon until smooth and shiny, not dull. It should be soft enough to pipe and hold a shape. If the ganache is too cold, leave it out on the kitchen counter or warm it very gently over a water bath. When it's smooth and pliable, transfer it to a piping bag fitted with a medium-size star tip.

CONTINUED

Milk Chocolate Chantilly

Put the chocolate in a bowl and break it into pieces. Pour the cream into a heavy saucepan and bring it to a boil. Pour the hot cream over the chocolate and whisk thoroughly to combine. Refrigerate the chocolate cream until it is completely chilled. You can do this the night before assembling the Noisette.

Once it is chilled, whip the chocolate cream to medium-to-firm peaks that just hold together and then transfer the mixture to a pastry bag fitted with a ½ inch (12–14mm) plain piping tip.

Caramel Sauce

Keep the cream warm in a heavy saucepan on a back burner of the stove. Don't let it reduce; it should just be warm.

Melt the sugar over medium heat in another heavy saucepan to make a dark caramel. Stir as needed, otherwise the sugar can burn in spots. Turn down the heat when all the sugar has melted, as it cooks very quickly.

Add the butter to the pan and take it off the heat. Stir the butter into the caramel until it is completely homogeneous, and then add the warm cream. Let the caramel sauce cool and then transfer it to a piping bag to use later.

Assemble

Working from bottom up, place the Dacquoise on a cake board or plate.

With a small palette knife, spread the Praline Feuilletine on the cake all the way to the edges.

Next, pipe concentric rings of Praline Ganache on the layer of Praline Feuilletine. Repeat to create another level of ganache to give it some height.

Then pipe the Milk Chocolate Chantilly on the ganache.

Finally, garnish the cake with the reserved caramelized hazelnuts and a drizzle of Caramel Sauce.

praline ganache

milk chocolate chantilly

praline feuilletine

dacquoise

STRAWBERRIES AND CREAM CHEESECAKE
WITH PISTACHIO SHORTBREAD

When we can resist the temptation to eat every last sweet summer strawberry right out of the basket from the farmers' market and make the effort to do something other than whipping vanilla Chantilly cream, we like to make this delightful strawberry and cream cheesecake, which gets a lovely tang from the cream cheese. And if you're not up for making the entire dessert, you can just bake yourself the pistachio shortbread and dip it into your Hazelnut Hot Chocolate (page 153).

PREP TIME 45–60 minutes + overnight rest   COOK TIME 30 minutes   SERVES 10

Pistachio Shortbread
½ cup + 2 tablespoons (140g) unsalted butter
⅔ cup + 1 teaspoon (140g) superfine sugar
1 egg yolk
1½ cups (180g) all-purpose flour
1½ cups (200g) hulled pistachios, coarsely chopped

Cheesecake
2½ sheets of gelatin or 1 teaspoon (5g) powdered gelatin
1½ egg yolks
¼ cup (50g) superfine sugar
1 tablespoon water
6 ounces (170g) Philadelphia cream cheese
1 cup (240g) whipping cream
2 teaspoons (5g) confectioners' sugar

Vanilla and White Chocolate Cream
3 ounces (85g) white chocolate
1 cup (240g) whipping cream
1 vanilla bean, split, and seeds scraped out
½ tablespoon (10g) honey

Vanilla Glaze
1 sheet of gelatin or ½ teaspoon (2g) powdered gelatin
⅓ cup + 1 teaspoon (75g) sugar
1 vanilla bean, split, and seeds scraped out
⅓ cup (75ml) water

Garnish
1 pound (450g) strawberries, hulled
Chopped pistachios, gold leaf, or silver dragées

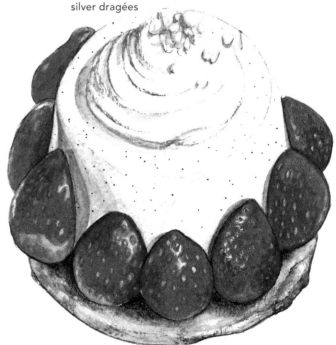

Pistachio Shortbread

Beat the butter in a bowl until smooth.

Add the sugar and continue to beat until light and fluffy.

Next, add the egg yolk and beat for another few minutes until the color becomes paler.

Stir in the sifted flour, followed by the pistachios.

Flatten the dough, wrap it snugly in plastic, and chill for 1 to 2 hours or at least 30 minutes.

Preheat the oven to 325°F (160°C).

Roll out the dough on a sheet of parchment paper to a diameter of about 9 inches (22cm) and then use a cake ring to cut it into a perfect circle of 8 inches (20cm). Slide the paper on a baking tray and prick the dough with a fork. Freeze the dough for a few minutes, then bake for about 20 minutes or until golden.

Using a spatula, transfer to a cooling rack and let cool completely.

Cheesecake

If you are using sheet gelatin, soak it in a bowl of cold water for 15 minutes. If you are using powdered gelatin, soak it in 3–4 tablespoons of cold water for 15 minutes, until all the moisture has been absorbed and it fluffs up.

Add the egg yolks to a bowl and break them up with a whisk.

In a saucepan, heat the sugar and a tablespoon of water and bring the mixture to a boil until the temperature reaches 250°F (120°C). It's important to use a thermometer and reach this temperature, otherwise the syrup may be too watery and the cheesecake may not set.

Pour the hot sugar syrup over the yolks in a gentle stream while constantly whisking the yolks (preferably using an electric beater) so that they don't cook with the heat from the sugar. Continue to beat the mixture until it cools.

In a bowl set over a pan of simmering water, melt the cream cheese. Squeeze the excess water from the gelatin, if using sheet gelatin, and add it to the cream cheese. Stir until the gelatin has completely dissolved into the cream cheese. Take it off the heat.

In another bowl, whisk the whipping cream with the confectioners' sugar.

Once the cream cheese is cool—but not cold (otherwise it will be too firm)—fold in the whipped cream, a third at a time. Do it quickly because the cold whipped cream will begin to set the mixture.

Pour the mixture into an 8-inch (20cm) round, silicone cake pan and freeze overnight.

Vanilla and White Chocolate Cream

Chop the chocolate into pieces and put them in a bowl.

Add ⅓ cup (80g) of the whipping cream, vanilla seeds, and honey to a saucepan and bring it to a boil. Pour the mixture over the chocolate. Let it sit for a minute, then whisk gently until the mixture is smooth.

Stir in the remaining whipping cream. Chill the mixture thoroughly overnight.

The next day, whip the cream with an electric mixer until it forms soft peaks. Reduce the speed and whip until firm. Be careful not to overwhip. Transfer the whipped cream to a piping bag fitted with a ½-inch (12mm) pastry tip.

CONTINUED

Vanilla Glaze

If you are using sheet gelatin, soak it in a bowl of cold water for 15 minutes. If you are using powdered gelatin, soak it in 3–4 tablespoons of cold water for 15 minutes, until all the moisture has been absorbed and it fluffs up.

In a saucepan, add the sugar and vanilla seeds. Rub the vanilla into the sugar with your fingertips so that it is evenly distributed. Add the water to the pan and bring it to a boil over medium heat.

When the mixture has boiled, remove it from the heat and stir in the soaked gelatin, squeezing off any excess water first if using sheet gelatin. Stir the mixture well and then pour it through a sieve into a jar. Use it when it has cooled to about 95°F (35°C), but not set.

Assemble

Unmold the frozen cheesecake on a wire rack set over a shallow tray. Pour the vanilla glaze over the top of the cake so that it flows smoothly and any excess drips into the tray. Put the cheesecake back into the freezer to let the glaze set.

Put the pistachio crust on a plate. Place the glazed cheesecake on top of it with the help of an offset spatula.

Cut the strawberries in half and place them along the side of the cheesecake, pushing them gently so that they stick to the glaze.

Pipe the Vanilla and White Chocolate Cream on top of the cheesecake.

Garnish with chopped pistachios, gold leaf, or silver dragées.

SOME OF OUR FAVORITES PÂTISSERIES IN PARIS

- **Christophe Michalak**
16, rue de la Verrerie, 75004 Paris

- **Pierre Hermé**
72, rue Bonaparte, 75006 Paris

- **Des Gateaux et du Pain**
63, Boulevard Pasteur, 75015 Paris

- **Mori Yoshida**
65, Avenue de Breteuil, 75007 Paris

- **Jacques Genin**
133, rue de Turenne, 75003 Paris

- **Gérard Mulot**
76, rue de Seine, 75006 Paris

- **La Patisserie des Rêves**
93, rue du Bac, 75007 Paris

- **La Goutte d'Or**
183, rue Marcadet, 75018 Paris

HAZELNUT HOT CHOCOLATE

Use quality chocolate and your best cups and you will feel like you're sitting in Angelina (226, rue de Rivoli, 75001 Paris), a gilded tea room known to serve the most decadent hot chocolate in Paris. The idea of using hazelnuts as a topping was inspired by a memorable visit to a gelato shop in Rome.

PREP TIME 10 minutes   COOK TIME 20 minutes   MAKES 2 cups

¼ cup (30g) hazelnuts, divided

1 cup (240g) whole milk

½ cup (120g) heavy whipping cream

½ vanilla bean, split, and seeds scraped out

4 ounces (120g) dark chocolate

Whipped cream

Toast the hazelnuts in the oven at 300°F (150°C), until they are fragrant and light golden brown, about 15 minutes. Rub off the papery skins. Reserve 1 tablespoon of the toasted hazelnuts for garnish and coarsely chop the rest.

Heat the milk and cream together in a pan with the vanilla bean and seeds. Once the mixture comes to a simmer, turn off the heat and cover the pot, so that the vanilla can be infused into the milk. Let the mixture rest for 20 minutes or so and then bring it back to a simmer. Take the pan off the heat. Place the dark chocolate in a bowl and pour the hot milk mixture over it. Let it sit for a minute, remove the vanilla bean and then use an immersion blender to thoroughly combine the ingredients. Pour the hot chocolate into cups and top with soft whipped cream and the whole toasted hazelnuts.

HAZELNUT CREAM BUNS

This is a choux bun version of the iconic French dessert, Paris Brest. It's a choux pastry that is baked until puffed and golden then filled with the most luxurious butter-laden hazelnut-flavored pastry cream, called *crème mousseline*. It does take a few different steps, but the easiest way to do it is to break up your work and make the praline paste and the *crème mousseline* a day before so that the cream is thoroughly chilled for when you need it. Make extra praline, you'll regret it if you don't.

PREP TIME 30 minutes   COOK TIME 1 hour   SERVES 10

Praline Paste
- 1 cup (130g) hazelnuts + some for garnish
- ½ cup (100g) superfine sugar

Praline Crème Mousseline
- ¼ cup (50g) superfine sugar, divided
- 2 egg yolks
- 1 tablespoon (15g) all-purpose flour, sifted
- 1 tablespoon (17g) cornstarch
- 1 cup (240g) whole milk
- 1 vanilla bean, split, and seeds scraped out
- ½ cup + 2½ tablespoons (150g) unsalted butter
- 3 ounces (85g) praline paste

Craquelin (Crumble Topping)
- ¼ cup (55g) unsalted butter, softened
- ⅓ cup (67g) demerara sugar or light brown sugar
- ½ cup (60g) all-purpose flour

Choux Pastry
- ½ cup (120g) whole milk
- ½ cup (112g) unsalted butter, cut into small cubes
- ½ teaspoon (2g) superfine sugar
- 1 teaspoon (5g) fine sea salt
- 1¼ cups (150g) all-purpose flour
- 4 eggs, beaten

Praline Paste
Toast the hazelnuts in at 300°F (150°C) oven until they are fragrant and light brown, about 15 to 17 minutes.

In a heavy-bottomed saucepan placed over medium heat, add all of the sugar. As the sugar heats up, it will begin to melt and then turn light golden. If you see bits of dry sugar in the pan, stir it lightly with a wooden spoon. Turn the heat down and continue to cook until all of the sugar is dark golden. Add the toasted hazelnuts. Stir them into the caramel for another minute, coating them thoroughly.

Transfer the hazelnuts to a silicone mat to cool slightly. Reserve a few for garnish and grind the rest in a food processor. The hazelnuts will grind down to a powder and then to a paste with the consistency of a runny nut butter.

Praline Crème Mousseline
In a bowl, mix together half of the sugar and egg yolks, then add the flour and cornstarch.

In a large saucepan, boil the milk with the vanilla seeds and the remaining half of the sugar and pour it over the yolk mixture in the bowl, whisking it as you go along. Pour the milk-and-egg mixture back into the saucepan and whisk over medium heat until the cream thickens and comes back to a boil.

Transfer the cream to a clean bowl, stir in the butter and the praline paste, and whisk until the mixture is homogeneous. Refrigerate the cream for at least 3 hours or, preferably, overnight.

Whip the cream until the texture is as light and airy as a mousse, and then transfer it to a pastry bag fitted with a star-shaped piping tip. Keep it refrigerated until the choux is ready.

Craquelin (Crumble Topping)

Knead all the ingredients together in a bowl until they're fully combined.

Roll out the dough between sheets of parchment paper to a thickness of ¹⁄₁₆ inch (1.6mm). Refrigerate the dough until it is firm. Using a round pastry cutter, mark the dough to be cut into 1-inch (2.5cm) circles, but do not pop out the circles. Freeze the sheet of dough until hardened, about 15 minutes. Working quickly with the help of palette knife, carefully pop out the discs. Reserve them in a container and place it back in the fridge until ready to bake.

Choux Pastry

Preheat the oven to 400°F (200°C). Line a baking tray with a silicone sheet or parchment paper.

In a saucepan, bring the milk, butter, sugar, and salt to a boil.

Take the pan off the heat and add all the flour at once. Stir the mixture vigorously with a wooden spoon, put the pan back on the heat, and cook until the mixture clumps up around the spoon and begins to stick to the bottom of the pan.

Remove the pan from the heat and transfer the dough to a mixing bowl.

Begin to beat the dough, and then pour in the eggs a little at a time until they're completely incorporated and the batter is smooth and shiny.

Transfer the choux pastry dough to a piping bag fitted with a ½-inch (12mm) tip and pipe it into 1 inch (2.5cm)

wide circles. Leave a 2-inch (5cm) space between the rounds of dough because they will rise quite a bit. Make sure they are all the same size so that they bake evenly.

Remove the discs of crumble topping from the fridge. Place one disc on top of each circle of piped choux dough and bake in the oven for 20 to 30 minutes. Do not open the oven door at all after putting the choux into the oven—if you do, the pastry will collapse and not rise again. You can turn the temperature down to 360°F (180°C) after the pastry has turned golden brown and looks like it has puffed up to nearly three times its original volume. Continue to bake the pastry until it is an even, dark golden brown.

Assemble

Place the choux buns on a cutting board and, using a small serrated knife, carefully slice off the top third of each bun.

Pipe the hazelnut mousseline cream into the bottom half of the choux buns. Place the tops back on the buns, dust with confectioners' sugar, and then gently push the reserved caramelized hazelnuts into the hazelnut mousseline cream.

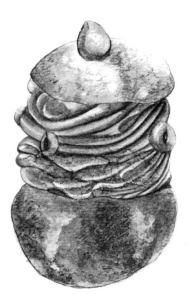

DRINKS

Instead of serving just water or resorting to artificially flavored drinks, we wanted to offer our picnic club guests an entire meal made from scratch, including the beverage. We took special care to create uncommon blends with fresh fruits, herbs, teas, spices, and flowers.

We've divided our drink recipes into nectars, syrups, and cordials. Nectars are thick, fruit pulp bases that are meant to be diluted. Syrups are simple herb or spice infusions that are easy enough to make as needed and are used in small quantities. And, finally, a cordial is citrus-based and can be diluted either with sparkling water, to play on the citrus flavor, or mixed with another fruit juice to change things up. You can use either citric acid, which helps in preservation, or fresh lemon juice to give the cordial its characteristic tart kick.* We hope that you take these recipes as a guide and work with whatever fresh fruit you might find in season around you.

* If you plan to store your cordial for several weeks, be sure to let it "burp" every once in a while, to let the naturally collected carbonation escape and relieve pressure on the bottle.

GREEN MANGO, FENNEL, AND MINT

Before the arrival of the indiscriminate mango-eating season in summer, Indian homes have a lot to accomplish with raw mangoes: mainly pickling and sun-drying them—and making enough of this refreshing green mango drink to last through the scorching summer. In its concentrated form, it makes a pretty amazing salsa for tacos.

PREP TIME 10 minutes   COOK TIME 30 minutes   MAKES 3 cups (750ml) nectar

Toast and grind **1 teaspoon fennel seeds** to a powder. Peel and then cut **3 unripe mangoes** into medium-size chunks, avoiding the pit. Combine the ingredients with **2 cups (500ml) water, 1 cup (200g) sugar**, and the ground fennel in a medium saucepan. Bring the mixture to boil and then reduce the heat to a simmer. Cook until the mangoes are very soft, about 20 to 30 minutes. Blend the mixture to a smooth pulp. You can bottle this to use over the course of a month.

To serve, blend **one part mango pulp** with **fresh mint leaves** to taste. Stir together with **three parts water**, strain, and serve over crushed ice. Season with a **pinch of salt** and garnish with **fresh mint leaves**.

GUAVA, CHILI, AND LIME

I n this recipe, we simmer the guava with water and sugar, much like a compote, to soften the flesh around the seeds, which makes it easier to extract the pulp. We recommend adding a little cayenne pepper for a nice strong kick, but you could also use freshly ground black pepper.

PREP TIME 10 minutes   COOK TIME 30–40 minutes   MAKES 1 quart (1 liter) nectar

Peel **2 pounds (1kg) ripe guavas** and cut them into small cubes. In a medium saucepan set over medium heat, combine the guava with **2 cups (500ml) water**, **1 cup (200g) sugar**, and **¼–½ teaspoon cayenne pepper**. Bring the mixture to a boil and then let it simmer until the fruit is well softened (at least 30 minutes). Once the mixture is cool, strain it through a fine mesh sieve, pressing the fruit firmly with the back of a large spoon to release as much pulp as possible. Whisk in the **juice of 3–4 limes**. You can bottle this to use over the course of a week.

To serve, combine equal parts of the guava nectar and cold water. Serve over ice.

PLUM AND CINNAMON

Sometimes we like to make this nectar with cinnamon and, at other times, with star anise. Pick perfectly ripe plums and make sure to blend them really well so that all the fibrous bits are broken down and the drink has a smooth mouthfeel.

PREP TIME 10 minutes   COOK TIME 15 minutes   MAKES 1 quart (1 liter) nectar

Pit **2 pounds (1 kg) ripe plums** and purée in a blender with the **juice of 4 lemons** until smooth. Place **½ cup (100g) sugar** in a small saucepan over medium heat and caramelize the sugar until it takes on a deep amber color, or when a thermometer reads 350–360°F (175–180°C). Do not turn away from the pan— the sugar can cook and burn very quickly. Once the sugar has caramelized, take the pan off the heat and add **½ cup water** to keep the caramel from cooking any further. Be careful; the sugar will bubble and seize up, so make sure to pour in the water, little by little. Return the pan to the heat, add **2 cinnamon sticks**, and bring it back to a boil. Reduce the heat to low and simmer for 5 minutes. Remove from the heat and let the cinnamon syrup come to room temperature. Once the mixture is cool, remove the cinnamon sticks and whisk in the blended plums. You can bottle this to use over the course of two weeks.

To serve, combine equal parts of cold still or sparkling water and the plum mixture. Serve over ice.

PEACH AND ROSEMARY

Occasionally, we like to swap out rosemary for lemon verbena in this infusion. When using verbena, we stir it into the syrup after turning the heat off, so that that it steeps like a tisane instead of cooking in the syrup. Rosemary, on the other hand, is hardier and benefits from cooking in the syrup.

PREP TIME 5 minutes   COOK TIME 10 minutes + overnight rest   MAKES 1½ quarts (1.5 liters) of the drink

In a medium saucepan over medium heat, combine ¼ cup (50g) sugar with ¼ cup (60ml) water. Once the sugar has dissolved and the mixture begins to boil, reduce the heat to low and add 1 sprig rosemary. Simmer the mixture for 5 minutes and then remove the pan from the heat. For the best results, let the rosemary infuse in the syrup in the refrigerator overnight. You can bottle this to use over the course of a month.

To serve, combine ¼ cup (60ml) rosemary syrup with 4 cups (1 liter) cold peach juice, 2 cups (500ml) sparkling water, and the juice of 2 lemons.

PINEAPPLE AND MINT LEMONADE

The most important thing to remember when making this recipe is to steep the mint for only 15 to 20 minutes. That's the best way to capture its fresh taste. If you steep it any longer the syrup gets cloudy, and the smell becomes overpowering.

PREP TIME 10 minutes   COOK TIME 5 minutes active, 20 minutes rest   MAKES 1 quart (1 liter) lemonade

Combine **¼ cup (50g) sugar** and **¼ cup (60ml) water** in a small saucepan over high heat. Bring the mixture to a boil. When all of the sugar has dissolved, remove the pan from the heat. Stir in **a handful of fresh mint leaves** (no stems) and set the pan aside to cool. Once the mixture is cool, strain out the mint and add the **juice of 1 lemon** to the syrup. You can bottle this to use over the course of a month.

To serve, combine **3 cups pineapple juice** with the lemon-mint syrup to taste. Add **1 cup cold water** and serve over ice.

SYRUPS

ORANGE, BAY LEAF, AND MAPLE

The use of bay leaf in this syrup may be unexpected, but its warmth really works with the brightness of the orange. Use a fresh bay leaf, rather than a dried one, and if you don't want to use maple syrup, use orange blossom honey instead—it makes the syrup taste particularly good.

PREP TIME 5 minutes   COOK TIME 10 minutes   MAKES 1 quart (1 liter) juice

Combine **½ cup (100g) sugar** and **¾ cup (180ml) water** in a small saucepan and set it over medium heat until the mixture comes to a boil. Once the sugar has dissolved, reduce the heat to a simmer, and add **1 bay leaf** and the **peel of 1 orange**. Continue to simmer the mixture for 5 minutes. Remove the saucepan from the heat and let it cool. Strain the mixture to remove any solids and then add **1 cup (300g) pure maple syrup**. You can bottle this to use over the course of two weeks.

To serve, combine the syrup to taste with **3 cups (750ml) freshly squeezed orange juice** and top with **sparkling water** for a hint of fizz.

PASSION FRUIT, RASPBERRY, AND VANILLA

P assion fruit and raspberry in a dessert work so well together. The sweetness of ripe raspberry and the tartness of passion fruit in a mousse cake from a pastry shop in Paris made us want to rethink the dessert as a drink.

PREP TIME 10 minutes   COOK TIME 5 minutes   MAKES 1½ quarts (1.5 liters) sparkling drink

Combine ⅓ cup (70g) sugar with ⅓ cup (80ml) water in a medium saucepan over medium heat. Split and scrape the seeds out of 1 vanilla bean. Add both the seeds and the bean to the pan of sugar syrup. Simmer for 5 minutes and let the syrup cool completely before straining and bottling it. Blend 2½ cups (300g) fresh or frozen raspberries to a purée. You can pass them through a sieve if you don't want to have any seeds. You can bottle this to use over the course of a month.

When ready to serve, combine with 1 cup (240ml) unsweetened passion fruit pulp, the blended raspberries, and 3 cups (750ml) sparkling water.

CARAMEL, APPLE, AND GINGER

This drink, which is perfect for autumn, is our version of a classic tarte tatin (French apple pie) in a glass. You could also make a hot version of the drink, spiced with cloves and cinnamon, for a cozy evening indoors.

PREP TIME 5 minutes　COOK TIME 10 minutes　MAKES 1½ quarts (1.5 liters) juice

Place ½ cup (100g) sugar in a small saucepan over medium heat and caramelize the sugar until it takes on a deep amber color 350–360°F (175–180°C). Do not turn away from the pan—the sugar can cook and burn very quickly. Once the sugar has caramelized, take the pan off the heat and add ½ cup apple juice to keep the caramel from cooking any further. Be careful: the sugar will bubble, so make sure to pour the juice in, little by little. If the sugar has hardened, place the pan back on a low heat so that the sugar can melt again. Next add a 2½-inch (7cm) piece of ginger that has been cut into slices and let it infuse with the caramel apple syrup by simmering the mixture for 5 minutes. Remove the pan from heat, add the juice of 2 lemons, and let it cool completely. Remove the ginger slices. You can bottle this to use over the course of two weeks.

To serve, combine the mixture with an additional 4 cups (1 liter) apple juice and 2 cups (500ml) cold sparkling water.

VANILLA, RHUBARB, AND BLOOD ORANGE

Rhubarb is commonly known to be a summer treat, but London is abundant with neon pink stalks in the wintertime. This bright type of rhubarb is "forced"—grown without any sunlight—which arrests chlorophyll development. As a result, it is more slender and less fibrous than conventionally grown rhubarb. It's excellent poached with orange juice and vanilla and served warm with spoonfuls of cream.

PREP TIME 20 minutes + overnight rest   COOK TIME 15 minutes   MAKES 1 quart (1 liter) cordial

Cut **1 pound (450g) rhubarb** into 2-inch (5cmm) pieces and place it in a medium saucepan with **2 cups (500ml) water** and **2 tablespoons (30g) sugar**. With a peeler, zest strips of **1 blood orange** and add it into the pan with the rhubarb. Next, split and scrape the seeds out of **1 vanilla bean** and add them to the saucepan. Bring the rhubarb mixture to a boil and then turn the heat down and simmer gently until the rhubarb has softened. It will look like a gloopy mush. Turn off the heat and let the mixture rest for 20 minutes. Line a colander with a muslin cloth, set it over a bowl, and pour the rhubarb and juice into it to strain. Place the bowl in the fridge and let the rhubarb juice drip into it overnight. The next morning, pour the juice and **1 cup (200g) sugar** into a saucepan and bring the mixture to a boil. You could also squeeze the bundle of rhubarb if you want to get more juice and don't mind if it's cloudy. Skim off any foam that gathers on the surface of the syrup. Turn off the heat and stir in the **juice of 3 lemons or 1 tablespoon citric acid** to dissolve. Add the **juice of 1 blood orange.** You can bottle this to use over the course of a month.

To serve, fill each glass with ice and add **1 part Vanilla, Rhubarb, and Blood Orange Cordial** and **4 parts sparkling water.** Stir to combine and serve with a curl of **blood orange zest.**

ELDERFLOWER AND GREEN GRAPE JUICE

We once spent an entire afternoon looking for elderflowers—a delicate, elusive flower that comes into bloom only in late spring, and often unpredictably—at the Buttes Chaumont park. We suggest that you get your hands on as much elderflower as possible and make a large batch of this syrup to last well beyond the summer. When making the cordial, make sure to keep the green stems to a minimum—snipping to the base of the tiny flowers takes a bit more time, but is well worth the effort, since the stems really distract from the flavor of the delicate flowers and also tend to discolor the cordial.

PREP TIME 15 minutes COOK TIME 10 minutes + overnight infusion MAKES 1 quart (1 liter) cordial

To prepare the elderflowers for the cordial, hold the stems of **6–8 elderflower heads** and dunk very briefly in cold water to give them a quick rinse. Into a large bowl, snip off the flowers, avoiding as much of the green stem as possible. Add the peel of **1 lemon** (making sure to avoid the white pith). Combine **2½ cups (500g) sugar** and **2 cups (500ml) water** in a medium saucepan. Over medium heat, bring the mixture to a gentle boil and make sure that all of the sugar has dissolved. Stir in the juice of **3 lemons or 1 tablespoon citric acid** to dissolve. Pour the syrup over the elderflowers. Cover and let the

mixture infuse at room temperature overnight. The next morning, strain and store refrigerated. You can bottle this to use over the course of 2 to 3 months.

To serve, combine **1 part elderflower cordial** with **3 parts green grape juice** and **3 parts sparkling water**. Serve over ice.

CLEMENTINE with HIBISCUS and CINNAMON

We discovered dried hibiscus flowers while scouring through the spice isles in the Middle Eastern stores in Ménilmontant. We were told to pour hot water over the flowers and enjoy it as a tisane. This blend is bright and floral with festive warmth from the cinnamon—you can also swap out the clementine for tropical juices such as pineapple, passion fruit, or mango.

PREP TIME 20 minutes   COOK TIME 10 minutes   MAKES 1 quart (1 liter) cordial

Pour **2½ cups (600ml) boiling water** over **20–30 dried hibiscus flowers**, and then cover and steep the flowers for 20 minutes. Remove the flowers and then pour the liquid, along with **2½ cups (500g) sugar**, into a small saucepan over medium heat. Once the sugar has dissolved and the mixture comes to a gentle boil, reduce the heat to a simmer and add **2 4-inch (10cm) sticks of cinnamon**. Simmer the mixture for 10 minutes, until fragrant. Remove the saucepan from the stovetop and stir in the **juice of 3 lemons or 1 tablespoon citric acid** to dissolve. Strain the cordial when it is cool and transfer it to a bottle. You can bottle this to use over the course of a month.

To serve, combine **1 part syrup** with **3 parts freshly squeezed clementine juice** and top with **sparkling water** for a hint of fizz.

MOROCCAN MINT TEA

The waiters at the café in the Grande Mosquée de Paris (2bis, place du Puits de l'Ermite, 75005 Paris), constantly hover with trays of sugary-sweet mint tea served in jeweled glasses that are perfectly in keeping with the ornate tiles and intricate architecture of the beautiful mosque. Only a simple gesture is needed to summon one of the attentive waiters for a glass of piping hot tea served with syrup-drenched, sticky North African pastries.

PREP TIME 5 minutes   COOK TIME 5 minutes   MAKES 1½ quarts (1.5 liter) tea

In a large teapot, place **1 heaping tablespoon of loose green tea (4 tea bags)** and **2 large handfuls of fresh mint leaves** (or as many as will fit). Fill the teapot to the brim with **6 cups (1.5 liters) hot water** from the kettle and let the tea and mint steep for 3 to 5 minutes. In a teacup or a small tea glass, place about **¼ cup (50g) sugar.**

The traditional Moroccan method of dissolving the sugar involves a dynamic movement of pouring the hot tea into the cup from a height. You could pour the tea back and forth into the kettle a couple of times to mix it, or you can simply stir the sugar into the tea with a spoon. Serve immediately.

DUTCH MINT TEA

On a weekend trip to Amsterdam we discovered the simple mint tea that the Dutch make so beautifully. We were fascinated by its simplicity. On returning to Paris, we made it for days on end.

PREP TIME 5 minutes   COOK TIME 5 minutes   MAKES 1 tall glass

Spoon **1 tablespoon honey** into the bottom of a tall clear glass and then plunge **3–4 sprigs fresh mint** "leaf down" (stalk up) into the glass. Fill the glass with **hot water**, making sure to submerge all of the leaves, and let the mint infuse for a minute before serving.

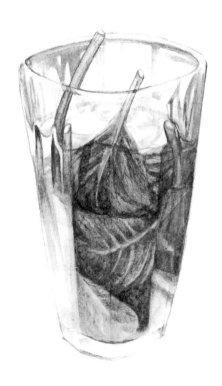

WINE

No meal—and certainly no picnic—in France is complete without a bottle of wine. My fondest memories of Paris are permeated with the jovial circles of bistro glasses scattered across a kitchen counter or coffee table. It's hard to go wrong with French wine in France, and even harder to tire of the selection—from the four-euro bottle you find on the bottom shelf at the local supermarket to the carefully curated selection at a specialty shop like the small Parisian chain Le Repaire de Bacchus.

In *A Moveable Feast*, Ernest Hemingway describes the subtleties of one of the most perfect marriages of French food and wine:

> *"As I ate the oysters with their strong taste of the sea and their faint metallic taste that the cold white wine washed away, leaving only the sea taste and the succulent texture, and as I drank their cold liquid from each shell and washed it down with the crisp taste of the wine, I lost the empty feeling and began to be happy and to make plans."*

To make a truly perfect pairing, you'll probably need to taste your way through several bottles of wine from all different nooks and crannies of the country. French wine abides by the rule of the land, or *terroir*, which holds that the soil, water, sun exposure, wind, and weather are among the many things that give a wine its most defining characteristics. The region, the town, and even the estate are specified to distinguish one wine from its neighbor down the road. For that reason, there's an incredible amount of variety, and it's worth the effort to figure out which town or side of the river is your favorite. In general, though, we use the following guide to pair wine with a specific menu or occasion:

CÔTES DU RHÔNE

Split in two by the Rhone River that rushes down from the Alps and empties out into the Mediterranean, the two "cotês" (or sides) of the river define its characteristics. Wines from the Northern Rhone are composed primarily of Syrah grapes, giving them their signature peppery bite. The wines of the Southern Rhone, however, are typically a combination of three grapes, making for a smooth complement to rich, meat-heavy dishes. Saint-Joseph wines, which come from the southern part of the Northern Rhone, are exposed to both cool continental and temperature Mediterranean weather systems. With a strong Syrah base, they are robust wines with varying nuances of spices or fruit depending on the exact location and exposure of the vineyard. We like to pair them with wild game or meats like our Slow-Roasted Rosemary Lamb (page 52).

BOURGOGNE

I will never forget the day that my friend Lauren introduced me to her neighborhood wine bar, L'Ambassade de Bourgogne. A tiny tasting room that's just a stone's throw away from the Luxembourg gardens, L'Ambassade offers an impressive variety of Bourgogne wine and one single item on its food menu—freshly baked gougères, heavenly cheese popovers from the same region. I've been a fan of Bourgogne ever since.

Dry red wines, reminiscent of New World Pinot Noir, are best to complement a night of cheese and charcuterie. White Chablis, from Northern Bourgogne, is made entirely from Chardonnay grapes but is dry and has a mineral, rather than an oaky finish, compared to other Chardonnay wines from around the world. It's fantastic with oysters, seafood, and spicy sausage.

BORDEAUX

Medium- to full-bodied reds from Bordeaux are perfect for rich dishes that are focused on red meat, such as our

Turkish Pot Roast (page 64). Some of the most famous and expensive Bordeauxs come from the Médoc region, but we are particularly fond of those from Saint-Emilion, known for a unique soil composition that lends the grapes a strong mineral finish.

BEAUJOLAIS

On the third Thursday of every November, villages and cities across France (and now in Tokyo, too) celebrate the long-awaited release of the annual Beaujolais Nouveau from the most recent harvest. This young wine is not intended for tasting per se, but rather for drinking as an excuse for merrymaking. The other wines from the Beaujolais region of southern Bourgogne are known to be light, refreshing, and versatile. They are a great go-tos for an impromptu picnic of a Smoked Ham, Brie, and Onion Jam tartine (page 104).

ALSACE

Unlike its German counterpart across the border, French Riesling from the Alsace region is only faintly sweet and is dominated by crisp, citrus notes. We love to pair it with our Caramelized Onion, Thyme, and Marjoram Tart (page 44) or to balance the kick of some of our spicier dishes, like Korean Chicken Salad (page 50) and Coconut Fish Stew (page 46).

CHAMPAGNE

The most delicate sparkling wines, known for their heady floral notes and miniscule bubbles, hail from the Champagne region. If you're celebrating or looking to make your dinner party a little more elegant, we recommend springing on the real stuff to accompany an amuse bouche of Oysters with Pickled Rhubarb (page 18). Otherwise, a Crémant uses the same classic in-bottle fermentation technique, *la méthode champenoise*, and can serve as a beautiful complement to smoked or cured fish, such as a Salmon Gravlax Salad with Pomelo Segments (page 14).

PROVENCE

Famous for its dry, blush-pink rosés, Provence is the region of summer. At my favorite wine bar, Le Baron

Rouge (1, rue Théophile Roussel, 75012 Paris), where overturned oak barrels are tables and the regulars start rolling in at 10 A.M., rosé flows by the liter and offers the perfect excuse to host an afternoon picnic. If you have time to hang around, you can enjoy your wine along with an *assiette mixte* (charcuterie, Tomme de Savoie, and crisp cornichons).

LANGUEDOC-ROUSSILLON

Soaked in the temperate Mediterranean climate and inching toward the Spanish border, the Languedoc region produces wines that are considered to be the most reminiscent of New World wine, being full bodied and fruit forward. The Vin de Pays from the Languedoc, denoted as Pays d'Oc, is particularly recognized as a great quality wine at a good price. This is our pick for a laid back, no frills night of roasted Cold-Oven Chicken (page 20).

VAL DE LA LOIRE

In the form of Chinon or Nicolas de Bourgueil, red wines from the Loire Valley are known for being earthy and light to medium in body. They are great accompaniments for poultry and vegetarian dishes, as they don't aim to overwhelm. White wine from La Loire, most notably in the form of Sancerre and also Pouilly-Fumé, is dry and highly aromatic with notes of summer fruits. It makes for a wonderful pairing for buttery seafood dishes and cheese plates (page 79).

On our first trip together, when we were still dating, my husband and I traveled to La Loire to do a little wine-tasting, and we spent a single night in the quaint village of Chinon. After dinner, we came across an alleyway café and sat down to have a bottle of wine and soak up the last days of summer. At midnight, the owners chaperoned a bunch of us inside for fear of complaints from their neighbors. We pushed aside the heavy velvet drapes and found ourselves in a bustling 1960s-style brasserie packed with people playing cards, a Serge Gainsbourg tune blaring from the organ, and a spirited bunch of sexagenarians dancing away near the bar. We stayed until closing, revelling among the locals and admiring the charming, quirky ways of La Loire.

—Jennie

LE PIQUE-NIQUE

HOW TO PICNIC LIKE A PARISIAN

Le pique-nique. When you're in Paris, you can picnic almost anywhere. You can turn any place into a picnic spot by buying a few oysters or a baguette and cheese while you watch boats go by on the banks of the Seine or chance upon a little square tucked away from the bustle of the Marais. It could be in the park or by the steps of the Sacre Coeur or while watching people play *pétanque* at Place Dauphine. Wherever you are, chances are you'll always end up sharing your baguette with a pigeon.

FILL YOUR BASKET

Depending on how elaborate you want your spread to be, you can pick up your picnic staples from your local Monoprix or plan it all out a day before by stopping for cute plates and accessories at Merci (111, boulevard Beaumarchais, 75003) or Hema in Les Halles (118-120, rue Rambuteau, 75001) for the prettiest affordable picnicware that can be used many times over.

For a quick-fix picnic, you can fill your basket at Rue du Nil with a baguette, cheese, charcuterie, and fresh fruits from Terroir d'Avenir and pick a menu on the following pages to make yours the most enviable picnic in the park.

PICNIC STYLE LUNCHES

CANAL SAINT-MARTIN

SPECK, ROASTED FIGS, GOAT CHEESE, AND PINE NUTS WITH ARUGULA TARTINE
PAGE 102

TONKA BROWN BUTTER MADELEINES PAGE 128

VANILLA, RHUBARB, AND BLOOD ORANGE CORDIAL PAGE 167
DRY SPARKLING WINE (CHAMPAGNE OR CRÉMANT)

PIGALLE

SMOKED HAM, BRIE, AND ONION JAM TARTINE PAGE 104

PISTACHIO AND VANILLA LOAF PAGE 134

PASSION FRUIT, RASPBERRY, AND VANILLA FIZZ PAGE 165
LIGHT RED (BEAUJOLAIS OR BEAUJOLAIS-VILLAGES)

PLACE D'ITALIE

PROSCIUTTO AND BUFFALO MOZZARELLA WITH ARUGULA
AND RED PEPPER MAYONNAISE PAGE 100

RYE, CHOCOLATE, AND SEA SALT COOKIES PAGE 120

PEACH AND ROSEMARY FIZZ PAGE 161
DRY CHARDONNAY (WHITE CHABLIS)

PICNIC STYLE LUNCHES

LE MARAIS

GRAVLAX, CAPERS, SORREL, AND CERVELLE DE CANUT TARTINE PAGE 88
ALMOND, ORANGE, AND OLIVE OIL CAKE PAGE 141

ELDERFLOWER AND GREEN GRAPE JUICE PAGE 168
ROSÉ (CÔTES DE PROVENCE)

JARDIN DU LUXEMBOURG

CHEESE PLATE PAGE 79

BAVETTE AND TAPENADE TARTINE PAGE 112

CHOCOLATE MOUSSE WITH CARAMELIZED PECANS PAGE 135

CLEMENTINE WITH HIBISCUS AND CINNAMON CORDIAL PAGE 169
DRY WHITE (SANCERRE) OR LIGHT TO MEDIUM-BODIED RED
(CHINON OR NICOLAS DE BOURGUEIL)

MONCEAU

ROASTED CHICKEN, BACON, TOMATOES, AND AVOCADO TARTINE PAGE 94

CHOCOLATE BROWNIE COOKIES PAGE 130

ORANGE, BAY LEAF, AND MAPLE SYRUP FIZZ PAGE 164
DRY WHITE (SANCERRE OR POUILLY-FUMÉ)

INTIMATE SUPPERS

POISSONIÈRE

BRETON ARTICHOKES PAGE 4

MARINATED SCALLOPS PAGE 11

CARAMELIZED ONION, THYME, AND MARJORAM TART PAGE 44

LATIN KARA'AGE PAGE 21

RASPBERRY AND GERANIUM TART PAGE 118

PINEAPPLE AND MINT LEMONADE PAGE 162
DRY WHITE (SANCERRE) OR
SLIGHTLY SWEET WHITE (ALSACE RIESLING)

OBERKAMPF

CHESTNUT TAGLIATELLE PAGE 6

CRUNCHY CHICKPEAS AND JERUSALEM ARTICHOKES PAGE 8

ROAST BEEF WITH ROSEMARY PEPPERCORN CRUST PAGE 62

CHOCOLATE AND HAZELNUT BUTTER CAKES PAGE 138

VANILLA, RHUBARB, AND BLOOD ORANGE CORDIAL PAGE 168
MEDIUM-BODIED RED (CÔTES DU RHÔNE)

INTIMATE SUPPERS

PLACE MONGE

FRENCHIE AREPAS PAGE 2

COCONUT FISH STEW WITH SPICY PIRÃO PAGE 46

CHOCOLATE AND PASSION FRUIT TART PAGE 122

GUAVA, CHILI, AND LIME CORDIAL PAGE 159
SUBTLY SWEET WHITE (ALSACE RIESLING)

MENILMONTANT

ASPARAGUS, GREEN GARLIC, HAZELNUTS, AND FETA PAGE 31

ROASTED SPICED EGGPLANT PAGE 40

CASABLANCA COUSCOUS PAGE 42

FIG AND HAZELNUT TART PAGE 124

MOROCCAN MINT TEA PAGE 170
LIGHT- TO MEDIUM-BODIED RED (CHINON OR NICOLAS DE BOURGUEIL)

INTIMATE SUPPERS

COURONNES

PINK SALAD PAGE 10

SLOW-ROASTED ROSEMARY LAMB PAGE 52

BRILLAT-SAVARIN, HONEY, PISTACHIO, AND PEAR PAGE 114

NOISETTE PAGE 146

PLUM AND CINNAMON FIZZ PAGE 160
MEDIUM- TO FULL-BODIED RED (BORDEAUX)

RUE CLER

CURED SEA BASS WITH ELDERFLOWER VINEGAR PAGE 12

POULET BASQUAISE PAGE 48

ESCOFFIER POTATOES PAGE 63

APPLE, FENNEL, AND KOHLRABI SALAD PAGE 36

HAZELNUT CREAM BUNS PAGE 154

CARAMEL, APPLE, AND GINGER FIZZ PAGE 166
DRY CHARDONNAY (WHITE CHABLIS) OR
FULL-BODIED RED (LANGUEDOC-ROUSSILLON)

LES BONNES ADDRESSES
OUR FAVORITE PICNIC SPOTS IN PARIS

PARC MONCEAU
Set up on one of the rolling hills, tucked among the park's winding pathways, for a picnic spot that feels regal and yet somewhat secluded.

JARDINS DU LUXEMBOURG
Watch children sail their vintage toy boats in the fountain. If you have a little one in tow, you can catch a classic French puppet show. Check schedule on: marionnettesduluxembourg.fr.

PARC DES BUTTES CHAUMONT
The steep hillsides of this landmark in the 19th make for a picnic challenge, but it's well worth it to appreciate the view of the city below.

BANKS OF THE SEINE
Don't forget your picnic blanket, as the stone banks can get cold at dusk. We prefer the spots on the edge of the 5th arrondissement, where you can find an occasional patch of grass and can also enjoy a view of Notre Dame as it lights up for the evening.

CHAMPS DE MARS
This park by the foot of the Eiffel Tower gets busy on a sunny day, but you'll always find a spot to call your own.

CANAL SAINT-MARTIN
You'll be close to incredible bread and viennoiserie (Du Pain et des Idées, 34, rue du Yves Toudic, 75010) good coffee (Ten Belles, 10, rue de la Grange aux Belles, 75010), the cutest canvas shoes in every color (Bensimon, 83, quai de Valmy, 75010), and a bookshop (Artazart, 83 quai de Valmy, 75010) with the most engaging selection of art and design books.

JARDIN VILLEMIN
Just a few steps back from Canal Saint-Martin, is a perfect spot for plopping down for an impromptu picnic or watching locals play basketball, *pétanque*, and various card games.

INVALIDES
The vast lawns that splay out in front of Les Invalides offer a beautiful view of some of the most recognizable landmarks in Paris and the city's pick-up soccer leagues.

SQUARE MARCEL BLEUSTEIN BLANCHET
Perched at the top of Montmartre, this charming square in the shadow of the Sacre Coeur is pretty special.

PLACE DES VOSGES
On seeing us with a camera, an elderly man insisted we visit this square. Ever since, it's always been worth a detour when we're in the Marais.

VERT GALANT
A green spot at the tip of Ile de la Cité with the river on either side and the perfect spot to watch the sunset.

TUILERIES
Pull up a chair by the large fountain at the iconic park on Rue Rivoli.

SQUARE BOUCICAUT
Before heading to this tiny park with a secret garden feel, stop at La Grande Epicerie (38, rue de Sèvres, 75007) for anything you fancy for your picnic.

BASIC RECIPES

These are the recipes that form the basis of our cooking. You will find that they are used several times in the book. These basics can be differentiated as stocks, condiments, sauces, and doughs. Cooking with stock is infinitely more flavorful and worth the effort. You can make a big batch and use it in many different ways over the course of the next few days. Condiments bring our recipes alive. We like adding elements of flavors that pack a punch—be it the concentrated flavor of Tomato Confit (page 197) or the fiery spice in Harissa (page 191). Our sauces range from creamy (with three different types of mayonnaise and aïoli, no less) to the herb-and-nut-rich pestos. And finally, the doughs used in pasta and pastry. We hope you keep going back to them, just as we do.

STOCK

You can modify these basic stock recipes for any number of purposes. To imbue your stock with a rich, comforting umami flavor, throw in any extra Parmigiano Reggiano rinds you may have stuffed away in the bottom of your cheese drawer. Depending on the recipe, or what you have on hand, you can also give your stock an aromatic twist by tossing in fennel fronds or cilantro or basil stalks during the last 5 minutes of cooking.

BASIC VEGETABLE STOCK

PREP TIME 10 minutes   COOK TIME 1¼ hours

- 3 medium carrots, peeled
- 2 stalks of celery, leaves and base removed
- 2 medium onions or 1 leek
- 1 tablespoon extra-virgin olive oil
- 1 teaspoon black peppercorns
- 1 bay leaf
- 3-4 sprigs fresh thyme

Cut the carrots, celery, and onions into large chunks. Heat the olive oil in a large saucepan over medium heat and add the vegetables along with the peppercorns, bay leaf, and thyme. Cook for 5 to 7 minutes, until the vegetables are slightly softened. Add enough hot water to fill the saucepan. Bring the mixture to a boil and then reduce the heat to a simmer. Cook for 45–60 minutes, until the liquid is fragrant and the vegetables have become very soft. Skim off any scum that rises to the surface. Strain the stock. It will keep in the fridge for up to 5 days and in the freezer for about 3 months.

Stock recipes featured in Fennel, Leek, Puy Lentils and Sausages with Basil Pistou (page 56), Potato and Leek Soup with Shredded Garlic Chicken (page 22), Poulet Basquaise with Butter Rice (page 48), Quinoa Salad (page 38), Roast Beef with Rosemary Peppercorn Crust (page 62), Coconut Fish Stew with Spicy Pirão (page 46), and Turkish Pot Roast (page 64).

BEEF STOCK

PREP TIME 15 minutes   COOK TIME 1½ hours

- 3 medium carrots, peeled
- 2 stalks of celery, leaves and base removed
- 2 medium onions or 1 leek
- 2 tablespoons extra-virgin olive oil
- 1 pound (450g) inexpensive cuts of beef and bones
- 1 tablespoon extra-virgin olive oil
- 1 teaspoon black peppercorns
- 1 bay leaf
- 3-4 sprigs fresh thyme

Cut the carrots, celery, and onions into large chunks. Heat the olive oil in a large, heavy saucepan over medium heat. Cut the meat into cubes and add them to the saucepan. Brown the meat on all sides. To allow for adequate browning, avoid turning the cubes frequently. As you turn the pieces of meat, scrape up the bits that have stuck to the bottom of the pan with a wooden spoon or spatula. Prep and add the vegetables, peppercorns, bay leaf, and thyme along with the bones, and cook them with the browned meat for 5 to 7 minutes. Add enough hot water to fill the saucepan. Simmer for 75 to 90 minutes. Skim off any scum that rises to the surface. Strain the stock. It will keep in the fridge for up to 5 days and in the freezer for about 3 months.

CHICKEN STOCK

PREP TIME 15 minutes   COOK TIME 2 hours

  3 medium carrots, peeled

  2 stalks of celery, leaves and base removed

  2 medium onions or 1 leek

  1 pound (450g) chicken bones or chicken wings

  1 teaspoon black peppercorns

  1 bay leaf

3-4 sprigs fresh thyme

Cut the carrots, celery, and onions into large chunks.

Preheat oven to 350°F (175°C).

Place the chicken bones in a large cast iron pot. Roast until well browned, about 30 to 40 minutes, turning halfway through. Next, add the vegetables, peppercorns, bay leaf, and thyme. Roast for another 20 minutes, until they have softened slightly.

Transfer the pot to the stovetop and place it over a medium flame. Deglaze the pan with 1 cup of hot water, using a wooden spoon to scrape up any brown bits on the bottom. Add enough hot water to fill the saucepan. Simmer for 45 to 60 minutes. Skim off any scum that rises to the surface. Strain the stock. It will keep in the fridge for up to 5 days and in the freezer for about 3 months.

FISH STOCK

PREP TIME 25 minutes   COOK TIME 45 minutes

  3 medium carrots, peeled

  2 stalks of celery, leaves and base removed

  2 medium onions or 1 leek

  ½ pound (225g) fish bones

  1 tablespoon butter

  1 teaspoon black peppercorns

  1 bay leaf

3-4 sprigs fresh thyme

  1 cup (50g) mushrooms, sliced

  ¼ cup (60ml) dry white wine

Cut the carrots, celery, and onions into large chunks.

Rinse the bones in cold water until the water runs clear, then soak them in cold water for an additional 10 minutes. Finally, rinse the bones again and pat them dry.

Heat the butter in a large saucepan set over medium heat. Cook the bones in the butter until all the water from the bones has evaporated.

Add the vegetables, peppercorns, bay leaf, and thyme with the mushrooms and continue to cook until the mushrooms have softened.

Add enough hot water to fill the saucepan and bring the mixture to a boil. Reduce the heat and simmer for 20 minutes. Skim off any scum that rises to the surface. Strain the stock. It will keep in the fridge for up to 5 days and in the freezer for about 3 months.

BASIL PESTO

We never added anchovies to our pesto until Shaheen picked up this little trick at cooking school. You won't know it's there, but it adds a rich umami flavor.

PREP TIME 15 minutes   COOK TIME 5 minutes   MAKES ⅔ cup

1 or 2 cloves garlic, germ removed and chopped

3 tablespoons pine nuts, toasted

⅓ cup (20g) Parmigiano Reggiano

1 anchovy fillet in oil

Zest of 1 lemon

½ cup (120ml) extra-virgin olive oil

1 bunch basil leaves (20–30g), chopped

Sea salt and freshly ground black pepper

With a mortar and pestle, or in food processor, blend together the garlic, pine nuts, cheese, anchovy, and lemon zest. Add a glug of the olive oil to loosen the mixture slightly.

Add the chopped basil and drizzle in more olive oil until the basil has incorporated with the rest of the ingredients. Add salt and pepper to taste.

Transfer the pesto to a container and cover it with a thin layer of olive oil, if you plan to store it. Keeps up to a week in the refrigerator.

Recipe featured in Zucchini, Roasted Peppers, Artichokes, Basil Pesto, and Tomato Confit Mayonnaise (page 82).

TIP If you want your pesto to have a nuttier flavor, toast the pine nuts in a pan over a low flame for 4 to 5 minutes. Swirl the pan frequently to ensure an even golden color. Take the pan off the heat and pound the pine nuts immediately as they're softer when they're warm.

CLASSIC MAYONNAISE

We love this rich emulsion just the way it is, but we also use it as a vehicle to carry more flavors by adding garlic confit, tomato confit, roasted peppers, or chopped olives and anchovies. You can make the mayonnaise either by hand or with the whisk attachment of a mixer.

PREP TIME 10 minutes   MAKES 1⅓ cup

2 egg yolks

½ teaspoon Dijon mustard

1 teaspoon red wine vinegar

1 garlic clove, germ removed and finely minced

1 cup (240ml) grapeseed or other neutral oil

Sea salt and freshly ground black pepper

In a bowl, mix together the yolks, mustard, vinegar, garlic, and a pinch each of salt and pepper.

Whisk the mixture vigorously as you add the oil in a thin drizzle. As you add more oil and continue to whisk, the mixture will thicken into a shiny emulsion. You can stop adding the oil before using it all—the mayonnaise will become lighter in color and thicker in consistency with the addition of more oil.

Season to taste and then add additional salt and pepper as necessary. Stored in an airtight container in the refrigerator, the mayonnaise will keep for up to 3 days.

Recipe featured in Breton Artichokes (page 4), Latin Karaage (page 21), Prosciutto and Buffalo Mozzarella with Arugula and Red Pepper Mayonnaise (page 100), Roasted Chicken, Bacon, Tomatoes, and Avocado with Mayonnaise and Baby Gem Lettuce (page 92), Turkey and English Cheddar with Pumpkin Seeds and Tarragon Aïoli (page 94), Zucchini, Roasted Peppers, Artichokes, Basil Pesto, and Tomato Confit Mayonnaise (page 82).

TIP If your mayonnaise "breaks" (separates), it's probably the result of adding the oil too quickly or not whisking the yolks fast enough. The oil needs to be poured in very slowly, in a thin stream, so that the yolk and oil bond and emulsify. To fix a broken batch of mayonnaise, whisk a fresh egg yolk with ½ teaspoon Dijon mustard in a clean bowl and very slowly drizzle the broken mixture into it, whisking continuously. Once it comes together, add the remaining oil. Because of the extra yolk, you may need to add a little more oil if you want a really thick mayonnaise.

TIP ON CODDLING EGGS Also, if you prefer not to use a raw egg in your mayonnaise, coddle it first. Place the egg in boiling water for one minute and then in an ice bath for another minute. This method not only pasteurizes the egg but also makes the yolk firmer, allowing it to maintain its structure as you whisk in the oil.

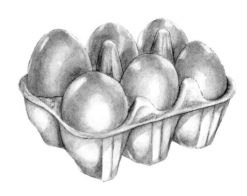

DUKKAH

Dukkah is a dry, aromatic mix of spices, seeds, and nuts. A little sprinkle of Dukkah perks up just about anything—salads, soups, vegetables, grilled fish, lamb. There are endless versions of Dukkah, and this is our take on the Egyptian blend.

PREP TIME 10 minutes   COOK TIME 15 minutes   MAKES 1½ cups

1½ cups (150g) hazelnuts

¼ cup (40g) sesame seeds

2 tablespoons cumin seeds

1 tablespoon coriander seeds

1 teaspoon fennel seeds

1 tablespoon dried oregano

¼ teaspoon ground clove

1 teaspoon coarse sea salt

1 teaspoon freshly ground black pepper

In an oven preheated to 325°F (160°C), place three separate trays of hazelnuts, sesame seeds, and the cumin, coriander, and fennel seeds. After 7 to 8 minutes, remove the sesame seeds and the spices. Leave the hazelnuts to toast for another 3 to 5 minutes (10 to 12 minutes, total).

Use a food processor to coarsely chop the hazelnuts. Combine the warm cumin, coriander, and fennel in a mortar and pound until crushed. Stir in the chopped hazelnuts and sesame seeds.

Crush the oregano between your fingers and add it to the mix along with the ground cloves and salt and pepper.

Recipe featured in Bresaola and Marinated Zucchini with Crunchy Almond Brown Butter (page 109).

ELDERFLOWER VINEGAR

To retain the maximum flavor of elderflowers, try to pick them away from city pollution and only give them a brief rinse before using. In this recipe we've used apple cider vinegar, which works beautifully, but honey or maple vinegar, if you can get your hands on them, will do an even better job in matching the sweet notes of the flower.

PREP TIME 20 minutes   MAKES 2 cups

20 elderflower heads
    Peel from 1 whole unwaxed lemon
2 cups (500ml) apple cider vinegar

Hold the elderflower heads by their stems and dunk them very briefly in cold water to give the flowers a quick rinse. With a small pair of scissors, snip the flowers off and avoid as much of the green stem as possible. Place them in a canning jar large enough to hold all of the ingredients.

Peel the lemon, avoiding the white pith. Drop the peel into the canning jar.

Cover the flowers with the vinegar. Seal the jar and leave it for about one week at room temperature. Shake the jar every other day.

After a week, the elderflower vinegar is ready to use. Either leave the flowers in the jar for display or drain the vinegar through several layers of cheesecloth for a clear liquid.

Recipe featured in Cured Sea Bass with Elderflower Vinegar (page 12).

GARLIC CONFIT

G arlic has several layers of skin. To make garlic confit, you need to peel off each layer until you reach the fine, shiny peel closest to the clove. The skin protects the garlic from direct heat and renders a tender texture and sweeter flavor.

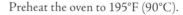

PREP TIME 15 minutes   COOK TIME 1 hour   MAKES 1½ cups

4 heads garlic

3 sprigs fresh thyme

1 sprig fresh rosemary

1 teaspoon coarse sea salt

4–6 black peppercorns

1 cup (240ml) extra-virgin olive oil

Preheat the oven to 195°F (90°C).

Break the head of garlic apart and peel the cloves down to the skin.

In a small saucepan, layer the garlic with the thyme and rosemary. Top with the salt and peppercorns and pour in the olive oil to cover all of the garlic.

Place the pan in the oven for one hour, until the garlic has softened completely.

Use the confit within 2 weeks or store it in the refrigerator for up to 2 months. You can use the garlic-infused oil for croutons, cooking potatoes, and sauteing vegetables, among other things.

Recipe featured in Cashew-Honey Goat Cheese (page 98), Onion Jam (page 104), Walnut Sauce (198).

HARISSA

Every Middle Eastern shop in the Ménilmontant neighborhood of Paris sells tubes and tubs of this hot paste. Le Phare du Cap Bon is the most common brand, but some shops make theirs in-house. Inspired by its inescapable presence in couscous restaurants, we set out to make our own harissa from scratch. Harissa is one of our favorite ingredients because of its sheer versatility—as a marinade, stirred into hummus, mixed in a vinaigrette, or tossed with roasted vegetables.

PREP TIME 40 minutes   COOK TIME 10 minutes   MAKES ½ cup

¼ teaspoon coriander seeds

½ teaspoon cumin seeds

¾ cup (25g) dried chiles or ½ cup (55g) Aleppo pepper

1 small roasted Roasted Pepper (page 194)

2 pieces Tomato Confit (page 197) or sun-dried tomato

1 garlic clove, peeled and germ removed

Zest of half a lemon

1 teaspoon lemon juice

½ teaspoon coarse sea salt

1 tablespoon fresh cilantro, chopped

3 tablespoons extra-virgin olive oil + extra for storage

Recipe featured in Aligot with Merguez Sausage and Harissa (page 54) and Za'atar Chicken, and Turkish Salad with Harissa Walnut Butter and Cumin-Cilantro Yogurt Sauce (page 92).

TIP When shopping for dried chiles, know your spice tolerance and how intense you want the final dish to taste. In North America, we typically use Colorado or Morita peppers for a milder version and chile de árbol or cayenne peppers for a strong kick. Use Aleppo chiles if you can find them. If you're not sure, opt for a Cascabel chile (medium hot) . . . or take your chances with whatever you find! Sometimes we also use fresh red chiles to give the harissa a nice vibrant hue. You can find an array of them in any African or Indian market.

On a baking sheet, toast the coriander and cumin seeds in an oven preheated to 325°F (160°C) for 5 to 7 minutes, until fragrant. Cool slightly and grind to a powder.

Remove the stems from the dried chiles and add them to a bowl. Cover with boiling water and let them soak for 20 to 30 minutes until softened. Drain off the water.

Put the roasted pepper, chiles, tomato confit or sun-dried tomatoes, garlic, toasted spices, lemon zest and juice, and salt in a blender or food processor with the olive oil and blend. Add cold water, 1 tablespoon at a time, if required, to bring it all together. Stir in the fresh cilantro just before using.

Store for up to two weeks in the fridge, topped with a thin layer of olive oil.

LEMON AND WALNUT OIL MAYONNAISE

This recipe starts out like a regular mayonnaise, but the walnut oil transforms it into a beautifully unctuous sauce. It works especially well with artichokes.

PREP TIME 10 minutes   MAKES ½ cup

1 egg yolk

Juice of ½ lemon

1 teaspoon Dijon mustard

Sea salt

¼ cup (60ml) grapeseed or other neutral oil

1 tablespoon (15ml) walnut oil

Sea salt and freshly ground black pepper

In a bowl, whisk together the egg yolk*, lemon juice, mustard, and a pinch of salt until smooth.

Add the grapeseed oil in a thin stream while whisking vigorously, until the mixture forms a smooth, shiny, thick emulsion. If at any point it looks like a lot of the oil is pooling, stop adding it and whisk until the mixture is well blended before going any further.

When the mayonnaise has thickened, season to taste with salt and pepper and whisk in the walnut oil. Transfer to a small serving dish and enjoy immediately.

Recipe featured in Breton Artichokes (page 4).

*If you prefer not to use a raw egg, you can coddle it first. For instructions, see Tip on Coddling Eggs (page 197).

PISTACHIO PARSLEY PESTO

We came up with this twist on conventional pesto when we had all the ingredients sitting around and wanted to rustle up a quick lunch. Olive oil brings together the parsley, pistachios, Pecorino cheese— and the garlic, for good measure. At other times, toasted almonds make an excellent substitute for the pistachios in this pesto.

PREP TIME 15 minutes   COOK TIME 10 minutes   MAKES 1 cup

¼ cup (40g) pistachios, toasted and chopped

½ cup (50ml) extra-virgin olive oil

2 or 3 cloves of garlic, germ removed and minced

1 big bunch (40g) flat-leaf parsley, leaves chopped

⅔ cup (50g) Pecorino Romano, grated

Sea salt and freshly ground black pepper

Toast the pistachios in a preheated 325°F (160°C) oven for 5 to 7 minutes until golden and fragrant. Skip this step if you're using roasted salted pistachios.

Add 1 tablespoon (15 ml) of the olive oil, and then the garlic, to a pan and heat it gently until fragrant. Turn off the heat and let cool. Stir in the parsley, cheese, and remaining olive oil. Make sure the mixture is well combined. Season to taste with salt and pepper. Transfer the pesto to a container and cover it with a thin layer of olive oil, if you plan to store it. Keeps up to a week in the refrigerator.

Recipe featured in Herb-Roasted Ham, Eggplant, and Tomato Confit with Almond Parsley Pesto, and Comté (page 101) and Pork Belly with Roasted Red Kuri Squash and Pistachio Parsley Pesto (page 28).

ROASTED PEPPERS

When you roast peppers, the hidden sweetness shines through and transforms this humble ingredient. You can use roasted peppers just the way they are, alongside a selection of cheese, or in salads and tartines.

PREP TIME 20 minutes   COOK TIME 40 minutes   MAKES 1 pint jar

3 pounds (1.4kg) red and yellow peppers

2 cloves garlic, germ removed and crushed

2 or 3 sprigs fresh thyme

Extra-virgin olive oil, enough to cover the roasted peppers in a jar

Preheat the oven to 400°F (200°C) and line a roasting tray with parchment paper.

Wash and dry the peppers and lay them on the tray.

Roast the peppers in the oven for 40 minutes, turning them over halfway through. At the end of roasting, they should look charred in spots and have softened completely.

Set them aside to cool slightly, then peel off the skin, remove the stem and seeds, and gently tear each pepper in half. Make sure no seeds remain inside.

When you're done, drain the peppers and discard the juices. Transfer the peppers to a jar and layer with the garlic and thyme, and then top with olive oil. Store in the refrigerator and use within 2 weeks.

Recipe featured in Zucchini, Roasted Peppers, Artichokes, Basil Pesto, and Tomato Confit Mayonnaise (page 82), Kale Salad with Red Pepper, Currants, and Pine Nuts (page 65), Meatballs in Amalfitana Sauce with Roasted Pepper and Gruyère (page 110), Prosciutto and Buffalo Mozzarella with Arugula and Red Pepper Mayonnaise (page 100).

SWEET PASTRY DOUGH

We've tried out many, many sweet pastry dough recipes, but there's no messing with this version of the classic formula from our pastry hero Pierre Hermé.

PREP TIME 15 minutes   MAKES about 1 pound

½ cup + 2 tablespoons (140g) unsalted butter

¾ cup + 1 tablespoon (90g) confectioners' sugar

Zest of 1 lemon

¼ cup + 1 teaspoon (30g) ground almonds

1 egg

2 cups (240g) all-purpose flour

Beat the butter until softened. Add the sugar, followed by the lemon zest and ground almonds.

Next, add the egg and beat until thoroughly incorporated. Scrape down the sides, mix again.

Finally, fold in the flour and mix until just combined.

Wrap the dough in plastic film and refrigerate for at least an hour.

Proceed as per recipe requirements.

Recipe featured in Caramelized Nut Tartelettes (page 139), Fig and Hazelnut Tart (page 124), Chocolate and Passion Fruit Tart (page 122), Raspberry and Geranium Tart (page 118), Apricot and Rosemary Tarte Tatin (page 127).

TARRAGON AÏOLI

With all the cooking we do, you might think we are good folks to have around. But you might want to first check with Jennie's neighbors on Rue Cler. Early one morning, we had to make some aïoli—just as the whisk began clicking on the steel bowl, creating a racket, we feared her flatmate might put our cooking session to a stop. So we just leaned out of the window and continued beating, and the courtyard echoed the din. One of us held the bowl and poured in the oil while the other whisked. When our arms got sore we'd alternate until our silky emulsion was ready. We're pretty certain some of our neighbors peeped through their curtains and were very confused by what they saw.

PREP TIME 10 minutes   MAKES ½ cup

1 egg yolk

½ teaspoon lemon juice

2 or 3 cloves garlic, germ removed and minced

¼ cup (60ml) grapeseed oil

¼ cup (60ml) extra-virgin olive oil

Pinch of sea salt

2 sprigs fresh tarragon, stems discarded and finely chopped

Zest of half a lemon

Place the egg yolk,* lemon juice, and half of the garlic in a mixing bowl.

Beat well with a whisk or electric mixer until well combined.

Combine oils and slowly drizzle into the mixture, whisking constantly and vigorously so that the yolk emulsifies with the oil. The mixture will thicken, take on a lighter, more opaque color, and retain the marks of the whisk for a few seconds.

Season to taste with remaining garlic and the salt. Stir in the fresh tarragon and lemon zest. The aïoli can be stored refrigerated for up to 3 days.

*If you prefer not to use a raw egg, you can coddle it first. For instructions, see Tip on Coddling Eggs (page 187).

Recipe featured in Breton Artichokes (page 4).

TOMATO CONFIT

Making tomato confit is a time-consuming job, but the intense fresh flavor and texture are well worth it. That's also why you should start with at least 4 pounds (1.8 kg) of tomatoes while you're at it, because they will reduce a lot in size and fit into a pint-size canning jar when finished.

PREP TIME 30 minutes   COOK TIME 3-4 hours   MAKES 1 pint jar

4 pounds (1.8kg) ripe, vine-ripened tomatoes

1 teaspoon sugar

4 sprigs fresh thyme

4 garlic cloves, crushed in their skin

1½ teaspoons sea salt

Freshly ground black pepper

2 tablespoons extra-virgin olive oil + enough to cover the tomatoes in a jar

Bring a large pot of water to a boil and set up a bowl of ice cold water next to it.

Pull the tomatoes from the vine, wash them, and cut an incision in the shape of a cross at the base of each tomato.

Once the water comes to a boil, fit as many tomatoes as you can in a single layer in the pot. Blanch the tomatoes for 20 to 30 seconds, then immediately place them in the cold water. Repeat with the rest of the tomatoes.

Once all the tomatoes have cooled, use your hands to peel, halve, and deseed them. The skin should slip off easily; if it doesn't, return the tomato to the boiling water and repeat the process.

Place the tomato halves in a bowl and toss with the sugar, thyme, garlic, salt, and pepper to taste. Set aside for 10 minutes to let the flavors meld.

Preheat the oven to 195°F (90°C). Line 3 baking trays with parchment paper. Lay the tomatoes, insides facing up, in a single layer spaced evenly across the trays, making sure to scatter any remaining thyme, garlic, and juices from the bowl onto the tomatoes.

Cook for 3 to 4 hours, turning the tomatoes over halfway through. Remove the tomatoes that cook faster to prevent them from singeing.

Let the tomatoes cool completely. Transfer to a sterilized jar and top with olive oil to preserve. Use within 2 weeks or store in the refrigerator for up to 2 months.

Recipe featured in Harissa (page 191), Herb-Roasted Ham, Eggplant, and Tomato Confit with Almond Parsley Pesto and Comté (page 101), Meatballs in Amalfitana Sauce with Roasted Pepper and Gruyère (page 110), Moorish Tomato Sauce with Cumin, Orange Zest, and Cinnamon (page 41), Slow-Roasted Rosemary Lamb with Late Harvest Riesling Yogurt-Feta Sauce (page 52), Zucchini, Roasted Peppers, Artichokes, Basil Pesto, and Tomato Confit Mayonnaise (page 82).

TIP Peel, halve, and deseed the tomatoes and place them in a strainer set over a bowl to collect the tomato juice. Combine the juice with a pinch of salt and ground cumin and serve over ice for a refreshing drink.

WALNUT SAUCE

S *alsa di Noci* from Liguria in Italy is traditionally meant to be a creamy walnut sauce, but you can make it as smooth or as chunky as you'd like. In this recipe, we've left it chunky for a good bite. If you're making it creamy, you might need to add a little water (or pasta water if you have some on hand) to loosen it up slightly.

PREP TIME 20 minutes   MAKES 1½ cups

1 or 2 cloves of garlic, germ removed, or 4–6 cloves Garlic Confit (page 190), peeled

2 cups (200g) walnuts, shelled and chopped

½ cup (35g) Parmigiano Reggiano, grated

½ cup (100ml) extra-virgin olive oil

2 sprigs fresh marjoram, chopped

Sea salt and freshly ground black pepper

With a mortar and pestle or in a food processor, grind the garlic and walnuts to a paste.

Add the grated cheese and drizzle in a bit of the olive oil until it's liquid enough to form a smooth paste. Season with salt and pepper and stir in the marjoram.

Once the paste is fairly smooth, drizzle in the remaining olive oil and give it a good stir. The walnut sauce can be kept refrigerated for up to 3 days.

Recipe featured in: Chestnut Tagliatelle with Chestnut and Rosemary Cèpes and Walnut Sauce (page 6).

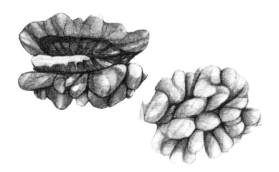

FRESH EGG PASTA

Making pasta by hand takes time but is well worth the effort, especially when you can get your hands on fresh eggs with bright yellow yolks. You don't even need anything special to dry the pasta—just use hangers!

PREP TIME 30-40 minutes active, 30 minutes rest   SERVES 4–6

2¾ cups (300g) sifted flour (⅓ semolina, ⅔ all-purpose)

Sea salt

2 eggs

3 egg yolks

1 tablespoon extra-virgin olive oil

Mix together the flour and a pinch of salt in a large bowl. Combine the eggs and egg yolks in a separate bowl and beat them together gently.

Make a well in the flour and pour the eggs into it. Begin to incorporate the flour by drawing it from all around the sides of the bowl. Whisk with a fork until the flour and eggs hold together as a rough mass.

Once the mixture is mostly combined, use your hands to gather together pieces of the dough and add the olive oil, kneading all the while.

Turn the dough out onto a floured countertop and knead for 10 minutes until it is firm and elastic. (If your dough is way too dry, add small amounts of water. If it's too sticky and wet, add more flour. The dough should be very firm.)

Wrap the dough in plastic and let sit for 30 minutes at room temperature or at least 1 hour refrigerated.

Divide the dough into 4 portions and flatten them slightly with a rolling pin. Run the first portion through a pasta machine on the widest setting. While you're working, keep the other portions of dough covered in plastic wrap to prevent them from drying out.

Once you've run the first portion of dough through the machine, fold it into thirds and run it through again, open side first. Repeat. Run the dough through a fourth time without folding it. Continue to flatten the dough, using a thinner setting each time you run it through the machine. If you're planning to use your dough to make ravioli, run the dough through the pasta machine all the way to the last, very thinnest setting.

TIP When rolling out the dough in the pasta machine, avoid using flour unless it's absolutely necessary, as it will make the dough stiff and hard to work with.

THE BELLY OF PARIS

Whenever anyone visits us in Paris, we have to take them to Emile Zola's belly of Paris at Les Halles. We usually start at Métro Sentier and take a walk on Rue du Nil, which is now home to a butcher, a fishmonger, a boulangerie, and our favorite produce shop, Terroir d'Avenir (7, rue du Nil, 75002 Paris). This shop brings the best produce of Europe to Paris. You will often find unexpected ingredients there, like Castelfranco radicchio, crosnes (Chinese Artichokes), pink caviar lime, Italian bergamot, and Japanese yuzu. After exploring this street, walk back to Sentier and go down the bustling rue Montorgueil, packed with food shops, bars, boulangeries, pâtisseries, and florists. Turn right on Rue Tiquetonne and in a few steps you will arrive at G. Detou (58, rue Tiquetonne, 75002 Paris), the only shop you need for all of your baking ingredients. This tiny space is packed with goods from floor to ceiling. Around Christmas, there's a line of people just waiting to get into the shop. There you can buy large bags of Valrhona chocolate, honey of every hue, pearl sugar, gianduja (hazelnut chocolate), pistachio paste, feuilletine, and anything else you wish to realize your baking fantasies. Next, head to Déco Relief (6, rue Montmartre, 75001 Paris) if you are into specialized patisserie equipment and decorating ingredients. Finally, walk to E. Dehellerin (18-20, rue Coquillière, 75001 Paris) for cake molds, carbon steel pans, and gleaming copperware. It's unlikely you won't find what you're looking for here, but just in case, you can also go to Mora (13, rue Montmartre, 75001 Paris) and A. Simon (48, rue Montmartre, 75002 Paris) for equipment. After this you're going to need a taxi.

INDEX

ACKNOWLEDGMENTS

To Friday Lunches, the original Paris Picnic Club,
and to everyone who helped us along the way—thank you.

Photo by David Graham

ABOUT THE AUTHORS

SHAHEEN PEERBHAI is a chef, teacher, and writer who has worked in Mumbai, Paris, and London at establishments ranging from *terroir*-driven bistros to Michelin three-star restaurants. She has been awarded prestigious scholarships from The Culinary Trust and The James Beard Foundation that turned her cooking school dreams into a reality, sending her to Le Cordon Bleu Paris and London and to Alain Ducasse Education in France. Shaheen teaches baking classes to thousands of enthusiasts and professionals across India and in London, where she lives. She documents her love for crusty breads and delicate pastries at purplefoodie.com.

JENNIE LEVITT is a chef, artist, and food entrepreneur who began her culinary career in rural Italy. Applying the foundations of Mediterranean cuisine to local ingredients and food culture, she opened a boutique catering company that has curated events in cities such as Aspen, Paris, Rio de Janeiro, and Bogotá. Her latest endeavor is Corelia, all-natural sparkling fruit juices that capture the lush flavor and freshness of the tropics (www.corelia.co). In *Paris Picnic Club*, Jennie brings food and art together with her watercolor illustrations inspired by the natural beauty of the ingredients themselves. She is a graduate of Williams College and HEC Paris.

Share photos of your creations by tagging them #parispicnicclub